The Hatherleigh Guide

to

Treating
Substance Abuse

Part I

The Hatherleigh Guides series

The Hatherleigh Guide

to

Treating Substance Abuse

Part I

Hatherleigh Press • New York

Gary Holmes, PhD, CRC
Emporia State University (Emporia, KS)

John Homlish, PhD
The Menninger Clinic (Topeka, KS)

Sharon E. Robinson Kurpius, PhD
Arizona State University (Tempe, AZ)

Marilyn J. Lahiff, RN, CRRN, CIRS, CCM
Private practice (Englewood, FL)

Chow S. Lam, PhD
Illinois Institute of Chicago (Chicago, IL)

Paul Leung, PhD, CRC
University of Illinois at Urbana-Champaign (Champaign, IL)

Carl Malmquist, MD
University of Minnesota (Minneapolis, MN)

Robert J. McAllister, PhD
Taylor Manor Hospital (Ellicott City, MD)

Richard A. McCormick, PhD
Cleveland VA Medical Center-Brecksville Division (Cleveland, OH)

Thomas Miller, PhD, ABPP
University of Kentucky College of Medicine (Lexington, KY)

Jane E. Myers, PhD, CRC, NCC, NCGC, LPC
University of North Carolina-Greensboro (Greensboro, NC)

Don A. Olson, PhD
Rehabilitation Institute of Chicago (Chicago, IL)

William Pollack, PhD
McLean Hospital (Belmont, MA)

Keith M. Robinson, MD
University of Pennsylvania (Philadelphia, PA)

Susan R. Sabelli, CRC, LRC
Assumption College (Worcester, MA)

Gerald R. Schneck, PhD, CRC-SAC, NCC
Mankato State University (Mankato, MN)

George Silberschatz, PhD
University of California-San Fransisco (San Fransisco, CA)

David W. Smart, PhD
Brigham Young University (Provo, UT)

Julie F. Smart, PhD, CRC, NCC
Utah State University (Logan, UT)

Joseph Stano, PhD, CRC, LRC, NCC
Springfield College (Springfield, MA)

Anthony Storr, FRCP
Green College (Oxford, England)

Hans Strupp, PhD
Vanderbilt University (Nashville, TN)

Retta C. Trautman, CCMHC, LPCC
Private practice (Toledo, OH)

Patricia Vohs, RN, CRRN, CRC, CIRS, CCM
Private practice (Warminster, PA)

William J. Weikel, PhD, CCMHC, NCC
Morehead State University (Morehead, KY)

Nona Leigh Wilson, PhD
South Dakota State University (Brookings, SD)

The Hatherleigh Guide to Treating Substance Abuse, Part I

Project Editor: Joya Lonsdale
Assistant Editor: Stacy Powell
Indexer: Angela Washington-Blair, PhD
Cover Designer: Gary Szczecina
Cover photo: Christopher Flach, PhD

© 1996 Hatherleigh Press
A Division of The Hatherleigh Company, Ltd.
420 East 51st Street, New York, NY 10022

This book is printed on acid-free paper.

Compiled under the auspices of the editorial boards of *Directions in Mental Health Counseling, Directions in Clinical Psychology,* and *Directions in Rehabilitation Counseling.*

Library of Congress Cataloging-in-Publication Data

The Hatherleigh guide to treating substance abuse, part I —1st ed.
        p.   cm. — (The Hatherleigh guides series ; 7)
    Includes bibliographical references and index.
    ISBN 1-886330-48-4 (alk. paper)
    1. Substance abuse.   I. Series.
    RC456. H38 1995 vol. 7
    [RC564]
    616.89 s—dc20
    [616.86]   96-26093
                                                         CIP

First Edition: October 1996

10 9 8 7 6 5 4 3 2 1

About the photograph and the photographer

Alley, San Fransisco, 1996
These city streets are home to much susbtance abuse.

Christopher Flach, PhD, is a psychologist in private practice in southern California. An avid photographer for more than 20 years, his favorite subjects include people and nature. He has studied photography with Ansel Adams, and his work has been on display in public galleries and in private collections.

Table of Contents

Illustrations

Introduction

The use of alcohol and other drugs is ubiquitous in contemporary society. A huge economic toll is exacted annually through lost wages, criminal prosecution and imprisonment, and expenses for social and health services. From the clinical standpoint, habitual alcohol or drug use places the consumer at risk for severe psychiatric disturbances, workplace maladjustment, manifold life-threatening diseases, and traumatic injuries. Violence, victimization, and suicide also are more common among patients with a substance problem. Moreover, a lifestyle that includes habitual alcohol or drug consumption often results in global deterioration in the capacity and motivation to fulfill social and domestic roles.

Epidemiologic findings underscore the seriousness of the problem. Research suggests that the average age of individuals who qualify for the first time for a diagnosis of alcohol/drug abuse or dependence is getting lower over time (Robins & Regier, 1991). In a representative sample of twelfth graders, 28% consumed five drinks in a single session in the 2-week period before the survey and 46% had used an illegal drug at least once (Johnston, O'Malley, & Bachman, 1994). In effect, a more rapid development of addiction exists today than in the past. The reasons for this are not entirely clear but may be due in part to the greater availability and wider assortment of addictive compounds. Hybridization of plants, potent synthetic drugs, and increased purification methods augment addiction liability.

The societal problems caused directly or indirectly by alcohol or drugs are enormous. Commensurate with this, approximately two dozen scientific journals are devoted specifically to reporting the results of research on alcohol and drug use, abuse, and dependence. A vigorous research commitment is supported by two agencies within the National Institutes of Health, which allocate approximately $500 million for research directed at elucidating the causes, course, and consequences of alcohol and drug use and devising innovative prevention and treatment methods. The Public Health Service disburses several hundred million dollars annually for direct costs of intervention through the Substance Abuse and Mental Health Services Administration. Surprisingly, however, only small portions of research findings are disseminated to practitioners. Often many years elapse before counselors become aware of new methods that can improve the efficiency, quality of assessment, and effectiveness of intervention.

The Hatherleigh Guide to Treating Substance Abuse, Part I and *Part II* fill a large void. The counselor, as a member of the health or social delivery system, has a key contribution to make in the treatment of alcohol and drug abuse; however, the field of substance abuse has not received the level of interest from counselors that is warranted based on the prevalence of the problem. These two *Hatherleigh Guides* offer counselors thorough reviews of the most recent empirical research on which improved evaluation and treatment of substance abuse can be based. Accomplished experts demonstrate how to use emerging scientific findings in practical settings; chapters include useful case examples from their own clinical experience to illustrate the day-to-day application of theory and research.

The Hatherleigh Guide to Treating Substance Abuse, Part I addresses general issues in the diagnosis and treatment of addictions and substance use disorders, and *Part II* focuses on treating specific populations of individuals with addictions to alcohol or other drugs. This volume, *Part I*, discusses a range of treatment modalities, including pharmacologic, nutrition, family, and psychosocial approaches.

Chapter 1 describes how to identify, screen, and evaluate adolescents and adults who are known or suspected to have a problem involvement with drugs or alcohol. The method of information gathering is systematic; severity of problems associated with substance use are objectively ranked and quantified. This information is then used to devise a treatment program, monitor the client's progress in treatment, and document treatment gains during aftercare. The information gathered from this assessment allows the clinician to prioritize treatment interventions according to the type and severity of problems. Chapter 1 also outlines the range of assessment instruments that can be used for comprehensive evaluation and provides a schema for applying this information to a treatment plan. Because counselors are becoming increasingly accountable for their services by third-party payers, this chapter informs the reader how to efficiently and inexpensively monitor the course of intervention, particularly to prevent florid relapse.

Chapters 2, 3, and 4 focus on pharmacotherapy. Drug therapy is increasingly accepted as a primary therapeutic modality in the present era of diminishing resources for psychosocial intervention; thus, the information contained in these three chapters is timely and important. Chapter 2 provides an excellent overview of the medications currently used in substance abuse treatment. Characteristic side effects and methods for evaluating and monitoring the efficacy of medications are described, and basic pharmacologic concepts are presented. The fact that alcohol and drug consumption commonly occurs in conjunction with psychiatric or emotional disturbance underscores the importance of pharmacotherapy as a component of contemporary practice. Counselors must have a basic understanding of pharmacotherapy to know when to make a medical referral, how to differentiate drug- or alcohol-related disturbances from those caused by the medication, and when the client may be weaned from pharmacotherapeutic agents during treatment.

Chapter 3 examines the overlooked role that nutrition can play in detoxification from drugs and alcohol. Because inpatient detoxification is less available as an option, the use of pharmacologic agents and nutrition is especially significant. Substance abuse has an adverse effect on the body's detoxification mechanisms, especially those that occur in the liver. This chapter outlines a simple and effective nutritional intervention program to assist in detoxifying the liver and reducing the effects of withdrawal.

Chapter 4 focuses on the efficacy of naltrexone, the most recent beneficial compound receiving widespread attention. Naltrexone reduces the likelihood of relapse and craving for alcohol. Because craving is a critical predisposing factor for relapse, the use of naltrexone as an adjunct to counseling cannot be overemphasized. However, naltrexone is only one medication in an emerging family of pharmacotherapies; a review of its effectiveness informs the reader of an emerging emphasis in the treatment of addictions to also include consideration of the biologic substrate.

Chapter 5 contrasts the relative advantages of inpatient versus outpatient treatment for alcoholism. The author concludes that, in contrast to the belief of the 1970s and 1980s that inpatient treatment is the gold standard, intensive outpatient treatment can be as effective as inpatient treatment for some individuals. For others, however, inpatient intervention is necessary. The goal, therefore, is to match the client's needs with the appropriate treatment. A decision tree format is provided to assist counselors in determining the optimum treatment strategy. This type of information is clearly of substantial value for justifying to third-party payers an objective and cost-effective treatment strategy.

The role of marital and family therapy in the treatment of alcohol abuse is discussed in Chapter 6. Used in conjunction with other treatment modalities, family therapy methods strengthen the early gains obtained from medication by providing support to the client and by enabling the development of new skills required for achieving lasting sobriety. According to recent research, utilizing marital and family therapy is effective at all stages of the alcoholism recovery process. In addition to a comprehensive review of the literature, this chapter contains numerous examples of situations that arise in family therapy and gives the reader practical ways to address them.

Chapter 7 reviews the clinical ramifications of two halluci-nogenic drugs, lysergic acid diethylamide (LSD) and 3, 4-methylenedioxymethamphetamine (MDMA; also known as "Ecstasy"). After a decrease in hallucinogenic drug use in the 1980s, the renewed popularity of LSD and Ecstasy is part of an apparent resurgence in drugs previously associated with the 1960s. LSD and Ecstasy are commonly taken at "raves," all-night dance parties packed with young participants fueled on hallucinogenic drugs. This chapter discusses the social, legal, and health consequences of these drugs; prolonged and ha-bitual use can be as detrimental as alcoholism or narcotic addiction. In extreme cases, an overdose of hallucinogens can end in death. An awareness of the consequences of these drugs is important for counselors who work with adolescents.

Chapter 8 examines the toxic and pharmacologic effects of caffeine and reviews the association between caffeine and panic disorder and insomnia. These two disturbances are common among heavy caffeine users. Because emotional dis-tress mitigates treatment progress, an understanding of the most commonly used psychotropic substance in the world is especially informative because of the need to distinguish symp-toms that are caused by caffeine from those caused by other factors.

Chapters 9 and 10 outline two intervention approaches that are in the vanguard of innovative treatment for addictions, cognitive behavior therapy and motivation enhancement mod-els. Chapter 9 reviews the theories of addiction to cocaine from the cognitive-behavioral perspective and describes various interventions that can be used in group settings and family therapy. Cognitive behavior therapies have received wide-spread acceptance among practitioners; however, their spe-cific application to addiction is less known. In the treatment of cocaine addiction, these interventions have had success in retaining users in treatment and achieving initial cocaine abstinence.

Motivation enhancement models, described in Chapter 10, utilize brief interventions to break through denial and resistance to treatment and elicit the client's active involvement to reduce or ameliorate problematic alcohol or drug use. Implicit in this approach is a recognition of the client's capacity to learn new behaviors, adapt new attitudes, and, in a coercion-free context, accept responsibility for self-guided improvement. The client and counselor collaborate as active partners in the client's recovery program.

The treatment of addictions has expanded; however, relapse rates remain unacceptably high. Chapter 11 addresses relapse prevention as a central goal of treatment; it should not merely be an addendum attached after treatment is completed. Contemporary models of relapse prevention are reviewed, including cognitive behavioral, biopsychosocial, and psychoeducational approaches. These intervention methods encompass specific processes, such as skill building and cognitive remediation, as well as more global processes involving lifestyle modification.

The success of treatment ultimately depends on our capacity to synchronize a network of service delivery professionals. Therefore, the book concludes with a discussion in Chapter 12 of how counselors can enhance interagency collaboration between clinical and social service agencies to help patients gain access to the range of human services needed to support recovery. Because alcohol and drug use, abuse, and dependence invariably have an impact on multiple spheres of functioning, counselors must be able to expeditiously navigate among the various disciplines and delivery systems to effectively apply their specialty skills.

Because 25% of the U.S. population will have an alcohol or drug abuse disorder at some time in their life (Robins & Regier, 1991), this book will become an indispensable *Guide* for counselors who require practical, up-to-date information on diagnosing and treating patients who use and abuse substances. With access to these necessary tools, effective treatment of this underserved population can become a reality.

Ralph E. Tarter, PhD
Pittsburgh, Pennsylvania

Dr. Tarter is Professor of Psychiatry and Neurology, University of Pittsburgh [PA] Medical School; and Director, Center for Education and Drug Abuse Research (CEDAR). CEDAR is a consortium between St. Francis Medical Center and the University of Pittsburgh.

REFERENCES

Johnston, L., O'Malley, P., Bachman, J. (1994). National survey results on drug use from the monitoring the future study, 1975–1993. Rockville, MD: U.S. Department of Health and Human Services, National Institute on Drug Abuse.

Robins, L., & Regier, D. (1991). *Psychiatric disorders in America: The epidemiological catchment area study.* MacMillan, NY: The Free Press.

1

An Integrative Approach for the Evaluation and Treatment of Alcohol and Drug Abuse

Ralph E. Tarter, PhD

Dr. Tarter is Professor of Psychiatry and Neurology, University of Pittsburgh [PA] Medical School; and Director, Center for Education and Drug Abuse Research (CEDAR). CEDAR is a consortium between St. Francis Medical Center and the University of Pittsburgh.

KEY POINTS

- Health care providers are currently faced with increasing demands on their accountability while having to treat difficult problems with limited resources. A strategy that addresses both accountability and cost-effective service provision is the "decision-tree" approach to evaluation and treatment.

- The decision-tree model involves three stages: two for assessment and one for intervention.

- The first stage involves administering the *Drug Use Screening Inventory* (DUSI-R), a 159-item questionnaire that identifies 10 domains to quantify severity of disturbance. The second stage entails comprehensive assessment in the disturbed domains the DUSI-R has identified. The third stage, intervention programming, consists of developing an individualized intervention program targeted to the specific areas of disturbance.

- Two essential responsibilities of therapists and counselors are to (a) monitor the treatment process and objectively quantify changes occurring during the intervention and (b) conduct periodic checkups after treatment to prevent relapse.

This chapter was supported by the center grant PO-05605 from the National Institute on Drug Abuse.

INTRODUCTION

The success of treatment for drug and alcohol abuse depends on the accuracy of the information derived from a comprehensive evaluation early in treatment. Targeting the precise determinants of the disorder and identifying environmental contributors to its course are essential for designing an effective treatment plan. In an unrestricted environment, where cost and access to the client are not concerns, an evaluation may take several days or even weeks. However, in the present era of increasingly fiscal-conscious third-party payers, pressure is mounting on health care providers to offer only those services documented to be cost effective.

The evaluation of persons known or suspected to abuse psychoactive substances requires the acquisition of both quantitative and qualitative information so that interventions can be targeted to identified areas of disturbance. This intervention strategy generally is referred to as *client-treatment matching*. Intervention is directed at ameliorating the underlying etiologic determinants of the disorder in addition to eliminating or modifying the factors that maintain or reinforce consumption of psychoactive substances.

With respect to the population of persons who are at high risk for substance abuse (e.g., children of substance-abusing parents, youth and adults with psychological and behavioral disorders) and persons whose substance use is beginning to cause adverse health or psychosocial consequences, evaluation is directed toward disaggregating the components of the predisposition so that the person can be redirected to normative adjustment before developing a full-blown substance abuse disorder. Whether the intervention focuses on prevention or treatment, the goal is to maximize prognosis by implementing remediation tailored to the client's needs.

THE PSYCHOMETRIC CONTEXT OF AN EVALUATION

A comprehensive evaluation involves sampling psychological

processes by using reliable and valid methods. The three major parts of psychometric validity are construct validity, predictive validity, and incremental validity. *Construct validity* refers to whether the instrument used obtains information that accurately describes the client's current condition. Construct validity ensures that the inventory, test, or interview actually measures what it claims to measure. *Predictive validity* refers to whether the results obtained from an instrument can predict the person's future course accurately with respect to the process measured. *Incremental validity* refers to whether the instrument provides more and superior information than that obtainable from casual observations.

In the practice of medicine, laboratory tests are useful to the extent that the patient's history and results of the physical examination are capable of yielding a correct diagnosis to guide treatment. Therefore, laboratory tests are performed to elucidate specific facets of organ-system pathology (construct validity) and to identify the course and prognosis of disease (predictive validity) beyond that afforded by observation or examination alone (incremental validity). Similarly, in the applied behavioral sciences, a psychometric evaluation yields clinically important information that cannot be accrued readily or accurately from routine examination and client history.

Whether the evaluation is biochemical, physiologic, or psychological, it is limited by time and fiscal constraints. It is clearly not feasible to attempt to measure everything about a person. Hence, a critically important practical issue concerns the selection of processes to be evaluated that optimally satisfy construct, predictive, and incremental validity requirements. Furthermore, the client's treatment must be identified expeditiously and an effective intervention implemented.

In addition to satisfying validity criteria, the evaluation must yield reliable information. Three types of reliability are interrater reliability, test-retest reliability, and internal reliability. *Interrater reliability* refers to the extent to which assessment results obtained by one examiner are equivalent to the results obtained by another. The evaluation should have high *test-retest reliability*: the results obtained must have temporal stability. This is somewhat problematic in the context of ongoing intervention because the client typically is changing over time. Nonetheless, based on findings obtained from nonclinical samples, an evaluation instrument should yield consistent results over time. *Internal reliability* means that the items of a test measuring a particular process should be highly intercorrelated. For example, on a scale evaluating family interaction, the inclusion of items measuring an irrelevant process would yield a summary score that obscures the process being assessed. High internal reliability reflects strong cohesion or unidimensionality of the process assessed.

DECISION-TREE APPROACH TO EVALUATION

The objectives of a psychological evaluation are to yield (a) comprehensive and (b) practical information. A decision-tree format is ideally suited to fulfilling these two objectives in a cost-efficient manner.

Figure 1.1 depicts a multistage evaluation paradigm. The process begins with a multidimensional screening for problems. Based on the results of this brief assessment, a formal diagnostic evaluation is performed in one or more areas to characterize comprehensively the natural history, severity, and, where possible, the etiology of disturbances previously identified in the screening assessment. The third stage involves using the information derived from the first two stages to design and implement interventions tailored to the client's problems. The advantage of this multistage approach is that it reduces the labor-intensive assessment procedure by narrowing the focus of evaluation successively to pinpoint and elaborate the client's problems. Therefore, at the conclusion of the evaluation, prioritizing the type and intensity of required interventions is possible.

Stage 1:

The first stage of the evaluation procedure consists of a

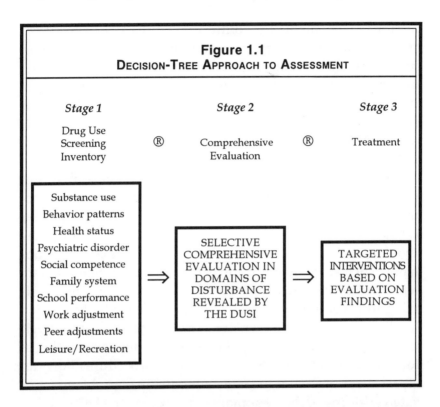

Figure 1.1
DECISION-TREE APPROACH TO ASSESSMENT

Stage 1   *Stage 2*   *Stage 3*

Drug Use Screening Inventory   ®   Comprehensive Evaluation   ®   Treatment

Substance use
Behavior patterns
Health status
Psychiatric disorder
Social competence
Family system
School performance
Work adjustment
Peer adjustments
Leisure/Recreation

⇒

SELECTIVE COMPREHENSIVE EVALUATION IN DOMAINS OF DISTURBANCE REVEALED BY THE DUSI

⇒

TARGETED INTERVENTIONS BASED ON EVALUATION FINDINGS

multidimensional screening of problems accompanied by documentation of the client's personal and medical history. The personal history informs the counselor about the client's family, school context (if appropriate), and medical history. The medical history provided by a physician, nurse clinician, or physician assistant documents health status (Tarter, 1990).

Following acquisition of this preliminary information, the revised *Drug Use Screening Inventory* (Gordian Group, P. O. Box 1587, Hartsville, SC 29550) is administered. The Drug Use Screening Inventory (DUSI-R), a 159-item questionnaire, contains a section to document frequency of drug use and drug preference for approximately 20 different classes of psychoactive substances. A 10-item "lie scale" estimates the likelihood of deliberate deception by the respondent.

The DUSI-R was designed to be applicable to those with at least a fifth grade reading level. (At the present time, English and Spanish language versions are available; homologous versions are available for youths and adults.) The severity of problems during the past year, month, or week can be determined with this inventory. The short intervals of "past month" and "past week" enable monitoring and quantifying changes that occur commensurate to treatment. To document changes in status occurring during follow-up, the past-month or past-year versions can be administered. The DUSI-R takes approximately 20 minutes to complete.

The DUSI-R quantifies severity of disturbance in 10 domains (Table 1.1). Two different profiles are generated: absolute problem density scores and relative problem density scores. Absolute problem density scores, which quantify the severity of the problems, are obtained in each of the 10 domains. Each score then is transformed into a relative problem density score. This scoring method is advantageous for prioritizing intervention resources by ranking the extent to which the client's problems in each domain contributed to the overall pattern of severity. Hence, the sum of scores across the 10 domains equals 100%. This latter scoring procedure allows an appreciation of the unique interrelationship of problems associated with any of the 10 domains assessed by the DUSI-R. For example, although the client may present for treatment of substance abuse as the most salient or obvious problem, other aspects of behavior or adjustment are frequently disrupted more severely. The relative problem density profile provides information regarding the unique configuration of problem severity for each person. Figure 1.2 presents a case example of the absolute and relative problem density profiles of a 17-year-old woman arrested for driving while under the influence of alcohol. Figure 1.2 illustrates that the woman's behavior patterns scored highest on her absolute problem density profile. However, according to the woman's relative problem density profile, her behavior patterns represent the *sixth* most important factor contributing to the overall severity of pathology.

An overall problem density index is obtained by counting the number of endorsements on the whole DUSI-R protocol (with the exception of the lie-scale items) and dividing the

Table 1.1
THE MEASUREMENT DOMAINS OF THE REVISED DRUG USE
SCREENING INVENTORY

Domain IA – Drug and Alcohol Use	Frequency of use of 20 substances, drug preferences
Domain IB – Substance Use	Degree of involvement, severity of consequences
Domain II – Behavior Patterns	Social isolation, anger, acting-out, self-control
Domain III – Health Status	Accidents, injuries, illnesses
Domain IV – Psychiatric Disorder	Anxiety, depression, antisociality, psychotic symptoms
Domain V – Social Competence	Social interactions, social skills, refusal skills
Domain VI – Family System	Dysfunctional conflict, parental supervision, marital quality
Domain VII – School Performance	Academic performance, school adjustment
Domain VIII – Work Adjustment	Work competence, motivation
Domain IX – Peer Relationships	Social network, gang involvement, quality of friendships
Domain X – Leisure/Recreation	Quality of activities during leisure time

Note: The DUSI-R also contains a 10-item lie scale to estimate the likelihood of deliberate deception by the respondent.

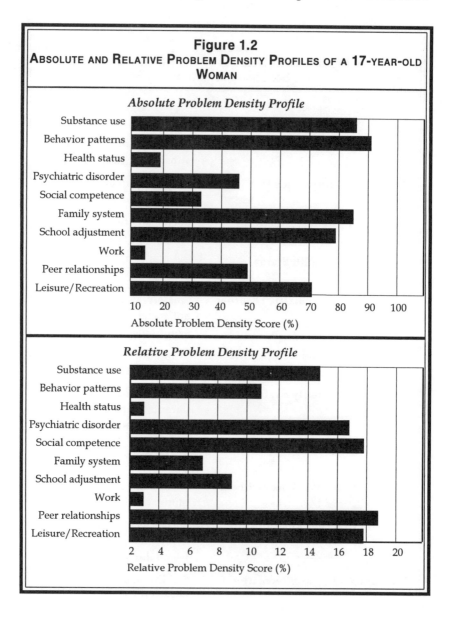

Figure 1.2
ABSOLUTE AND RELATIVE PROBLEM DENSITY PROFILES OF A 17-YEAR-OLD WOMAN

total by 149. The resulting score is multiplied by 100 to obtain the overall problem density index. This score, ranging from 0%–100%, summarizes problem severity across all 10 domains of the DUSI-R. As a rule, a score exceeding 15% indicates the need for intervention.

To document profile validity, the DUSI-R also contains a lie scale, composed of the last item from each of the 10 domains. A score of five or more "no" responses suggests deceptive reporting by the client.

The psychometric properties of the DUSI-R have been documented (Kirisci, Mezzich, & Tarter, 1995; Tarter & Kirisci, in press). Each domain appears to measure one major factor. A single second order factor, indexing overall severity, also has been documented. In the adolescent version, internal reliability correlations and test-retest reliability have been shown to be highly significant statistically; psychometric studies are ongoing in adult samples. In adolescents, 91% of cases are correctly classified as either normal or qualifying for a diagnosis of psychoactive substance use disorder based on the revised third edition of the *Diagnostic and Statistical Manual of Mental Disorders* (DSM-III-R) (American Psychiatric Association, 1987).

Stage 2:

The second stage of the decision-tree model of evaluation entails comprehensive assessment in the domains the DUSI-R has revealed to be suggestive of disturbance. This aspect of the evaluation essentially protects against false-positive results; that is, the incorrect inference of the presence of a disorder where none actually exists. In stage 2 of the assessment, information is gathered in sufficient detail to formulate a diagnosis.

The assessment instruments used in stage 2 ideally should be standardized and possess proven validity and reliability. However, this is not always possible because certain domains covered by the DUSI-R do not have complementary established instrumentation. Therefore, the counselor must rely on instruments that, although not standardized, serve the purpose of comprehensive examination. Thus, interpretation of the findings must be advanced cautiously and in conjunction with documented clinical impressions as well as, where possible, informant reports.

Depending on the age, ethnicity, cognitive capacity, and

motivation of the client, the counselor should exercise a "best judgment" approach in the selection of measures for this phase of the evaluation.

Domain I—Substance Use

The first requirement in comprehensive assessment is to characterize substance use behavior. The onset of each type of substance consumed must be documented so that the progression of drug use and pattern of involvement can be described explicitly. For each type of substance use in the client's history, it is essential to ascertain whether it reached problematic severity so as to warrant a diagnosis of abuse or dependence. In addition, the occurrence of remission and number of lifetime episodes should be described. The quantity and frequency of consumption within a typical 30-day period should be recorded for each episode so that a picture of the client's total involvement with alcohol and drugs can be obtained.

Multiple drug use should be investigated because of the substantial lethal risk posed by the synergistic effects of the simultaneous use of psychoactive drugs. For example, conjointly using alcohol and benzodiazepines (antianxiety medications) is especially dangerous because of the risk of respiratory arrest.

Drug problem severity can be quantified using the Teen Addiction Severity Index (McClellan, Luborsky, Woody, & O'Brien, 1980). This semistructured interview yields an evaluation of the impact of drug use on six spheres of daily living. This version of the Addiction Severity Index designed to assess teenagers with addiction problems is currently undergoing psychometric validation (Kaminer, Bukstein, & Tarter, 1991). The Alcohol Use Inventory for adults is another well-established multidimensional questionnaire (Wanberg & Horn, 1985).

Psychometric techniques that encompass the measurement of all aspects of alcohol and drug use have not yet been developed. The instruments mentioned herein only document and quantify current use pattern and problem severity; it is important to obtain other pertinent information. During the course of the examination, the following should be determined: pattern of substance use (episodic versus continuous); context of substance use (solitary versus social consumption); availability of drugs in the social environment; perceived importance of drugs in the client's life; expected and experienced effects of drugs on mood and behavior; family history of drug and alcohol abuse; and access to drugs (dealer versus consumer).

Domain II—Behavior Patterns

Certain dispositional behaviors or personality traits are commonly associated with the etiology and maintenance of alcohol or drug abuse. The extent to which certain personality traits presage the onset of substance use, or are shaped by the long-term consequences of drug abuse, must be ascertained on a case-by-case basis. Features such as low self-esteem, impulsivity, aggressiveness, behavioral disinhibition, and sex-role conflict are more prevalent in drug abusers than in normal persons.

No single instrument currently assesses all dimensions of personality relevant to understanding drug use behavior. The Minnesota Multiphasic Personality Inventory (MMPI) traditionally has been useful for profiling psychopathology and behavior disorders (Hathaway & McKinley, 1951). More recently, the Multidimensional Personality Questionnaire (Tellingen, unpublished data, 1982) has been developed, which contains scales that measure traits salient to drug and alcohol abuse (e.g., aggression, alienation, negative affect, and social potency). For children and adolescents, the Child Behavior Checklist is the most widely used assessment tool (Achenbach & Edelbrock, 1983). One important advantage of the Child Behavior Checklist is that convergent information can be obtained from the parent and teacher as well as directly from the child.

Domain III—Health Status

Health can be compromised by the direct effects of chronic drug use and by the associated effects of a neglectful or irresponsible lifestyle. Physical examination, supported by appropriate laboratory assessment, is mandatory as part of a comprehensive diagnostic work-up. Self-report measures of health status can provide additional useful information that otherwise may be overlooked (Schinka, 1984). The Millon Behavioral Health Inventory evaluates health status insofar as it bears on psychological well-being, habits, and attitudes (Millon, Green, & Meagher, 1982).

Domain IV—Psychiatric Disorders

Structured diagnostic interviews have been used increasingly for the objective formulation of substance-use disorders as well as other psychological diagnoses. Several instruments, all with good reliability, are currently available. The Structured Clinical Interview for DSM-III-R is the most recent comprehensive interview available (Spitzer, Williams, & Gibbon, 1987).

The Kiddie Schedule for Affective Disorders and Schizophrenia (Orvaschel, Puig-Antich, Chambers, Tabrizi, & Johnson, 1982) and the Diagnostic Interview for Children and Adolescents (Wellner, Reich, Herjanic, Jung, & Amado, 1987) are used most often for children and adolescents. These interviews also have a version that can be administered to a parent to obtain convergent validity of the findings accrued from the youngster.

Domain V—Social Competence

Social skills deficits are common in persons suffering from alcoholism or drug abuse. Deficiencies in assertiveness skills, refusal skills, and compliment-giving skills have been documented. A poor ability to manage conflict in interpersonal situations also may be linked to alcohol or drug abuse. Moreover, the exacerbation of poor social skills by ensuing stress or anxiety may lead to substance use as an acquired coping response. Thus, coping style must be determined as one component of the assessment of social skills.

At this time, no psychometrically standardized instrument is available for evaluating social skills. Although lacking standardization, various self-rating scales have been used for identifying social skills deficits and targeting behaviorally focused interventions. The same limitations exist with respect to coping style; however, two measures are informative – the Ways of Coping Scale (Folkman & Lazarus, 1980) and the Constructive Thinking Inventory (Epstein, 1987).

In addition to social skills, the comprehensive evaluation should document the person's capacity to exercise the skills required for everyday living. As society becomes more techno-logically complex, it is important to determine whether the client is capable of performing everyday tasks required for adaptive social adjustment. For example, can the person man-age a bank account, use bank-card machines, access directo-ries, obtain appropriate service information, use public trans-portation, satisfy personal needs with respect to food and clothing, and apply for a job? Deficiencies in any of these areas may exacerbate the level of experienced stress and thus pro-mote alcohol or drug abuse.

Furthermore, during the course of an evaluation, social skills can be inferred to some extent from the client's eye contact with the counselor, appropriateness and frequency of smiling, duration and lapses of verbal responses, affect, body gestures, and spontaneous communications.

Domain VI—Family Adjustment

Family organization and interactional patterns contribute to the etiology and maintenance of substance abuse. The transmission of alcoholism across generations is influenced, to some degree, by familial attitudes and rituals surrounding alcohol consumption and the meanings attached to alcohol ingestion (Steinglass, Bennett, Wolin, & Reiss, 1987). Two self-report instruments quantifying the severity of family prob-lems are the Family Environment Scale (Moos & Moos, 1981), which assesses family values and behaviors across 10 dimen-sions, and the Family Assessment Measure, which emphasizes interactional patterns among family members (Skinner, Steinhauer, & Santa Barbara, 1983).

From the standpoint of clinical diagnosis, four major issues must be addressed. First, it is essential to characterize the contribution of psychological disorders — including substance abuse — in the family. The greater the density of psychological disorder in family members of the client undergoing evaluation, the more problematic the family and the client are likely to be. Among young substance-abusing clients, it is especially important to record past as well as present physical or sexual abuse of the clients as a critical index of family dysfunction. Second, the causal relationship between family dysfunction and drug use behavior must be ascertained. How drug use precipitated the family problems — or, conversely, how family problems triggered drug use — must be investigated in the course of the diagnostic evaluation. Third, the reinforcement contingencies, if any, exercised by the family on the member having the drug use problem must be analyzed. For example, is the drug use ignored, punished, or positively reinforced? Fourth, the roles and status of each family member must be understood to the extent that maladjustment, conflict, or instability contributes to the family dysfunction that propels one member to seek alcohol or drugs as a means of coping with the resulting stress.

Domain VII—School Performance

For young alcohol or drug abusers, it is important to document school adjustment and performance. The school is the primary social environment during adolescence. Drug accessibility in or near school and, particularly, the peer-affiliation network of the adolescent are especially influential determinants of drug use initiation. Conduct problems and deviance from normal behavior commonly are associated with current substance abuse and future psychopathology.

An important aspect of school adjustment is the extent to which an adolescent participates in athletics and other extracurricular activities. These types of activities indicate how well the adolescent is socially integrated and accepted by peers. In addition, it is essential to evaluate academic achievement and learning aptitude in the basic skills. For example, learning disability, compounded by low self-esteem, may be a major factor propelling the teenager toward drug use as well as other nonnormative behavior. Standardized learning and achievement tests may be required to document the extent to which cognitive impairment and low achievement are involved in the motivation to use alcohol or drugs. A quick indication of whether such testing is needed is whether the client has been held back at least two grades or cannot master specific subjects.

Domain VIII—Work Adjustment

The rapid expansion of employee assistance programs illustrates the extent to which alcohol and drug abuse affects the workplace and, in turn, to which the workplace may influence alcohol or drug use. Stress in the workplace can have a multifactorial basis. For example, stress may occur as a consequence of the inability to meet performance standards, conflicts with other employees or supervisors, disruptive work schedules, and low job satisfaction. In the most extreme cases, unemployment as well as underemployment must be evaluated as a factor underlying substance abuse. Also, extensive travel and associated social obligations may place some persons in social situations where alcohol consumption is expected. No single factor in the workplace predisposes a person to substance abuse. Therefore, it is necessary to analyze, in detail, performance and adjustment in the workplace as an etiologic determinant of substance abuse.

Besides evaluating the job demands and workplace environment, it is necessary to evaluate the client's behavioral disposition. For example, premorbid personality disorders (particularly antisocial personality disorder or social phobias) may contribute to job failure, which in turn may predispose the person to a substance use disorder. Furthermore, it is imperative to evaluate the particular job in the context of normal behavior with respect to alcohol and drug use. For example, persons who work in the entertainment industry, the military, or bars and lounges are more inclined to use alcohol and drugs. Access to addictive substances places the person at an increased risk simply by virtue of easy availability. Therefore, the vocational evaluation must not only identify specific job-related characteristics that predispose a client to alcohol or drug abuse, but it must also elucidate the personality and behavioral characteristics of the person. In particular, it should clarify how the vocational maladjustment resulted from an interaction between the person and the job environment. (For a more extensive discussion on substance abuse in the workplace, see Thomas [1996].)

Domain IX—Peer Relationships

A social network where drug use is commonplace will increase the likelihood that the person will engage in this behavior as well. Therefore, the availability of drugs and alcohol is important to evaluate in the context of peer relationships because ameliorating the substance use disorder may require abandoning long-standing friendships; changing the peer environment may be necessary to prevent relapse after treatment. The extent to which peer relationships are embedded in a pattern of nonnormative or antisocial behavior also must be evaluated because such maladjustment interacts with other aspects of role performance at work, at school, and in family life. However, standardized psychometric instruments for evaluating peer affiliation patterns have not been developed. As a consequence, this information must be accrued during the course of the diagnostic interview.

Because the social environment is a major source of reinforcement, it is essential to learn about the reward contingencies, role models, and social contextual characteristics associated with alcohol or drug use for the client. The client not only responds to a particular social environment but also seeks out an environment that has reinforcing value. Accordingly, during the course of the psychometric assessment, attempts should be made to learn why the client seeks out social interactions that have maladaptive consequences. From such an evaluation, social needs and motivational patterns that bear directly on the etiology and persistence of substance abuse for the client can be elucidated.

Domain X—Recreation and Leisure Activities

Alcohol and drug use is commonly associated with recreational and leisure activities. A person who does not have socially satisfying recreational activities, hobbies, or other leisure opportunities may resort to the use of alcohol or drugs as a means of passing time or to cope with stress or boredom. This may be particularly problematic among the elderly who are no longer gainfully employed and have not developed adequate, productive, or satisfying substitute behaviors. A somewhat similar problem may confront adolescents who have substantial free or unstructured time.

Assessment and counseling related to recreational and leisure activities constitute a newly developing specialty. No standardized evaluation procedure is presently available. Therefore, the counselor must obtain this information informally. Once it is determined that the absence of positively reinforcing pastimes is associated with substance abuse, or that recreational activities involve peers who use psychoactive substances, the client's lifestyle may be restructured.

Neuropsychological Assessment

In addition to the 10 domains, on occasion it is important to evaluate the cognitive capacities of chronic alcohol and drug abusers. Because cognitive capacity is prognostic of academic success, social adjustment, and vocational level, it is valuable to assess the client in this respect to develop a comprehensive rehabilitation program. This assessment typically falls within the purview of a neuropsychological evaluation. It should be conducted only *after* drug withdrawal has been completed, usually at least 1 month following detoxification.

Although neuropsychological testing to evaluate the integrity of the central nervous system (CNS) is time consuming, the unique contribution of such testing is that it enables determination of the presence and location of cerebral lesions and quantifies severity in the context of readily understood psychological processes (e.g., language, memory, abstracting, attention, and learning). By delineating the client's cognitive strengths and weaknesses, neuropsychological tests afford the important advantage of yielding information pertinent to vocational rehabilitation, educational planning, and psychosocial treatment.

A comprehensive neuropsychological evaluation must be balanced against the time and resources required to conduct such an evaluation. To be efficient, the neuropsychological evaluation should be conducted in three stages. As described by Tarter and Edwards (1987), the first stage of a comprehensive neuropsychological evaluation is an initial screening to determine whether evidence of a CNS disturbance is present. This stage of testing requires sensitive but nonspecific tests. Various brief instruments, such as the Mini Mental Status Exam (Folstein, Folstein, & McHugh, 1975), the Trail Making Test (Armitage, 1946), and the Symbol Digit Modalities Test (Smith, 1973) adequately serve this purpose.

The second stage of the evaluation includes the delineation of cognitive abilities and limitations. At this stage, standardized batteries, complemented where necessary by specialized tests, should be used to quantify the severity of cognitive impairment. The processes evaluated typically include speech and language, attention, psychomotor skills, learning and memory, and abstract reasoning ability. At this stage of the evaluation, hypotheses can be formulated about lesion localization and lateralization. Several standardized neuropsychological batteries are currently in wide use. The Halstead-Reitan Neuropsychological Test Battery (Reitan, 1955), the Luria-Nebraska Neuropsychological Test Battery (Golden, 1981), and the Pittsburgh Initial Neuropsychological Testing System (Goldstein, Tarter, Shelly, & Hegedus, 1983) are among the most comprehensive surveys of the major cognitive domains.

If significant impairment is noted in a specific cognitive domain, specialized comprehensive testing should be conducted to examine its severity and breadth; this is the third stage of the assessment. It is not only important for purposes of lesion localization, but perhaps is even more critical for posttreatment planning. Psychomotor impairments should be described in detail if the client works with power machinery or other safety risks exist. Visuoperceptual disturbances must be documented comprehensively if the person drives a car. Similarly, if a learning or memory deficit is identified, it should be evaluated further if the posttreatment plan includes educational or vocational rehabilitation. The end point of a neuropsychological assessment is a profile of cognitive strengths and weaknesses such that the resulting information can be applied to treatment or rehabilitation.

Stage 3:

Following assessment, coordinated intervention (prevention or treatment) that responds to the client's identified needs is implemented. Because of the complexity and common occurrence of health, psychological, and psychosocial disturbances concomitant with substance abuse, the resources of a multidisciplinary team frequently are required to address the client's needs effectively. In addition to the case manager, who can be any professional within a multidisciplinary team, the development of a coordinated and comprehensive intervention plan should encompass the contributions of persons with specialties in one or more of the 10 domains. In this multistage evaluation model, the intervention team is not a static entity. Rather, its composition is determined according to the findings accrued from the DUSI-R and the comprehensive assessment. In this manner, available personnel are used efficiently to lower the cost of intervention.

THE ROLE OF ASSESSMENT IN TREATMENT

Monitoring the Client During Intervention:

A disturbing shortcoming of many counselors is a failure to

recognize the value of periodic assessment during the course of intervention. An essential responsibility of the counselor is to monitor the treatment process and objectively quantify changes occurring during the intervention. Monitoring change in the client during intervention is increasingly becoming a requirement for reimbursement from third-party payers.

The need to obtain objective quantitative information must be balanced against using time that otherwise could be allocated to conduct treatment. One strategy for resolving this dilemma is to readminister the DUSI-R on a regular basis to chart changes. The DUSI-R versions that document severity of disturbance during the past month or past week can be used for this purpose. The culmination of periodic evaluations is a graphic portrayal of the intervention course with respect to changes that have occurred in the 10 domains assessed by the DUSI-R.

Relapse Prevention:

It is common that, after discharge from substance abuse treatment, the client is not seen again unless a florid relapse occurs. Initiating treatment after relapse is both difficult and costly; therefore, the potential for relapse should be addressed proactively. This is accomplished easily by a periodic checkup to assess the presence of prodromal indicators of relapse. Used as a measure of posttreatment monitoring, the DUSI-R can be mailed to the client and returned in the mail to the counselor. For only nominal cost, maintenance of intervention gains can be documented and, if necessary, "booster" treatment can be provided when the findings point to incipient relapse.

SUMMARY

All practitioners involved in health care are faced with increasing demands on their accountability while having to treat difficult problems with limited resources. A strategy that simultaneously addresses accountability and cost-effective service provision is to use a decision tree for evaluation and treatment. Such an approach involves three stages: two for assessment and one for intervention. This three-stage model was developed for suspected and known substance abusers, although in view of the 10 domains covered by the DUSI-R, this method probably also is applicable to other behavioral and psychosocial problems.

The central principle underlying the decision-tree assessment model is that the evaluation should be cost-efficient and practical. In addition, the evaluation also must provide the basis for prevention or treatment intervention targeted to the client's identified needs.

The first stage involves administering a 20-minute self-report (DUSI-R) to quantify problem severity across 10 domains of health and psychosocial adjustment. Based on the information accrued, the second stage consists of a comprehensive diagnostic examination in selected areas of disturbance identified by the DUSI-R. The third stage, intervention programming, connects assessment with intervention to develop an individualized intervention plan targeted to specific areas of disturbance. Finally, evaluation and intervention are linked in an ongoing basis by monitoring the course of an intervention and reducing the risk of relapse by periodic checkup evaluations conducted after treatment.

REFERENCES

Achenbach, T., & Edelbrock, C. (1983). *Manual for the child behavior checklist and revised child behavior profile.* Burlington, VT: University of Vermont, Department of Psychiatry.

American Psychiatric Association. (1987). *Diagnostic and statistical manual of mental disorders* (3rd ed., rev.). Washington, DC: Author.

Armitage, S. (1946). An analysis of certain psychological tests used for the evaluation of brain surgery. *Psychological Monographs, 60,* 277.

Epstein, S. (1987). *The constructive thinking inventory.* Amherst, MA: University of Massachusetts, Department of Psychology.

Folkman, S., & Lazarus, R. (1980). An analysis of coping in a middle-aged community sample. *Journal of Health and Social Behavior, 21,* 219–239.

Folstein, M. F., Folstein, S. E., & McHugh, P. R. (1975). Mini mental state. *Journal of Psychiatric Research, 12,* 189–198.

Golden, C. J. (1981). A standardized version of Luria's neuropsychological tests. In S. Filskov & T. J. Boll (Eds.), *Handbook of clinical neuropsychology.* New York: Wiley-Interscience.

Goldstein, G., Tarter, R., Shelly, C., & Hegedus, A. (1983). The Pittsburgh Initial Neuropsychological Testing System (PINTS): A neuropsychological screening battery for psychiatric patients. *Journal of Behavioral Assessment, 5,* 227–238.

Hathaway, S. R., & McKinley, J. C. (1951). *The Minnesota multiphasic personality inventory manual.* (Rev.). New York: Psychological Corp.

Kaminer, Y., Bukstein, O. G., & Tarter, R. E. (1991). The Teen Addiction Severity Index: Rationale and reliability. *The International Journal of the Addictions, 26,* 219–226.

Kirisci, L., Mezzich, A., & Tarter, R. (1995). Norms and sensitivity of the adolescent version of the drug use screening inventory. *Addictive Behaviors, 20,* 149-157.

McClellan, A., Luborsky, L., Woody, G., & O'Brien, C. (1980). An improved diagnostic evaluation instrument for substance abuse patients: The Teen Addiction Severity Scale Index. *Journal of Nervous and Mental Disease, 168,* 26–33.

Millon, T., Green, C., & Meagher, R. (1982). *Millon behavioral health inventory manual.* Minneapolis, MN: National Computer Systems.

Moos, R., & Moos, B. S. (1981). *Family environment scale manual.* Palo Alto, CA: Consulting Psychologists Press.

Orvaschel, H., Puig-Antich, J., Chambers, W., Tabrizi, M. A., & Johnson, R. (1982). Retrospective assessment of prepubertal major depression with the Kiddie-SADS-E. *Journal of the American Academy of Child and Adolescent Psychiatry, 2,* 392–397.

Reitan, R. (1955). An investigation of the validity of Halstead's measures of biological intelligence. *Archives of Neurology and Psychiatry, 73,* 28–35.

Schinka, J. A. (1984). *Health problems checklist.* Odessa, FL: Psychological Assessment Resources.

Skinner, H. A., Steinhauer, P. D., & Santa Barbara, J. (1983). The family assessment measure. *Canadian Journal of Community Mental Health, 2,* 91–105.

Smith, A. (1973). *Symbol digit modalities test.* Los Angeles, CA: Western Psychological Services.

Spitzer, R. L., Williams, J. B. W., & Gibbon, M. (1987). *Instruction manual for the structured clinical interview for* DSM-III-R *(SCID, 4/1/87).* (Rev.). New York: New York State Psychiatric Institute.

Steinglass, P., Bennett, L., Wolin, S., & Reiss, D. (1987). *The alcoholic family.* New York: Basic Books.

Tarter, R. (1990). Evaluation and treatment of adolescent substance abuse: A decision-tree method. *American Journal of Drug and Alcohol Abuse, 16,* 1–46.

Tarter, R. (1995). Rationale and method of client treatment matching. *The Counselor, 56,* 99–103.

Tarter, R., & Edwards, K. (1987). Brief and comprehensive neuropsychological assessment of alcoholism and drug abuse. In L. Hartlage, M.
Ashen, & L. Hornsby (Eds.), *Essentials of Neuropsychological Assessment*
(pp. 138–162). New York: Springer.

Tarter, R., & Kirisci, L. (in press). The drug use screening inventory for
adults: Psychometric structure and discriminative sensitivity. *American
Journal of Drug and Alcohol Abuse.*

Tarter, R., Laird, S., Bukstein, O., & Kaminer, Y. (1993). Validation of the
drug use screening inventory: Preliminary findings. *Psychological
Addictions Behavior, 6,* 223–232.

Tellingen, A. (1982). [Multidimensional personality questionnaire.]
Unpublished raw data. University of Minnesota, Minneapolis, MN.

Thomas, J. C. (1996). Substance abuse in the workplace: The role of
employee assistance programs. In *The Hatherleigh guide to treating
substance abuse, part II* (pp. 1-55). New York: Hatherleigh Press.

Wanberg, K., & Horn, J. (1985). *The alcohol use inventory: A guide to the use
of the paper and pencil version.* Fort Logan, CO: Multivariate Measurement
Consultants.

Wellner, Z., Reich, W., Herjanic, B., Jung, D., & Amado, K. (1987).
Reliability, validity, and parent-child agreement studies of the Diagnostic Interview for Children and Adolescents (DICA). *Journal of the American Academy of Child and Adolescent Psychiatry, 26,* 649–653.

2

Medications Used in Rehabilitation Settings: Considerations for Therapists and Counselors

Susan Gallagher-Lepak, RN, MSN, Fong Chan, PhD, Donald Kates, MS, Laura Dunlap, MA, Kristine M. Eiring, MS, and Joseph Cunningham, MS.

For a list of authors' affiliations, see page 47.

KEY POINTS

- A basic knowledge of pharmacology permits therapists and counselors to assess the effects of medications on client functioning, the work environment, and job interviews. It can also help professionals recognize cases of improper dosage, noncompliance, and atypical reactions to medications so they may alert prescribing physicians.

- This chapter reviews major medications applicable to many patients and describes a variety of new agents that have been introduced. The basic principles regarding pharmacologic treatment are described: drug function, drug concentration, absorption rates, distribution throughout the body, excretion, biotransformation, tolerance, and dependence.

- The three forms of side effects to medications are *expected side effects* (those that commonly occur in high concentrations or when drugs are taken for long periods), *idiosyncratic toxicities* (unpredictable effects that occur rarely), and *allergic responses* (adverse immunologic reactions).

Parts of this chapter were extracted from: Gallagher-Lepak, S., Chan, F., Roldan, R., Reid, C., Saura, K., & Kates, D. (in press.) Clinical pharmacology for vocational evaluators. In F. Chan, D. W. Wong, B. Richardson, K. H. Byon (Eds.), Vocational assessment and evaluation of people with disabilities. Lake Zurich, IL: Vocational Consultants Press.

INTRODUCTION

Counselors should possess a basic knowledge of pharmacology, particularly about the medications commonly prescribed to their clients who have disabilities, such as substance abuse disorders. This information permits the counselor to assess the effects of medications on client functioning, the work environment, and job interviews — from both performance and behavioral standpoints. Similar to disabilities, medications may produce functional limitations that consequently become important considerations in the rehabilitation planning process.

Knowledge about pharmacology can assist the counselor in determining functional limitations caused by not only the medication itself but also by factors such as improper dosage, noncompliance, and atypical reactions to a particular medication (Falvo & Maki, 1991). Some medications may produce sensory or communication deficits, whereas others may affect cognitive functioning, moods, and tolerance for physical activity.

Certain medications may affect a client's level of consciousness, thus affecting performance in environments where optimum awareness is a necessity. Alterations of consciousness produced by some medications may significantly affect functioning in a job interview, reduce performance on assessment measures, and preclude the client from operating various types of machinery. Medications also may produce difficulties in hand-eye coordination; diminish finger or hand dexterity; and affect speed, balance, and endurance.

Another factor the counselor must consider is how medications are managed in the client's environment. Certain medications may require a hospital setting for administration, whereas others may require modifications to the work schedule that allow the client to take medications at prescribed times. Counselors should be aware that such medications may have an impact on a client's social environment if they produce socially unacceptable side effects or physical/psychological dependency.

The purpose of this chapter is to provide counselors with a general review of major drug classes applicable to their clients. Over the past several years, a variety of new drugs that produce fewer side effects have been marketed. These medications are highlighted throughout this chapter.

PHARMACOLOGIC PRINCIPLES

Pharmacology is the scientific discipline dealing with the study of all aspects of drugs (e.g., properties and effects). A drug is any substance, other than food, that alters the structure or function of a living organism. The term *medication* often is used to refer to drugs intentionally used for health purposes. Psychopharmacology refers to drugs that are specifically used to treat psychiatric disorders. Medical pharmacology primarily pertains to drugs used to prevent and treat medical disorders (Murray, 1987).

Drugs are labeled with a chemical, generic, and brand (or proprietary) name. The chemical name provides a complete chemical description and is derived from the rules of organic chemistry for naming compounds. A generic name, such as diazepam, is the official and legal name of the drug. A brand name, such as Valium (for diazepam), connects the medicine to a particular manufacturer. For the purposes of this chapter, medications are identified by the generic name with the trade name in parentheses at first mention.

Drugs exert a variety of effects. Effects of medications vary among individuals based on several factors: age, body weight, route of administration (e.g., orally or via injection), drug combinations, pathology, and compliance with taking the drug as prescribed (Falvo & Maki, 1991). Several groups of people, especially older adults, often show increased sensitivity to medications. In fact, older adults usually require lower doses of medications to avoid serious side effects (Hughes & Pierattini, 1992). No drug has only one mechanism of action. For example, the action of aspirin includes reduction of minor pain, fever, and inflammation in addition to prolonged bleeding time and gastric irritation.

Drug Function:

Although many of the physiologic mechanisms of drug action are known, these are rarely observed and are not used in the assessment of drug function. Drug function is determined by the concentration of the drug in the bloodstream and by the individual's reaction to the drug. Pharmacologic treatments are targeted to specific systems or processes. However, it is important to remember that the effect of a drug treatment may not be limited to the intended target area because many medications affect multiple systems.

Drug Concentration:

Drug concentrations are determined by the interaction of four processes: absorption, distribution, excretion, and biotransformation. Drug concentrations are generally assumed to affect functioning in a consistent way. However, three major concerns are associated with this assumption. First, continuous administrations of a medication can eventually lead to habituation and desensitization. If this occurs, larger doses will be required to achieve the same effect. Second, the presence of adequate drug concentrations does not necessarily equate with clinical responsiveness. Some medications require weeks before observable clinical changes are evident. Third, there are individual differences in reaction and response to drug treatments. Therefore, when discussing drug concentration and function, these three factors should be considered.

Absorption

Absorption is the process by which the drug enters the bloodstream. In order of increasing absorption speed, this can occur through oral, topical (through the skin), intramuscular, and intravenous administration. Each form has its own advantages depending on the type of drug and the desired absorption rate. For example, oral administration can be performed by the patients themselves and allows for a slower absorption. In contrast, intravenous injection allows for faster and more complete absorption but requires administration by a medical professional.

Distribution

This process occurs after the drug is absorbed into the blood. The blood, with the accompanying drug, is distributed throughout the body via the bloodstream. Large quantities of drugs often are absorbed into the body's cells for processing at a later time. The complete distribution of drugs can be affected by their physical or chemical characteristics because some bodily areas limit or prevent the passing of drugs. For example, the brain is protected from numerous chemicals by the meninges, which form the blood-brain barrier. Few drugs can penetrate this barrier, thereby protecting the brain from potentially adverse side effects.

Excretion

Drugs can be expelled from the body through feces, sweat, breath, and saliva, but the primary route of excretion is through urination by way of the kidneys. As blood is filtered through the kidneys, the drug is removed. The rate of excretion is determined by the drug's concentration and half-life (the time required for half of the drug to be removed from the body). Most drugs follow this exponential rate of decay; however, a few — most notably aspirin and the anticonvulsant phenytoin (Dilantin) — are excreted at a fixed rate. These drugs are removed from the body at a steady pace that does not vary with drug concentration levels.

Biotransformation

Biotransformation is the process by which the body converts chemicals into an alternate form. Some drugs are incompatible with kidney excretion in their administered form. As a result, such drugs must be transformed (usually by the liver) into another form so that they can be removed from the body. The drug biotransformation process can vary according to individual differences in metabolic rates and to multiple drug interactions. For example, alcohol alters the biotransformation of many drugs, thereby adversely affecting blood concentration levels and altering the drugs' effects. Without complete information regarding a client's use of prescribed and unprescribed drugs, the effectiveness of any pharmacologic treatment can only be hypothesized.

SPECIAL CONSIDERATIONS

When reviewing a patient's current pharmacologic treatment profile, the following should be considered: side effects, compliance, drug interactions, tolerance, dependence, and abuse of alcohol or other drugs.

Side Effects:

The potential side effects associated with different medications always must be considered when reviewing a client's medical status. In some circumstances, the side effects of a particular medication may be extremely severe but must be endured for the individual to receive the necessary treatment. In other situations, the side effects may only affect a limited area of functioning. Therefore, the range of possible side effects of a medication should be reviewed in detail with the client and the physician.

Three forms of side effects are associated with pharmacologic treatments: expected effects, idiosyncratic toxicities, and allergies. *Expected side effects* are the problems that commonly occur when drug levels or concentrations become too high or when some drug treatments are continued for extended periods of time. *Idiosyncratic toxicities* are unpredictable side effects that occur rarely in few persons. *Allergic responses* are adverse immunologic reactions to particular drugs.

Adherence/Compliance:

Adherence refers to how closely the client follows the prescribed pharmacotherapeutic regimen. This includes both the correct dosage and the designated time interval between administrations. Because absorption, distribution, excretion, and biotransformation rates vary, achieving optimal results depends on accurate drug dosage and administration intervals. In the hospital setting, compliance can be readily monitored. However, in outpatient cases, adherence is completely controlled by the client. In both circumstances, clients must understand why compliance with drug prescriptions is necessary.

Drug Interactions:

Although drug interactions are primarily the concern of the treating physician, counselors should be aware of this factor because the medical problems facing persons with disabilities often require multiple medications. These medications may interact not only with each other but also with over-the-counter drugs, other prescribed drugs, or alcohol to alter the treatment effect adversely. The interaction of different drugs usually results in an increase or decrease in the desired effects. For example, alcohol exaggerates the sedative effects of anxiolytics. All clients must be made aware of the possibility of drug interactions. Care also must be taken to ensure that all prescribed medications are known to the treating physician.

Tolerance:

Tolerance is a decrease in the effectiveness of a pharmacologic treatment caused by repeated administrations. As tolerance increases, so must the dosage of drug required to achieve the same therapeutic effect. Drug tolerance is believed to result from improved drug elimination processes and decreased sensitivity of body cells. This is the reason many long-term pharmacologic treatments lose their effectiveness with repeated administrations.

Dependence:

A serious concern for many pharmacologic treatments is the risk of dependence. Repeated exposure to some medications, such as the benzodiazepines, can lead to physical dependence. Long-term treatments also can result in psychological dependence on the drug. If left unchecked, physiologic and psychological dependencies can lead to drug addiction.

Drug and Alcohol Abuse:

The interactions between drugs and alcohol can greatly alter the effects of prescribed medications. The dual diagnosis of a physical disability (e.g., spinal cord injury, traumatic brain injury, mental disorder) and alcoholism or substance abuse is not uncommon. Alcohol and substance abuse problems frequently interfere with rehabilitation programs and often lead to poor outcomes. In assessing a client's medical history and status, information regarding alcohol or other drug use and abuse is vital.

Abbreviations:

Most prescribed medications have specific instructions (which take the form of a Latin abbreviation) regarding how the medication is to be taken. Counselors may encounter such abbreviations in referral information included in medical reports or hospital records. Prescription instructions usually follow the name of the prescribed medication. For example, the prescription for phenobarbital (Luminal) taken twice a day would be written *phenobarbital b.i.d.* Other commonly used abbreviations are listed in Table 2.1.

Table 2.1
ABBREVIATIONS FOR PRESCRIPTION INSTRUCTIONS

aa.	*ana*; of each
a. c.	*ante cibum*; before meals
b. i. d.	*bis in die*; twice daily
c	*cum*; with
gtt.	guttae (drops)
h. s.	*hora somni*; at bedtime
IM	intramuscularly
IV	intravenously
per os	by mouth
p. r. n.	*pro re nata*; as needed
q. d.	*quaque die*; every day
q. h.	*quaque hora*; every hour
q. i. d.	*quarter in die*; four times a day
q. l.	*quantum libet*; as much as desired
sub-q	subcutaneously

Source: Falvo, D., & Maki, D. R. (1991). Medications: Considerations for rehabilitation planning. *Journal of Applied Rehabilitation Counseling, 14*, 28–31.

PSYCHOPHARMACOLOGY

The major drug classes used to treat mental disorders are anxiolytics, antidepressants, and antipsychotics. These drugs primarily affect the function of the central nervous system (CNS; brain and spinal cord) and subsequently alter behavior.

Anxiolytics:

Anxiolytics, often called minor tranquilizers, depress the CNS, thereby exerting an anxiety-relieving or calming action. This type of medication is widely used to treat acute anxiety disorders and a variety of general medical disorders such as musculoskeletal conditions, convulsive disorders, alcohol withdrawal, and temporary sleep problems. Major types of medications within this category include barbiturates, benzodiazepines, and an entirely new class of drugs that includes buspirone (BuSpar).

Barbiturates are used less often than in the past because of their strong addictive and CNS depressant effects (such as respiratory depression), especially in cases of overdose. Benzodiazepines are the most frequently prescribed antianxiety agents; diazepam is the fourth most frequently prescribed medication in the United States (Holmes, 1991). Approximately 14 benzodiazepines are currently marketed; the most commonly used include diazepam (Valium), alprazolam (Xanax), lorazepam (Ativan), oxazepam (Serax), and chlordiazepoxide (Librium) (Spiegel, 1989).

All of the benzodiazepines are potentially addictive although less so than the barbiturates. Many benzodiazepines have a rapid onset of action (within 30–60 minutes) and achieve peak blood levels within 2–4 hours. This swift effect can produce a euphoric "rush" that may enhance the potential for abuse. After taking benzodiazepines for several days, life-threatening convulsions can occur if the medication is stopped abruptly. For this reason alone, it is recommended that patients always check with their physicians before altering the use of a benzodiazepine in any way.

Other common side effects of benzodiazepines include sedation, drowsiness, poor coordination, and dizziness. These drugs also have been implicated in attention, concentration, and memory deficits (Cope, 1986). Strong consideration should be given to these potential side effects when evaluating factors such as work performance and work environments that require attention to detail, driving, or operating potentially dangerous machinery. Finally, counselors should be aware that the sedative effects of benzodiazepines and barbiturates are potentiated (greater than addictive effect) when taken with CNS depressants such as alcohol or analgesics.

Buspirone, a new anxiolytic, differs from barbiturates and benzodiazepines in that it is nonsedating and nonaddictive.

However, buspirone is slow acting, requiring 2–6 weeks of treatment before therapeutic effects are seen. Individuals taking this medication need to be aware of this timing to avoid premature discontinuation of the drug due to perceived ineffectiveness.

Antidepressants:

Antidepressants prescribed for treatment of unipolar depression can be broadly classified into three categories: tricyclic antidepressants (TCAs), monoamine oxidase inhibitors (MAOIs), and selective serotonin reuptake inhibitors (SSRIs). Antidepressants are primarily prescribed for their mood-elevating effects and are effective in the treatment of depression and other conditions, such as panic disorder, agoraphobia, bulimia nervosa, and obsessive-compulsive disorder (OCD). (A comprehensive review of antidepressant medications by Delgado and Gelenberg [1994, 1996] is an excellent resource on this topic for interested readers.)

Commonly used TCAs include amitriptyline (Elavil), imipramine (Tofranil), nortriptyline (Aventyl, Pamelor), desipramine (Norpramin, Pertofrane), doxepin (Sinequan), maprotiline (Ludiomil), and protriptyline (Vivactil). All TCAs have a lag period of 2–4 weeks before therapeutic effects are apparent (Arana & Hyman, 1991). Common reasons for a lack of improvement in depressive symptoms include an insufficient duration of treatment, inadequate dosage, and failure to follow prescription instructions.

Side effects from these medications can significantly affect work performance and social interactions. Common side effects with TCAs include anticholinergic effects (dry mouth, constipation, and blurry vision). Weight gain and low blood pressure when standing, otherwise known as orthostatic hypotension, may occur. Amitriptyline and doxepin produce psychomotor sedation and are more often used to treat cases of agitated depression.

The MAOIs are frequently used when TCAs are not effective for a certain patient. In addition, MAOIs are more effective in the treatment of atypical depressions that present primarily with anxiety and phobic symptoms, masked depressions (e.g., hypochrondriasis), and anorexia nervosa (Preston & Johnson, 1990). Commonly used MAOIs include tranylcypromine (Parnate) and phenelzine (Nardil).

Greater caution must be used with MAOIs because of the possibility of serious side effects. The most serious problem that can occur is a rapid elevation in blood pressure, or hypertensive crisis, resulting from interaction between MAOIs and foods containing the amino acid tyramine. Foods such as fava beans, herring, many cheeses, red wine, and chocolate contain moderate to high amounts of tyramine. Other common side effects of MAOIs include weight gain and orthostatic hypotension.

Several new drugs known as second-generation atypical antidepressants have been developed and recently have received much publicity. Trazodone (Desyrel), nafazodone (Serzone), and amoxapine (Asendin) — for psychotic depression — are examples. Unlike TCAs, these medications are less likely to cause anticholinergic effects and weight gain, both of which are common reasons for noncompliance with TCAs. Side effects of these atypical antidepressants include overstimulation that may lead to nervousness, weight loss, and insomnia.

Among the various treatments for depression, the SSRIs have received the most attention in recent years because of their ability to affect specific sites in the brain (i.e., only at those synapses involved in the uptake of serotonin) and, therefore, to produce fewer side effects than other antidepressant agents. The medications in this category include fluoxetine (Prozac), sertraline (Zoloft), paroxetine (Paxil), and fluvoxamine (Luvox). Fluoxetine has received considerable attention, mostly because of anecdotal claims that it may induce suicidal ideation; however, counselors should know that these effects have not been substantiated in large clinical studies (Potter, Rudorfer, & Manji, 1991). The SSRIs have proved effective in the treatment of major depression, OCD, and panic disorder.

Clomipramine (Anafranil) and venlafaxine (Effexor) block the reuptake of serotonin but function as inhibitors of norepinephrine uptake as well. Clomipramine, widely prescribed for many years in Canada and Europe for the treatment of depression, was only recently approved (in 1989) by the Food and Drug Administration (FDA) for distribution in the United States. It is one of three drugs (in addition to fluoxetine and fluvoxamine) approved by the FDA for treating OCD. In 1994, the FDA approved venlafaxine for the treatment of major depression, and early reports indicate that it may be more effective than fluoxetine in patients suffering from major depression (Delgado & Gelenberg, 1994).

Another relatively new antidepressant is bupropion (Wellbutrin), which attained clinical infamy in the early 1980s when its phase III trials were suspended by the FDA due to a high incidence of seizures. This agent, which serves as a CNS stimulant and blocks the reuptake of dopamine, increases locomotor activity and may lead to restlessness, insomnia, anorexia, and psychosis. The risk of seizures with bupropion is substantially increased by certain predisposing factors (e.g., history of seizures, head trauma, brain tumor, anorexia nervosa, and bulimia nervosa); therefore, this medication should be avoided by patients who are taking antipsychotics, by alcoholic patients, or by patients known to be — or even suspected of — abusing benzodiazepines (Delgado & Gelenberg, 1994).

Medications for Bipolar Disorder

Lithium (Eskalith, Lithane) is the drug of choice for treatment of bipolar disorders. It exerts a mood-stabilizing effect in which the frequency and severity of manic episodes and depressive episodes are reduced. Lithium begins to normalize symptomatology within 1–3 weeks (Medical Economics Data Production Co., 1995). Blood monitoring must also be conducted regularly because of a narrow range between therapeutic and toxic blood levels. Common side effects of lithium include fine hand tremors, polyuria (increased urination), weight gain, and dry mouth.

Issues to Consider with Antidepressant Medications

Counselors should evaluate several issues with regard to persons taking antidepressant medications, including the potential for blurred vision secondary to anticholinergic effects, hand tremors, and sedation. Although antidepressants are used to elevate mood, specific drugs, such as amitriptyline, have sedating properties that should be avoided in patients with jobs requiring a high level of concentration and sustained mental vigilance (e.g., working with dangerous machinery and driving). In addition, the consumption of alcohol can be problematic in combination with any antidepressant. For example, the TCAs and lithium potentiate the effect of alcohol, thereby resulting in greater-than-expected intoxication and subsequent sedation (Arana & Hyman, 1991). All things considered, the counselor may want to suggest that vocational planning be postponed until the full effects of some medications are realized.

Antipsychotics:

Antipsychotics, sometimes referred to as major tranquilizers, are used for the symptomatic treatment of schizophrenia and states of agitation that accompany psychotic syndromes. They are also used to treat other syndromes such as mania, agitation following head injury, and depression with agitated symptoms. The therapeutic effects of these medications include sedation, calming, and antipsychotic effects — the latter of which is evidenced by reduced hallucinations, delusions, and confusion. Although sedative effects appear early after drug administration, the antipsychotic effects generally do not occur until after several weeks of treatment (Spiegel, 1989).

The side effects of antipsychotics can be visible and disturbing, which is frequently the reason why patients elect to discontinue these medications. Primary side effects of concern include sedation, anticholinergic effects, and extrapyramidal side effects (EPSs).

The EPSs result from drug effects on parts of the CNS that

control and coordinate movement. EPSs include dystonic reactions (muscle spasms of the head, neck, lips, and tongue), akathisia (a nervous feeling and involuntary motor restlessness), and parkinsonian effects (mask-like facial expression, shuffling gait, tremors).

Commonly used antipsychotics can be described with reference to their overall side effect profiles (Table 2.2). Bothersome side effects of antipsychotics can be treated by reducing the dose of medication, using a different medication within the class, or using an additional medication to treat the undesired effect. Antiparkinsonian agents, such as benztropine mesylate (Cogentin) and amantadine (Symmetrel), often are used to treat EPSs. Tardive dyskinesia, a long-term complication of antipsychotic drug administration, cannot be treated effectively and is characterized by involuntary rhythmic movements of the trunk, extremities, and mouth. Such side effects may be viewed as socially inappropriate in a work environment, thus interfering with successful integration into a job setting.

Clozapine (Clozaril), a relatively new antipsychotic medication, was released in the United States for general use in 1990 and has shown promise for individuals who do not respond to typical antipsychotics. The mechanism of action and pharmacologic profile are different from other antipsychotics in that clozapine blocks dopaminergic activity (at the DA_1 and DA_2 [dopamine] receptors) and, therefore, has a more pronounced effect on dopamine-related behaviors. Also, clozapine has been associated with significantly fewer side effects, including fewer EPSs and less tardive dyskinesia (Meltzer, 1988). Side effects do occur, however, and include sedation, anticholinergic effects, and the risk of agranulocytosis (low white blood cell count).

Risperidone (Risperdal) is the newest addition to the class of medications that aim to reduce symptoms of psychosis. Risperidone's pharmacokinetics set it apart from its sister medications because it is an antagonist of both serotonin and dopamine. In clinical trials thus far, this medication has been

Table 2.2
COMMONLY USED ANTIPSYCHOTICS AND THEIR SIDE EFFECT PROFILES

Drug	Sedation	Anticholinergic Effects	Extrapyramidal Side Effects
Chlorpromazine (Thorazine)	high	high	low
Thioridazine (Mellaril)	high	high	low
Haloperidol (Haldol)	low	low	high
Fluphenazine (Prolixin)	low	low	high
Thiothixene (Navane)	low	low	high
Trifluoperazine (Stelazine)	low	low	high

Adapted from: Preston, J., & Johnson, J. (1990). *Clinical psychopharmacology made ridiculously simple.* Miami: MedMaster, Inc.

effective in reducing both the positive symptoms (e.g., hallucinations, delusions, and catatonia) *and* negative symptoms (e.g., social deficits, apathy, and poor motivation) of schizophrenia (Davis, 1994).

The use of antipsychotics with sedative properties (e.g., chlorpromazine [Thorazine]) can affect job performance and is contraindicated in patients whose jobs require high mental acuity, work with dangerous machinery, and driving. Antipsychotics with high anticholinergic properties can cause difficulty with visual acuity, especially with reading. These medications potentiate CNS depressants such as alcohol, pain medication, and barbiturates, thereby causing a greater intoxicating or sedating effect than is obviously desired. Drugs such as amphetamines, cocaine, and caffeine can exacerbate symptoms associated with schizophrenia (Benowitz, 1990).

MEDICAL PHARMACOLOGY

Medical pharmacology involves the use of drugs in the prevention and treatment of illnesses such as seizure disorder, chronic pain, spinal cord injury, and traumatic brain injury. Medications used in the treatment of these conditions will be reviewed.

Anticonvulsants:

Anticonvulsants (or antiepileptics) are used to prevent epileptic seizures, but they also have beneficial effects on mood and behavior. Recent reports support the use of several anticonvulsants in treating manic-depressive illness and clients with aggressive or violent behaviors. For example, carbamazepine (Tegretol), valproic acid (Depakene), and divalproex sodium (Depakote) are used in patients with bipolar disorder who do not respond to lithium. The most commonly prescribed anticonvulsants include phenytoin, clonazepam (Klonopin), carbamazepine, phenobarbital, and valproic acid.

The most prevalent side effects of these medications are sedation, drowsiness, and poor motor coordination. Phenytoin can cause tremulousness and hirsutism (abnormal hair growth). Furthermore, phenytoin and phenobarbital can depress general cognitive processing, even at therapeutic blood levels (Cope, 1986). Not surprisingly, carbamazepine is preferred because of its minimal adverse effects on cognition. Given the nature of the side effects, avoiding tasks that require mental acuity or physical coordination may be necessary, thus restricting certain employment options. The aforementioned side effects may also seriously impair or endanger the client in work settings involving dangerous machinery.

Drugs Used to Alleviate Pain:

Pain medications, or analgesics, are used to decrease or eliminate pain without inducing loss of consciousness. Analgesics are used for a variety of conditions, including acute pain following injury or surgical interventions, pain syndromes found with spinal cord injury, and many other chronic illnesses (e.g., arthritis). Chronic pain, in contrast, is more often treated with psychotropic medications, most notably benzodiazepines and antidepressants (Walsh, 1991).

Analgesics are categorized as narcotic or nonnarcotic. The term *narcotic* or *opioid* is used to refer to a group of drugs with morphine-like action. Narcotic analgesics exert an effect on pain receptors located in the brain and spinal cord. Common examples include hydromorphone (Dilaudid), meperidine (Demerol), oxycodone (Percocet, Percodan, Tylox), and codeine.

These medications have many undesirable side effects, such as sedation, drowsiness, constipation, and dependency with repeated use. Because of a high potential for abuse, prescriptions for narcotic analgesics are regulated by the Federal Substances Act, which specifies that only a 1-month prescription can be given with limited or no refills depending on the specific type of narcotic. The use of these medications can significantly impair mental acuity, consequently affecting performance on the job or in an evaluation situation. As indicated with other types of medications, alcohol and other CNS depressants can produce additive sedation.

Nonnarcotic analgesics, in contrast, exert their effect by reducing inflammation and blocking the transmission of pain impulses at the nerve ending. As a result, pain impulses are not transmitted via the peripheral nerves into the CNS. Commonly used nonnarcotic analgesics include aspirin (Bufferin), ibuprofen (Advil, Motrin), acetaminophen (Tylenol), naproxen (Naprosyn), and diflunisal (Dolobid). Nonnarcotic analgesics are nonaddictive, have relatively few side effects, and interfere minimally with work performance; however, because these medications reduce pain, work activity should be monitored to avoid further injury.

Drugs Used in Spinal Cord Injury:

Spinal cord injury impairs motor functions and bodily regulation by the autonomic nervous system below the level of injury. The autonomic nervous system regulates many "automatic" processes such as blood pressure, body temperature, and bowel mobility. Clients with spinal cord injury can be susceptible to side effects of many medications that alter the autonomic nervous system, such as antidepressants (Murray, 1987). Moreover, antispastic agents such as baclofen (Lioresal), dantrolene (Dantrium), and the benzodiazepine diazepam often are used to control muscle spasticity and maintain bowel functions. Baclofen can cause sedation and, on abrupt withdrawal, can also precipitate nightmares and hallucinations.

Anticholinergic medications, such as oxybutynin (Ditropan) and propantheline bromide (Pro-banthine), are used to treat spasmatic bladder contractions in persons with spinal cord injury. Lederle (Fibercon) and docusate calcium (Surfak) are used as part of a bowel management program; these medications have relatively few significant side effects.

Drugs Used in Traumatic Brain Injury:

Individuals with brain injury may show a multiplicity of physical, cognitive, and behavioral sequelae. The impairments may include poor coordination; difficulties with memory, learning, and judgment; and personality changes. Pharmacotherapy may be used to prevent and treat seizures as well as ameliorate mood disorders and extreme behavior problems. Depression is common after head injury and generally is treated with antidepressants, particularly those with low anticholinergic properties (e.g., desipramine) (Bachman, 1992). Emotional lability, which is also common after head injury, can be distressing to individuals and their families. Fluoxetine and carbamazepine have been helpful in stabilizing mood swings after head injury (Kneale & Eames, 1991; Sloan, Brown, & Pentland, 1992).

Aggressive and disruptive behaviors may follow moderate and severe head injury. Although drugs such as benzodiazepines, antipsychotics, lithium, and propranolol (Inderal) reduce these behaviors in some patients (Bachman, 1992), no single drug has proved consistently effective in the treatment of such behaviors. Propranolol, a medication traditionally used for blood pressure control, has been helpful in reducing restlessness and symptoms of anxiety after brain injury. Anticonvulsants typically are used for prophylaxis or treatment of posttraumatic seizures. The weight of empirical evidence suggests that carbamazepine has fewer adverse effects than other anticonvulsants and a lesser effect on cognitive functioning (Cope, 1986; Glenn, 1991). The use of alcohol after head injury is generally discouraged because of the potentiating effects on other CNS depressants such as benzodiazepines. Moreover, evidence suggests an increased sensitivity to the CNS effects of alcohol among persons with posttraumatic brain injury (Zasler, 1991).

SUMMARY

Pharmacotherapy is a complex field involving the development and application of medications to improve functioning. Basic information has been presented in this chapter to provide the counselor with material applicable to professional practice in rehabilitation settings. Potential side effects of medications, especially cognitive and psychological effects, have been emphasized. This information may be useful in comprehensively evaluating the functional capacities of individuals and in assisting them in the development of a realistic rehabilitation plan. Moreover, this information can help the counselor anticipate the impact on work performance of side effects due to medication, thus assisting the client in the counseling and placement process.

For more detailed information about medications, the counselor is advised to consult the *Physicians' Desk Reference* (Medical Economics Co., 1995) and the *Physicians' Desk Reference for Non-Prescription Drugs* (Medical Economics Co., 1996). These resources are available at most libraries and rehabilitation clinics. They are updated each year and contain a list of all currently available pharmaceutical products and relevant information on side effects and dosing.

REFERENCES

Arana, G. W., & Hyman, S. E. (1991). *Handbook of psychiatric therapy.* Boston, MA: Little, Brown.

Bachman, D. L. (1992). The diagnosis and management of common neurologic sequelae of closed head injury. *Journal of Head Trauma Rehabilitation, 7,* 50–59.

Benowitz, N. L. (1990). Clinical pharmacology of caffeine. *Annual Review of Medicine, 41,* 277–288.

Cope, D. N. (1986). The pharmacology of attention and memory. *Journal of Head Trauma Rehabilitation, 1,* 34–42.

Davis, J. M. (1994). Risperidone: Properties, use, efficacy, and side effects. *Directions in Psychiatry, 14*(spec rep, Aug 24), 4.

Delgado, P. L., & Gelenberg, A. J. (1994). Decision making in the use of antidepressants, II: Choosing a medication. *Directions in Psychiatry, 14*(22).

Delgado, P. L., & Gelenberg, A. J. (1996). Decision making in the use of antidepressants: Treatment considerations. In *The Hatherleigh guide to managing depression* (pp. 265–280). New York: Hatherleigh Press.

Falvo, D., & Maki, D. R. (1991). Medications: Considerations for rehabilitation planning. *Journal of Applied Rehabilitation Counseling, 14,* 28–31.
Glenn, M. B. (1991). Anticonvulsants reconsidered. *Journal of Head Trauma Rehabilitation, 6,* 85–88.

Holmes, D. (1991). *Abnormal psychology.* New York: HarperCollins.

Hughes, J. R., & Pierattini, R. A. (1992). An introduction to pharmaco-therapy for mental disorders. In J. Grabowski & G. R. VandenBos (Eds.), *Psychopharmacology: Basic mechanisms and applied interventions* (pp. 101-125). Washington, DC: American Psychological Association.

Kneale, T. A., & Eames, P. (1991). Pharmacology and flexibility in the rehabilitation of two brain-injured adults. *Brain Injury, 5,* 327-330.

Medical Economics Co. (1995). *Physicians' desk reference.* (49th ed.). Montvale, NJ: Author.

Medical Economics Co. (1996). *Physicians' desk reference for nonprescription drugs* (17th ed.). Montvale, NJ: Author.

Meltzer, H. (1988). Dimensions of outcome of clozapine. *British Journal of Psychiatry, 160,* 4-53.

Murray, P. K. (1987). Clinical pharmacology in rehabilitation. In B. Caplan (Ed.), *Rehabilitation psychology desk reference* (pp. 501-525). Rockville, MD: Aspen Publishers.

Potter, W. Z., Rudorfer, M. V., & Manji, H. (1991). The pharmacological treatment of depression. *New England Journal of Medicine, 325,* 633-642.

Preston, J., & Johnson, J. (1990). *Clinical psychopharmacology made ridiculously simple.* Miami: MedMaster Inc.

Sloan, R. L., Brown, K. W., & Pentland, B. (1992). Fluoxetine as a treatment for emotional lability after brain injury. *Brain Injury, 6,* 315-319.

Spiegel, R. (1989). *Psychopharmacology: An Introduction.* New York: Wiley.

Walsh, E. M. (1991). Psychopharmacology of chronic pain. *Journal of Psychopharmacology, 5,* 364-369.

Zasler, N. D. (1991). Neuromedical aspects of alcohol use following traumatic brain injury. *Journal of Head Trauma Rehabilitation, 6,* 78-80.

AUTHORS' AFFILIATIONS

Dr. Chan is Professor and Co-Director of the Rehabilitation Research and Training Center on Career Development, Department of Rehabilitation Psychology and Special Education, University of Wisconsin-Madison.

Ms. Gallagher-Lepak, Mr. Kates, Ms. Dunlap, and Ms. Eiring are doctoral students in the Department of Rehabilitation Psychology and Special Education, University of Wisconsin-Madison.

Mr. Cunningham is a doctoral student in the Clinical Psychology Program, Department of Psychology at the Illinois Institute of Technology, Chicago, IL.

3

Improved Detoxification from Drugs and Alcohol Through Nutrition

Jeffrey S. Bland, PhD

Dr. Bland is Founder and Chief Executive Officer, HealthComm International, Inc., Gig Harbor, WA.

KEY POINTS

- Alcohol and other substances suppress appetite and alter food consumption patterns, which cause nutrition problems in many addicted patients. Poor nutrition further impairs the absorption of nutrients into the body and exacerbates nutritional deficiencies.

- Substance abuse has an adverse impact on the body's detoxification mechanisms, which occur principally in the liver. Detoxification enzymes in the liver called *cytochrome P-450* are produced to compensate for the exposure to the substance. However, the liver also produces toxins called *oxygen-free radicals*, which damage the addicted patient's liver, brain, digestive tract, and nervous system.

- The body requires proper nourishment to protect against the toxic effects of oxygen-free radicals and the breakdown products of alcohol and drug detoxification.

- Nutritional intervention is an overlooked tool in the management of substance abuse. Few therapists are trained in nutrition and its effects on detoxification.

- The author presents a simple and effective nutrition plan called *the detoxification diet*, which improves the detoxifying capability of livers that have reduced functional capacity. Therapists need not be experts in nutrition to use this program with their patients who abuse substances.

INTRODUCTION

Alcoholism and other substance abuse problems share many features, one of which is a relationship to poor nutrition. Because alcohol and other substances suppress appetite and alter food consumption patterns, the addicted person often displays poor nutritional status, which further impairs the proper absorption of nutrients and, in turn, exacerbates nutritional problems.

Furthermore, substance abuse has a distinctly adverse impact on the body's detoxification mechanisms, which take place principally in the liver. Derangement of the detoxification process can result in an exposure to *metabolites* (breakdown products) of alcohol and other chemical substances, which further contributes to the physiologic addiction process.

THE PATHOPHYSIOLOGY OF SUBSTANCE ABUSE

Alcohol and other substances of abuse are metabolized by the liver by a family of detoxification enzymes called *cytochrome P-450* (Ruckpaul & Rein, 1989). These liver enzymes are inducible: when a person is addicted to a specific substance, the body tries to compensate for the exposure by enhancing the level and activity of these enzymes. However, the liver simultaneously produces a class of secondary toxins called *oxygen-free radicals*. The production of these substances is associated with damage to the addict's liver, brain, digestive tract, and nervous system.

THE ROLE OF NUTRITION

To protect against the damaging effects of these toxic chemicals and the breakdown products of alcohol and drug detoxification, the body requires proper nourishment with various protector nutrients, such as vitamin C, vitamin E, and *carotene* (the orange-red pigment from fruits and vegetables such as carrots), as well as such minerals as zinc, manganese, and copper. Adequate intake of dietary protein is also important to help support the body's proper detoxification pathways (Anderson & Conney, 1979).

With proper nourishment, the damaging effects of the detoxification process are minimized, and the withdrawal effects during the "drying-out" period are reduced. Many therapists have found that those who are addicted to alcohol and other substances can experience improved success in a treatment program if they are properly nourished with the protector nutrients, the B-complex vitamins, and magnesium. Doses of nutrients that have been used for this purpose are listed in Table 3.1.

TABLE 3.1
NUTRIENTS APPROPRIATE FOR THOSE UNDERGOING DETOXIFICATION

200 IU vitamin E
1000 mg vitamin C
10 mg carotene
10 mg vitamins B_1, B_2, and B_6
50 mg vitamin B_3
20 µg vitamin B_{12}
400 µg folic acid
20 mg zinc
2 mg copper
5 mg manganese
400 mg magnesium
70 g high-quality dietary protein

Improvements in nutritional status enable the liver to perform its function in detoxification without damage to the body from the toxic effects of oxygen-free radicals. The reduction of toxic substances through improved detoxification also results in lowered addiction potential.

Nutritional intervention is an overlooked tool in the management of substance abuse. Because most therapists are not trained in nutrition and its effects on detoxification, application of this important adjunctive method of therapy is not included in the comprehensive client management plan.

Fortunately, the therapist need not be an expert in nutrition to apply this nutrition concept. Over the past 4 years, we have been involved in the development and evaluation of a simple and effective nutritional intervention program to assist in liver detoxification. Once understood, this program can easily be applied to clients who may suffer from a variety of substance abuse problems. It can be integrated within all traditional approaches to managing substance abuse to improve program success, lower recidivism, and reduce the adverse health effects associated with substance abuse and its treatment.

EVALUATING NUTRITIONAL STATUS

We have devised a method to evaluate liver function with regard to detoxification. With this information, the nutritional component of the treatment program can be implemented. Its success can be followed by an evaluation of the program's effect on the liver's ability to detoxify toxic substances and render them ready for excretion. The test requires the client to consume a standard dose of caffeine in purified form along with a measured dose of sodium benzoate, a common food preservative that retards mold growth. Saliva samples are taken at 2 and 14 hours after the caffeine administration, and urine is collected for 4 hours. The saliva samples are tested at the laboratory (Great Smokies Diagnostic Laboratory, Asheville, North Carolina) for caffeine levels and the urine for *hippuric acid*, the detoxification product from sodium benzoate. The more rapidly the caffeine disappears from the saliva and the more hippuric acid excreted in the 4-hour urine sample, the greater the rate of detoxification (Renner, Wiethholtz, Huguenin, Arnaud, & Presig, 1984; Tietz, 1976). This protocol has been used extensively in our studies to evaluate liver detoxification status and to follow the success of a nutritional intervention program designed to improve the effectiveness of a treatment program.

Altered test values for either caffeine or benzoate reveal modified or ineffective detoxifying function of the individual's liver. Indications of poor detoxification ability is predicative of a more difficult course and the potential for compliance or outcome. Recent studies (e.g., Rea, 1992) indicate that individuals who have multiple chemical or substance abuse exposure may have an even more difficult time in detoxification. Drugs, alcohol, cigarettes, and medications all work together to alter the detoxification ability of the liver; these complicating factors make it even more important to implement a nutrition intervention program.

THE DETOXIFICATION DIET

We have developed a specific diet that is high in nutrients known significantly to improve or "upregulate" the detoxifying capability of a liver that has reduced functional liver capacity. Earlier studies (e.g., Anderson & Kappas, 1991) had already shown that diet is important in the regulation of cytochrome P-450 and that it can also be affected by the amount and type of protein, fat, and carbohydrate in the diet. Other research (Bland, Barrager, Reedy, & Bland, 1995) had revealed that specific vitamins, minerals, and conditionally essential nutrients, such as glutathione and the amino acid L-cysteine, can influence liver detoxification.

We conducted a 21-day, placebo-controlled intervention trial to evaluate the effect of this nutrient-tailored diet on the liver's ability to process foreign substances and prepare them for excretion. The caffeine and benzoate tests were used to evaluate liver function during this study. The test and placebo diets were similar in calories but differed in the level of specific nutrients recognized to help support improved liver detoxification.

Participants were evaluated before and after the test diet or placebo intervention by the caffeine and benzoate tests. The physical signs and symptoms experienced by the participants in this study were evaluated using the Metabolic Screening Questionnaire (Figure 3.1). Scores greater than 100 points on the questionnaire indicate significant toxicity problems needing nutritional support, whereas scores between 50 and 99 points indicate moderate health problems associated with metabolic toxicity. The questionnaire is derived from the Cornell Medical Index, a respected medical evaluation instrument, and has now been used with several thousand people going through a detoxification program to follow the success of the program.

The results of this placebo-controlled diet intervention program were remarkable. Before the diet intervention, the liver detoxification ability of both the test and placebo groups was slightly abnormal. After intervention with the diet for 21 days, however, a statistically significant difference ($p < .05$) between the test diet group and the placebo group was seen. The test diet group showed improved liver detoxifying ability not seen in the placebo diet group. This improvement was also mirrored in the improvement in the self-rated symptoms, as measured from the questionnaire. The initial symptom scores from the questionnaire were the same in both the test and placebo diet groups, but after diet intervention, only the test diet group had a significant reduction in health complaints.

RELATIONSHIP OF TOXICITY TO HEALTH PROBLEMS

The study results point to an important relationship between improvement in liver detoxification ability and the decrease in chronic health problems and symptoms associated with toxicity. A number of contributions to toxicity symptoms may exist in the addicted. Long-term consumption of excessive alcohol,

Figure 3.1
METABOLIC SCREENING QUESTIONNAIRE

Rate each of the following symptoms based on your health profile for the past 30 days

> POINT SCALE
>
> 0 = Never or almost never have the symptom
> 1 = Occasionally have it, effect is not severe
> 2 = Occasionally have it, effect is severe
> 3 = Frequently have it, effect is not severe
> 4 = Frequently have it, effect is severe

DIGESTIVE TRACT	____ Nausea or vomiting ____ Diarrhea ____ Constipation ____ Bloated feeling ____ Belching or passing gas ____ Heartburn		Total ___
EARS	____ Itchy ears ____ Earaches, ear infections ____ Drainage from ear ____ Ringing in ears, hearing loss		Total ___
EMOTIONS	____ Mood swing ____ Anxiety, fear, or nervousness ____ Anger, irritability, or aggressiveness ____ Depression		Total ___
ENERGY/ ACTIVITY	____ Fatigue, sluggishness ____ Apathy, lethargy ____ Hyperactivity ____ Restlessness		Total ___
EYES	____ Watery or itchy eyes ____ Swollen, reddened, or sticky eyelids ____ Bags or dark circles under eyes ____ Blurred or tunnel vision *(not including near- or farsightedness)*		Total ___
HEAD	____ Headaches ____ Faintness ____ Dizziness ____ Insomnia		Total ___
HEART	____ Irregular or skipped heartbeat ____ Rapid or pounding heartbeat ____ Chest pain		Total ___
JOINTS/ MUSCLES	____ Pain or aches in joints ____ Arthritis ____ Stiffness or limitation of movement ____ Pain or aches in muscles ____ Feeling of weakness or tiredness		Total ___

for example, damages the sensitive lining of the intestinal tract, allowing absorption into the body of toxic substances that may further aggravate toxicity symptoms (Waals, 1991). Substance abuse can also alter the types and numbers of toxin-producing bacteria in the intestinal tract, which can contribute to alterations in brain function and cognitive behavior. The liver is important for "cleansing" the blood of these toxins before they can reach the brain and alter brain chemistry. Therefore, if the liver's detoxifying function is impaired, the result is increased damage to the nervous system (Allen, 1991).

Substance abusers may also become more "allergic" as a consequence of the damaging effects of toxins on the immune system. Health problems, such as irritable bowel syndrome, eczema, and arthritis, are all associated with the toxic burden that accompanies alteration in digestive and immune function in substance abusers. Avoiding foods that tend to produce food intolerance symptoms — such as dairy products, cereal grains other than rice, yeast, shellfish, and citrus fruits — may help relieve symptoms in those suffering from these disorders. Hunter (1991) pointed out that alteration of digestive function and intestinal bacteria may alter liver function as a result of the release from toxic bacteria of substances that alter immune function and could result in symptoms of arthritis. Even the appearance and progression of nervous system diseases may be the result of exposure of the nervous system to toxins that were not properly detoxified by the liver. Steventon, Heafield, Waring, and Williams (1989) found that those who had Parkinson's disease had significantly reduced liver detoxification ability. From their work, they concluded, "Parkinson's disease patients may be unusually susceptible to exogenous or even endogenous toxins" (Steventon et al., 1989).

The author found liver function in a group of nondiseased persons to vary widely when evaluated by the caffeine and benzoate tests. This variation of liver detoxifying ability may be linked to the susceptibility of a substance abuser to the secondary health effects associated with drug and alcohol problems (Lieber, 1991).

DIET COMPOSITION

Because a tailored diet can improve liver detoxifying ability, this nutritional intervention program is believed not only to help improve the success of a treatment program but also to reduce the health risks associated with substance abuse. By using a diet that supplies readily digestible high-quality nutrition that is high in specific nutrients supportive of detoxification, a significant improvement in both digestive function and liver detoxifying ability can be realized.

This unique detoxifying diet uses specific nutrients that improve digestion and assimilation of nutrients while providing the important nutrients in the correct level to help support the body's natural detoxification process. In a sense, this diet might fit the definition of a medical food. A medical food differs from traditional food by supplying specific tailored nutrients at levels that can support unique physiologic processes associated with certain health needs. The diet composition of the program for detoxification is shown in Table 3.2. This diet supplies not only adequate calories and levels of the essential vitamins and minerals but also special nutrients such as the amino acids L-cysteine, glutathione, and molybdenum, which are important for the liver's detoxification process (Ketterer, Coles, & Meyer, 1983). An example of the application of the diet is shown in the 4 days' menu plan described in Table 3.3. (A more complete description of the 21-day detoxification diet plan and nutritional formula can be obtained by writing HealthComm International, Inc., 5800 Soundview Drive, Building B, Gig Harbor, WA 98335, or calling them at 1-800-843-9660.)

The diet can help improve the conversion of toxic substances in the liver to nontoxic materials that are prepared for excretion in the urine or bile. Because this diet has been demonstrated to help in several of the liver's detoxification processes, including cytochrome P-450 as well as conjugation activity, it helps to convert substances to less toxic by-products. This is different from the effects of certain drugs or

Table 3.2
THE NUTRIENT COMPOSITION OF THE TWO BASE POWDERED MEAL SUPPLEMENT PRODUCTS

Nutrient	Test	Placebo
Calories	450	300
Protein	45 g	30 g
Carbohydrate	51 g	40 g
Fat	9 g	2 g
Fiber	6 g	8 g
Sodium	180 mg	320 mg
Potassium	1260 mg	1380 mg
Vitamin B_1	6 mg	1.1 mg
Vitamin B_2	6 mg	1.2 mg
Vitamin B_3	21 mg	14 mg
Vitamin B_4	10.2 mg	1.4 mg
Vitamin B_{12}	10.8 mg	4.2 mg
Folic acid	240 mg	200 mg
Pantothenic acid	10.5 mg	7 mg
Biotin	405 mg	210 mg
Vitamin C	900 mg	42 mg
Vitamin A	15,000 IU	3500 IU
Vitamin E	324 IU	22 IU
Calcium	600 mg	500 mg
Magnesium	420 mg	200 mg
Iron	10.8 mg	12.6 mg
Zinc	30 mg	10.5 mg
Copper	3 mg	1.4 mg
Phosphorus	600 mg	500 mg
Manganese	3.9 mg	2 mg
Selenium	120 mg	60 mg
Chromium	150 mg	134 mg
Molybdenum	360 mg	100 mg
Iodine	159 mg	105 mg
L-Glutathione	10 mg	—
L-Cysteine	5 mg	—
N-Acetyl Cysteine	5 mg	—

Table 3.3
SAMPLE DIET, DAYS 1 THROUGH 4

Day 1

Breakfast (8 AM)	Test diet formula
Snack #1 (10 AM)	Apple or papaya
Lunch (12 PM)	Test diet formula
	Carrot and celery sticks
Snack #2 (3 PM)	Test diet formula
Dinner (6 PM)	White rice
	Peas and zucchini
Snack #3 (8 PM)	Pears (fresh or canned without sugar)

Day 2

Breakfast	Test diet formula
Snack #1	Pear(s)
Lunch	Test diet formula
	White rice
Snack #2	Test diet formula
Dinner	Baked sweet potato or yam
	Green beans
	Sliced cucumber
Snack #3	Banana

Day 3

Breakfast	Test diet formula
Snack #1	Peach(es)
Lunch	Test diet formula
	White rice
Snack #2	Test diet formula
Dinner	Baked winter squash
	Steamed broccoli or cauliflower
Snack #3	Kiwi fruit

Day 4

Breakfast	Test diet formula
Snack #1	Melon
Lunch	Test diet formula
	Carrot and celery sticks
Snack #2	Test diet formula
Dinner	White rice
	Peas and zucchini
	Broccoli
Snack #3	Kiwi fruit

alcohol, which activate cytochrome P-450 but do not improve the function of the conjugation steps. Therefore, drugs and alcohol may increase the body's toxic reaction because the intermediate substances produced by the action of cytochrome P-450 may be more toxic than the initial substances (Caldwell, 1982). It is only through the proper balancing in the liver of all the steps of detoxification that a nontoxic substance is produced and the withdrawal symptoms are reduced. This is the advantage of a tailored nutritional approach to improving liver detoxification, because each of the liver's detoxification processes is normalized, resulting in improvement in the excretion of nontoxic substances.

Antioxidant nutrients, such as vitamins C and E and carotene, are important in minimizing damage to the body that might occur as a consequence of an increase in the rate of detoxification during drug or alcohol treatment. The overall beneficial effects of the diet on the liver's detoxifying ability, therefore, are a result of the combined influence of the easily digested white rice protein concentrate, the energy-efficient dietary fat source of medium-chain triglycerides, easily digested carbohydrates with a very low potential for fermentation in the gut to toxic substances (high molecular weight dextrins from rice), and the specific nutrients known to support the liver's effective detoxification processes, such as zinc, copper, manganese, iron, B vitamins, and the antioxidant vitamins.

The most significant improvement in toxicity-related symptoms seen within the first 10 days of the diet included reductions in "tired eyes," "pain behind the eyes," headaches, digestive disturbances, morning pain and stiffness, and chronic respiratory complaints.

SUMMARY

This author and his colleagues concluded from this research that a specific nutrient-tailored diet can be helpful in improving the potential for positive results in programs designed to treat alcohol and drug dependence. This 21-day diet, the first four days of which is outlined in Table 3.3, has demonstrated its ability to support improved liver detoxification. The remarkable difference between this dietary approach and traditional drug treatment to enhance liver function is that this diet improves both the first- and second-phase detoxification reactions, resulting in the excretion of fully detoxified substances. It is rewarding to witness the significant reduction of many of the chronic health complaints associated with toxicity during the 21-day diet intervention. This dietary approach is easily implemented and has demonstrated high compliance, resulting in improved program success. As a result of this work, we suggest that all clinical management programs for substance abuse would experience improved success and reduced recidivism by implementing the proper nutrient-tailored diet intervention program.

REFERENCES

Allen, F. E. (1991, October 14). One man's suffering spurs doctors to probe pesticide-drug link. *The Wall Street Journal*, p. A1.

Anderson, K. E., & Conney, A. H. (1979). Nutrition and oxidative drug metabolism in man: Relative influence of dietary lipids, carbohydrate and protein. *Clinical Pharmacology and Therapeutics, 26*, 493-501.

Anderson, K. E., & Kappas, A. (1991). Dietary regulation of cytochrome P-450. *Annual Review of Nutrition, 11*, 141-167.

Bland, J., Barrager, E., Reedy, R. G., & Bland, K. (1995). A medical food-supplemented detoxification program in the management of chronic health problems. *Alternative Therapies, 1*(5), 62-71.

Caldwell, J. (1982). Conjugation reactions in foreign compound metabolism: Definition, consequences and species variation. *Drug Metabolism Reviews, 13*, 745-777.

Hunter, J. O. (1991). Food allergy — or enterometabolic disorder? *Lancet, 338*, 495-496.

Ketterer, B., Coles, B., & Meyer, D. J. (1983). The role of glutathione in detoxification. *Environmental Health Perspectives, 49*, 59-69.

Lieber, C. S. (1991). Alcohol, liver, and nutrition. *Journal of the American College of Nutrition, 10*(6), 602-632.

Rea, W. J. (1992). *Chemical sensitivity* (vol. 1). Boca Raton, FL: Lewis.

Renner, E., Wiethholtz, H., Huguenin, P., Arnaud, M. J., & Presig, R. (1984). Caffeine: A model compound for measuring liver function. *Hepatology, 4*, 38-46.

Ruckpaul, K., & Rein, H. (1989). *Basis and mechanisms of regulation of cytochrome P-450.* New York: Taylor & Francis.

Steventon, G. B., Heafield, M., Waring, R. H., & Williams, A. C. (1989). Xenobiotic metabolism in Parkinson's disease. *Neurology, 39*, 883-887.

Tietz, N. (1976). *Fundamentals of clinical chemistry.* Philadelphia: Saunders.

Waals, V. (1991). Intestinal permeability, diet, and growth. *Lancet, 338*, 1403-1404.

4

Naltrexone Pharmacotherapy for the Treatment of Alcohol Dependence

Robert L. DuPont, MD, and Mark S. Gold, MD, FCP, FAPA

Dr. DuPont is President of the Institute for Behavior and Health Inc., Rockville, MD; Clinical Professor of Psychiatry at Georgetown University School of Medicine, Washington, DC; and First Director of the National Institute on Drug Abuse (NIDA). Dr. Gold is Professor in the Departments of Neuroscience, Psychiatry, Community Health, and Family Medicine, University of Florida Brain Institute, College of Medicine, Gainesville, FL.

KEY POINTS

- In 1995, naltrexone (ReVia) was approved by the Food and Drug Administration (FDA) for the treatment of alcohol abuse. Although not a "magic bullet," naltrexone promises to aid many patients in their struggle to overcome the relapses of the disease.

- This chapter reviews the current state of knowledge about naltrexone and provides guidelines for administering this medication.

- The goal of naltrexone pharmacotherapy is to reduce the craving for alcohol and the "brain reward" from alcohol use.

- Naltrexone is a long-acting com-

petitive antagonist of opioid receptors that blocks the subjective and objective effects of opioid drugs.

- Naltrexone reduces alcohol relapse when added to the standard treatment for alcohol dependence. It can be included in any outpatient treatment program or employee assistance program. This medication may be the harbinger of a new era in pharmacotherapy for addiction that emphasizes identifying new agents capable of reducing the rewards of addictive drugs.

INTRODUCTION

Although most people who drink alcohol have no problems associated with alcohol consumption, an estimated 15.3 million Americans meet the diagnostic criteria for alcohol abuse or alcohol dependence. The various costs to society that are linked to use and abuse of alcohol and other substances are mind-numbing. A recent *Wall Street Journal* op-ed piece (February 7, 1996) stated that we collect approximately $12 billion in taxes annually from tobacco sales, whereas the health costs associated with tobacco use is estimated to be $75 billion per year. Likewise, Americans spend $70.3 billion on alcoholic beverages each year, with nearly $20 billion going to the government in alcohol taxes; estimates for alcohol-related health costs run as high as $140 billion (National Institute on Alcohol Abuse and Alcoholism, 1994). The most recent figure from the National Institute on Alcohol Abuse and Alcoholism (NIAAA) on the economic cost of alcoholism was $85.8 billion (NIAAA, 1994). Of these costs, only 9% were for the treatment of alcoholism; illness and death resulting from alcohol use accounted for 73% of these costs (Rice, Kelman, Miller, & Dunmeyer, 1990).

Although the treatment of alcoholism has improved in recent years, especially as a result of the greater integration of Alcoholics Anonymous (AA) and the other 12-step programs into every aspect of care, the risk of relapse remains tragically high with this progressive and potentially fatal disease (Cross, Morgan, Mooney, Martin, & Rafter, 1990; DuPont & McGovern, 1994). This can be attributed partially to the fact that more than one third of persons who are dependent on alcohol also suffer from a comorbid mental health disorder, most often an affective or anxiety disorder (DuPont, 1995; NIAAA, 1994).

Approximately 1 million Americans seek treatment for alcoholism each year. For most of these persons, treatment is short lived and focused on acute abstinence. Physicians and the medical model took responsibility for evaluating patients for the consequences of alcohol and drug use, for the diseases commonly associated with the use or the lifestyle of the user, and for the prompt and safe medical treatment of withdrawal. Physicians then would either send patients on their way or encourage them to go to a 12-step meeting. We now recognize that the brain affected by alcohol or heroin comes to define a drug state known as the "new normal." This state, clinically referred to as tolerance, implies that more drug must be taken to achieve the same effect and that the brain has defined "normal" to include a certain amount of a particular substance. Rebound neural excitation after discontinuation of chronic drug self-administration is associated with withdrawal. Treatment of withdrawal generally has included medications that are similar to the addicting drug but of less abuse potential, medications that are cross-tolerant, and unrelated medications that interfere with the autonomic release accompanying many drug withdrawal states.

In 1995, the Food and Drug Administration (FDA) approved naltrexone (ReVia, pronounced rah-VEE-ah) for the treatment of alcohol abuse and dependence. Enoch Gordis, MD, Director of the NIAAA, sent a letter to physicians in the United States with the following remarks:

> Naltrexone appears to reduce craving in many abstinent patients and to block the reinforcing effects of alcohol in many patients who drink. The latter effect often enables patients who drink a small amount of alcohol to avoid full-blown relapse and lessens the likelihood of their return to heavy drinking. However, the mechanism of naltrexone's effect on alcoholism has not been demonstrated conclusively.

> The 3-month, NIAAA-supported trials conducted at the University of Pennsylvania and Yale University found that naltrexone cut the rate of patient relapse by nearly one half. In addition, patients who received naltrexone reported less alcohol craving, fewer drinking days, and less severe alcohol-related problems than patients treated with placebo. Both NIAAA-supported studies used naltrexone in combination with counseling, an important part of the treatment regimen.

The recently concluded 3-month, open trials (sponsored by the DuPont Merck Pharmaceutical Company) demonstrated that naltrexone is safe at the prescribed dose (50 mg/day) in a large, heterogeneous population of alcoholic patients (many of whom were concomitantly taking psychotropic medications) in diverse outpatient and inpatient settings.

Approximately half of alcoholic patients who are treated relapse within the first few months of treatment. Relapse to alcohol addiction is most likely to occur in the first 3–6 months of abstinence, a period characterized by physiologic abnormalities, mood dysregulation with common complaints of anxiety, depression, insomnia, and endocrine and sleep problems. Alcoholic patients who are recently abstinent suggest that they need alcohol to "feel normal" in terms reminiscent of the heroin addict asking for methadone. Although not a "magic bullet," naltrexone nevertheless promises to aid many of these patients in their struggle to overcome a chronic relapsing disease.

This chapter reviews the current state of knowledge about naltrexone and describes guidelines that clinicians should follow when integrating this drug into their treatment regimens for persons dependent on alcohol (Gold, 1994).

HISTORY OF TREATMENT OF ALCOHOL ABUSE

In 1948, disulfiram (Antabuse) was approved for the treatment of alcohol abuse. Until 1995, disulfiram was the only medication approved by the FDA for the treatment of chronic alcoholism (as opposed to the treatment of alcohol withdrawal, for which many drugs have been approved). Disulfiram poisons the enzymes that metabolize ethyl alcohol into carbon dioxide and water, causing a toxic accumulation of *acetaldehyde*, a metabolite that produces elevated blood pressure, flushing, nausea, and even death. Disulfiram has been received ambivalently by physicians and patients alike. Its biggest problems stem from poor patient compliance, which leads to poor long-term efficacy (Wright & Moore, 1989). (In addition, aversive consequences vary, and some patients report being willing to vomit for a drink.) These limited results with disulfiram (and the high relapse rates with all forms of treatment of alcoholism) led to a continued search for anticraving agents, specifically blocking agents for the neurotransmitter systems thought to be involved in reinforcement and craving: g-aminobutyric acid (GABA), serotonin, dopamine, and opioids.

In the course of the more than two generations since the search for pharmacologic treatments of heroin addiction began, one of the early successes was the identification of naloxone (Narcan). This agent reversed overdose, eliminating heroin's effects by occupying and blocking the opioid receptors, including those in the brain responsible for the heroin "high" (Jaffe, 1990). Naloxone has an important role in the treatment of heroin overdoses; people brought into hospitals near death can be revived within minutes by an injection of naloxone. However, the effects of naloxone last only a few minutes, and, to be most effective, it must be administered intravenously; thus, it has no role in the long-term, outpatient treatment of heroin addiction.

Changing Role for Naltrexone:

Two decades ago, naltrexone was developed as an orally effective, longer-acting opioid antagonist, sparking great enthusiasm for its use in the treatment of heroin addiction. Naltrexone not only prevented overdose deaths, but it also precipitated acute and severe withdrawal in opioid-dependent patients and blocked the euphoria induced by the use of heroin and other opioids. Marketed as Trexan at the time, naltrexone was administered orally, at doses of 50 mg a day or 150 mg every third day, to prevent opiate dependence. Although naltrexone initially seemed to be an attractive approach to opiate addiction, subsequent clinical experience dampened the original optimism, because long-term compliance with naltrexone treatment by heroin addicts was difficult to maintain. (Low long-term compliance also limited the value of disulfiram.)

Considerable evidence exists that the reinforcing effects of ethanol (alcohol) are mediated, at least in part, by the brain's endogenous opioid systems and that these systems may contribute to the adaptive neuronal responses provoked by ethanol intoxication (Nevo & Hamon, 1995). It is known, for example, that a number of the behavioral and pharmacologic effects of ethanol — such as hypothermia, euphoria, analgesia, and motor activation — as well as the development of tolerance and dependence, are similar to those produced by opiates. Clearly, these findings correspond with the idea that ethanol affects dopamine neurotransmission through the activation of an opioid intermediary link ending with the stimulation of δ– and/or μ–receptors.

Because opioid mechanisms were thought to play a role in alcohol reinforcement in animals and among persons with a family history of alcoholism, investigators who understood the basic literature began to turn their attention to the use of naltrexone for treating alcoholism. In 1980, the first animal studies showed a reduced alcohol usage after naltrexone treatment; the first human trials were reported in 1986 (Volpicelli, Davis, & Olgin, 1986). In 1992, the findings of two small, placebo-controlled, double-blind studies (referred to by Dr. Gordis in his letter to physicians) were published (O'Malley, Jaffe, Chang, Schottenfeld, Meyer, & Rounsaville, 1992; Volpicelli, Alterman, Hayashida, & O'Brien, 1992). In an unusually expedient action, the FDA cleared naltrexone for use in the treatment of alcohol-use disorders in 1995 based on these two 12-week studies.

The FDA's approval of naltrexone for alcoholism seems to have been expedited for three reasons: (a) naltrexone previously had been approved for another indication (showing that its long-term use by outpatients was safe); (b) alcohol abuse is a serious health problem for which there is no other effective pharmacologic treatment; and (c) the agency is incessantly criticized for its slow approval processes of pharmaceuticals. Naltrexone, now widely used in the United States and abroad for the treatment of alcoholism, is labeled ReVia to distinguish it from its earlier version, Trexan. ReVia is available in a 50-mg dose suitable for once-a-day oral administration.

Naltrexone is not a panacea for alcoholism; it does not adequately substitute for other forms of treatment (O'Malley et al., 1992). In fact, it is not a stand-alone treatment for alcoholism at all, but, rather, a promising part of the comprehensive, long-term treatment of alcohol-use disorders. Any physician who prescribes naltrexone to an alcoholic patient to solve a drinking problem is not only seriously misunderstanding both alcoholism and its treatment, but also shortchanging the patient (Volpicelli et al., 1992).

FINDINGS OF THE PENN AND YALE STUDIES

Volpicelli and colleagues (1992), from the University of Pennsylvania, reported the results of a 12-week, double-blind, placebo-controlled study; it involved 70 male alcoholic patients who took either placebo or 50 mg of naltrexone once a day as part of the treatment of alcoholism in the Substance Abuse Unit of the Philadelphia Veterans Affairs Medical Center. These patients participated in a 6-hour-a-day, partial hospitalization program for 1 month, followed by 11 months of after care composed of twice-a-week group therapy meetings. Study patients who took naltrexone reported less craving and drank less often than patients on placebo.

In this study, relapse was defined as a report of drinking five or more drinks in 1 week, drinking five or more drinks on one drinking occasion, or measuring a blood alcohol concentration above 100 mg/dL at one of the weekly study evaluations. ReVia doubled the success rate in this study. During the study, 23% of the 35 patients taking naltrexone relapsed, whereas 54% of the 35 patients taking placebo met the criteria for relapse. Perhaps most important is the finding that of the

20 patients who took placebo and drank alcohol during treatment, an astounding 95% relapsed, whereas only 50% of the patients who took naltrexone and consumed alcohol during the 12-week study went on to full-blown relapse (see Figures 4.1 and 4.2). Among the patients who took naltrexone, the only side effects reported were two complaints of nausea and one complaint of increased arthritic pain.

The study from Yale University reported the results of 97 alcohol-dependent patients who participated in one of two treatment protocols: a coping-skills relapse prevention therapy or a supportive therapy designed to reinforce patients' own efforts to achieve abstinence without teaching new coping skills (O'Malley et al., 1992). Patients were recruited through newspaper advertisements to participate in the outpatient treatments of the Alcohol Treatment Unit of the Connecticut Mental Health Center. Of the 97 participants, 74% were male, 93% were white, 66% were unmarried, and 73% were employed full time at the start of the study.

Patients were randomly assigned to receive either naltrexone, 50 mg a day, or identical placebo tablets. Naltrexone significantly outperformed placebo on the measures of drinking and relapse. Patients who received naltrexone and supportive therapy experienced the best results overall (Figure 4.3); furthermore, of the patients who drank during the 3-month study, those who used naltrexone while participating in the coping-skills therapy were the least likely to suffer a full relapse. Patients who received naltrexone reported drinking on half as many days as patients who received placebo, and they consumed only one third as many drinks during the study as those receiving placebo. Naltrexone was noted to be far more acceptable to alcoholic patients than was disulfiram. O'Malley and colleagues (1992) reported that only 26% of eligible persons declined to participate in the naltrexone study, whereas 62% declined to participate in an unrelated study using disulfiram.

Although the two studies were very small and lasted for only 3 months (a short period given that alcoholism is a

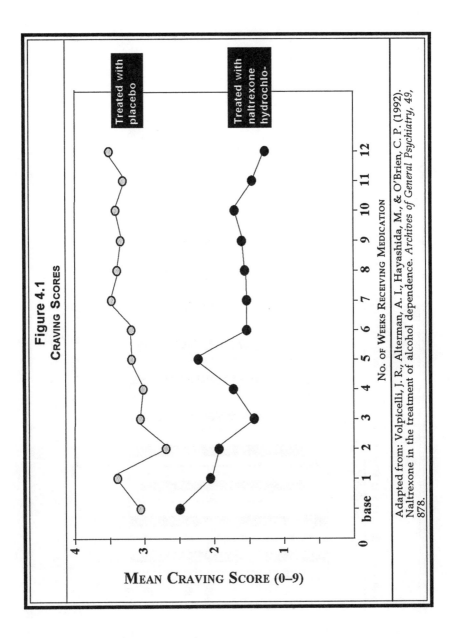

Figure 4.1
CRAVING SCORES

Adapted from: Volpicelli, J. R., Alterman, A. I., Hayashida, M., & O'Brien, C. P. (1992). Naltrexone in the treatment of alcohol dependence. *Archives of General Psychiatry, 49,* 878.

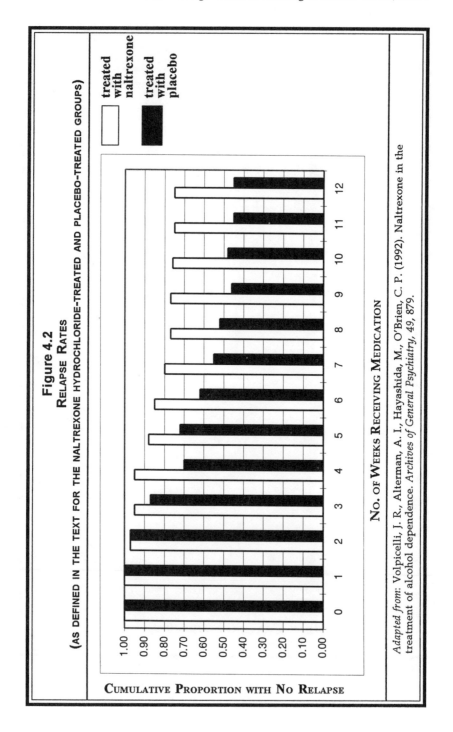

Figure 4.2
RELAPSE RATES
(AS DEFINED IN THE TEXT FOR THE NALTREXONE HYDROCHLORIDE-TREATED AND PLACEBO-TREATED GROUPS)

Adapted from: Volpicelli, J. R., Alterman, A. I., Hayashida, M., O'Brien, C. P. (1992). Naltrexone in the treatment of alcohol dependence. *Archives of General Psychiatry, 49,* 879.

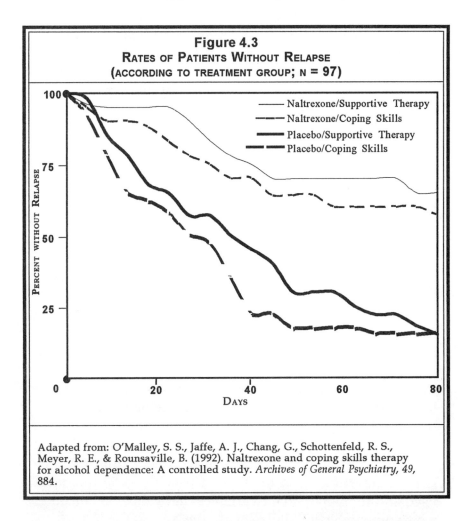

Figure 4.3
RATES OF PATIENTS WITHOUT RELAPSE
(ACCORDING TO TREATMENT GROUP; N = 97)

Naltrexone/Supportive Therapy
Naltrexone/Coping Skills
Placebo/Supportive Therapy
Placebo/Coping Skills

Adapted from: O'Malley, S. S., Jaffe, A. J., Chang, G., Schottenfeld, R. S., Meyer, R. E., & Rounsaville, B. (1992). Naltrexone and coping skills therapy for alcohol dependence: A controlled study. *Archives of General Psychiatry, 49,* 884.

lifelong affliction), they have proved remarkably influential because they were well-designed and expertly conducted. (Their publication led to FDA approval of naltrexone for the treatment of alcoholism a mere 2 years later.)

Follow-Up Results:

The two studies have been followed up by a wide range of studies in many settings, some of which extend over longer periods of time. In the two clinical trials of naltrexone for alcohol dependence, patients receiving naltrexone were less likely to relapse (O'Malley et al., 1992; Volpicelli et al., 1992). This effect is consistent with the hypothesis of naltrexone's inhibition of alcohol reward through endorphin mediation of alcohol-induced mesocorticolimbic dopamine release. In these trials, the relapse effect was most pronounced among alcoholic patients who actually had a drink or drinks. Naltrexone actually appears to block craving, which is induced by alcohol or alcohol-conditioned stimuli so that "loss of control" is somehow no longer as pressing an issue (Volpicelli et al., 1992).

When combined, these studies show that treatment with naltrexone results in improved rates of abstinence and reduction in rates of heavy drinking compared with placebo (O'Malley, Croop, Labriola, & Volpicelli, 1995). Compared with placebo, naltrexone is associated with a 50% reduction in the rates of relapse and a 36% reduction in rates of nonabstinence. Among patients who were nonabstinent during these studies, patients receiving naltrexone were less likely to relapse to heavy drinking and drank less frequently (O'Malley et al., 1995). The similarity in outcomes between the two studies, as confirmed by combined analyses, indicates that the benefit of adjunctive pharmacotherapy is not limited to a specific "brand" of therapy or treatment approach. The two studies differed in the type of psychological treatment used and in many patient variables; nevertheless, outcomes were comparable (O'Malley et al., 1995).

Our experience (DuPont & Gold, 1995), and the reports of other investigators (O'Malley, Jaffe, Sode, & Rounsaville, 1996; Volpicelli et al., 1992), suggests that naltrexone decreases intoxication. Alcoholic patients treated with naltrexone who do slip often state that "the high" does not feel the same: it is not as good, nor is it worth all the associated guilt (DuPont & Gold, 1995). In formal studies, social drinkers given a dose of alcohol reported lowered stimulation and more nausea and sedation when taking naltrexone as opposed to placebo (Swift, Whelihan, Kuznetsov, Buongiorno, & Hsuing, 1994). These data corroborated other findings that alcoholic patients taking naltrexone reported less perceived intoxication than usual (Volpicelli, Watson, King, Sherman, & O'Brien, 1995).

PHARMACOLOGIC PROFILE

Naltrexone is a long-acting competitive antagonist of opioid receptors that blocks the subjective and objective effects of opioid drugs, including morphine, codeine, methadone, and heroin. It does not produce opioid effects because it lacks agonist properties. Naltrexone precipitates opioid withdrawal in dependent patients within 1 hour of use; these effects may last up to 48 hours.

Naltrexone works quickly, unlike the 2–4-week latency for the therapeutic effects of antidepressants. The drug clears the body rapidly: its effects are gone within 2 or 3 days of the last dose. Its elimination half-life is approximately 10 hours.

ReVia is generally taken orally in a 50-mg tablet once a day to help alcoholic patients involved in comprehensive treatment reduce their craving for alcohol and the risk of relapse. Clinicians often start patients on 25 mg once a day and increase the dose to 50 mg, as indicated. When naltrexone is effective, patients report having an easier time "putting the drink back down" and genuinely participating in their recovery programs. Compliance with a naltrexone regimen to treat alcohol dependence is greater than with disulfiram for alcoholism and naltrexone for heroin addiction, because there is a clear benefit to the alcoholic patient in reduced alcohol craving. Disulfiram in the treatment of alcoholism and naltrexone in the treatment of heroin do not curb the craving; instead, they block the ability of addictive substances to satisfy — an action that frequently leads to patients' failure to use the medications for their respective indications. We have observed three major effects of naltrexone treatment in alcohol-dependent patients: (a) reduction of craving, (b) reduction in anticipatory ("happy hour") reward, and (c) reduction in alcohol reward.

Most patients using naltrexone for the treatment of alcoholism experience no side effects. Side effects, however, are obviously possible. The most common side effects include difficulty sleeping, anxiety, nervousness, abdominal pain, nausea and/or vomiting, low energy, joint and muscle pain, and headache. (Nausea, the most common side effect, is generally managed by reducing the dosage to 25 mg/day or taking naltrexone with a meal.)

Danger of Opioid Withdrawal:

Naltrexone should not be used for alcoholic clients who may be simultaneously dependent on heroin or other opioids (including methadone) because even a single dose of naltrexone can precipitate severe opioid withdrawal. Patients who are dependent on opioids can be treated with naltrexone once they are free of opioid dependence (e.g., once they have undergone detoxification) or, experimentally, as part of a rapid detoxification protocol.

Patients taking naltrexone should be informed that if they require opioid analgesia for any reason, they should try alternative pain relief. However, anesthesiologists and other pain experts can safely use opiates in patients taking naltrexone — but these patients will probably require higher doses of the opioid (such as codeine or morphine) to achieve pain relief. If patients develop a need for opioid analgesia, they can stop naltrexone treatment, and their response to the opioids will return to normal in 2 or 3 days.

Dosage:

Some alcoholic patients report good results from 25 mg of naltrexone (or one half of a tablet) once a day. The goal of therapy with ReVia is to reduce the craving for alcohol and the "brain reward" from alcohol use. If this goal can be achieved successfully on 25 mg of naltrexone for a particular patient, there is no reason to use 50 mg. Obviously, decreasing the dose lowers the cost of treatment. On the other hand, many patients require 50 mg a day to obtain the drug's full benefit. The personal experience of each patient with naltrexone is the best guide for whether a 25- or 50-mg dose is indicated.

Hepatic Effects:

Liver function tests (e.g., serum glutamic oxaloacetic transaminase and alkaline phosphatase) can reveal liver injury that is a consequence of heavy drinking. Elevations of lipid levels in the blood (e.g., triglycerides and lipoprotein cholesterol) can be observed, resulting from decreases in gluconeogenesis associated with heavy drinking. High fat content in the blood also contributes to the development of fatty liver. In very high doses, naltrexone can be toxic to the liver; therefore, it should be used with caution in patients with acute liver dysfunction or failure. According to the FDA-approved package insert for ReVia, "It has the capacity to cause hepatocellular injury when given in excessive doses. ReVia is contraindicated in acute hepatitis or liver failure, and its use in patients with active liver disease must be considered carefully in light of its hepatotoxic effects." This is more often a problem with the higher doses used in opioid addiction treatment than it is with the 50-mg dose used to treat alcoholism.

Liver damage is extremely unlikely with naltrexone at the 50-mg dose, but it can be seen at doses 5–10 times higher. Patients with blood alcohol levels of 100 mg/dL (or even 200 mg/dL) with no apparent signs of intoxication may express concern about naltrexone and their livers. In such situations, it is appropriate to inform patients that although excessive doses of naltrexone *may* be associated with liver damage, alcoholism definitely *is* associated with this outcome. Because alcoholism is hereditary and is often associated with liver disease, some patients resist using naltrexone because they fear liver disease on the basis of their tragic family experiences. Clinicians can help patients overcome this resistance to using naltrexone by reassuring them that the 50-mg daily regimen of naltrexone has not been associated with liver damage.

Furthermore, any concerns about liver disease that patients

may have can be handled directly by conducting occasional blood tests for liver function while they are taking naltrexone. For worried patients, a liver function test should be conducted before starting naltrexone to ensure that there are no or inconsequential abnormalities; after 1 month of treatment, routine liver function testing should be performed every 6–12 months during long-term treatment with naltrexone. Nevertheless, liver function tests are not required on a routine basis for patients taking naltrexone because there is no reason to expect problems unless the patient has preexisting liver disease or is concerned about liver disease. Naltrexone often is given to patients awaiting liver transplantation because the alcohol — not the naltrexone — is hepatotoxic. Moreover, it has been the experience of one of the authors (Gold) that naltrexone may reduce pruritus.

THE ROLE OF NALTREXONE IN THE TREATMENT OF ALCOHOLISM

It appears that naltrexone blunts the brain's endogenous neuropeptide-dopamine response to drinking, thereby curbing the rewarding effects of drinking alcohol. Unlike methadone, naltrexone is not a controlled substance. Because it does not cause a "high" and is not an abusable substance, it has no "street" value. Naltrexone does not make alcoholic patients sick if they consume alcohol (as does disulfiram), nor does it block the intoxicating and other effects of alcohol use (as naltrexone blocks the effects of opioids such as heroin). Therefore, alcoholic patients can drink and get "high" from using drugs other than opiates while on naltrexone without fear of becoming sick as a result of the naltrexone. Many patients who try alcohol after taking naltrexone say that alcohol is not as satisfying as it was before taking the medication and that they lose interest in drinking (craving) over time with naltrexone.

Naltrexone is not merely a novel approach to the treatment of alcoholism. It may be the harbinger of a new era in pharmacotherapy for addiction which emphasizes the identification of new agents to reduce the rewarding properties of alcohol and other drugs. We have reviewed the neurobiology of nicotine, opiate, alcohol, and other drug dependencies and concluded that naltrexone may play a role in reducing relapse in patients addicted to alcohol, opiates, and nicotine (Johnson & Gold, 1996). Such data are also consistent with basic science data (Hodson, Davenport, Price, & Burden, 1993).

Indeed, reward has been shown to be the principal force behind addictive behavior over the long term (DuPont & Gold, 1995). Naltrexone decreases alcohol craving and consumption in alcohol-dependent patients. Nalmefene is a newer opiate antagonist that has some potential advantages. Twenty-one alcohol-dependent subjects were randomly assigned to 12 weeks of double-blind treatment with 40 mg of nalmefene, 10 mg of nalmefene, or placebo. The 40 mg group had significantly lower rate of relapse and greater number of abstinent days than the other groups (Mason, Ritvo, Morgan, Salvato, Goldberg, Welch, & Mantero-Atienza, 1994).

Agents like ReVia will not replace other forms of therapy, such as psychological treatments and especially the uniquely valuable 12-step programs. However, they may prove useful in tipping the balance for some addicted patients in that these programs will have a higher probability of success (Miller & Gold, 1991). Naltrexone can be included in any outpatient treatment program or employee assistance program (EAP) (McMichael, 1995). To be sure, naltrexone reduces relapse in patients who attend AA meetings and/or are concurrently participating in other forms of behavioral therapy.

In general, naltrexone should be considered for any alcoholic patient who is experiencing craving for alcohol or who has had a prior history of relapse to alcohol use after treatment. Because the results of using ReVia are evident within a few days, a trial period of a few weeks may be desirable to assess a particular patient's response to the drug. A good response is seen when a patient reports reduced or eliminated craving and/or a reduced reward with increased ability to stop drinking once started. A poor response to naltrexone is seen when a patient reports no benefit from its use or relapses to sustained alcoholic drinking while taking the medication. Nonresponders to daily naltrexone dosages of 50 mg increasingly are being treated with higher doses of naltrexone or augmentation with a selective serotonin-reuptake inhibitor.

CLINICAL GUIDELINES FOR USING NALTREXONE

Although our experience and the initial findings on naltrexone use in the treatment of alcoholism are positive, the history of alcoholism treatment is littered with hopeful interventions that simply do not meet the test of time, especially pharmacologic treatments. Therefore, an attitude of cautious optimism toward the use of naltrexone in the treatment of alcoholism is best at this time. A trial period of at least 3 months seems reasonable to determine whether a patient truly benefits from naltrexone. Available research does not offer guidance as to the optimal duration of naltrexone treatment, but prudence suggests that daily use of naltrexone be continued as long as the patient and physician deem it useful and are concerned about the potential for relapse.

One of the critical aspects in the clinical decision to use naltrexone is its cost. Naltrexone is not inexpensive, with a retail cost of nearly $4.00–$5.00 a tablet. (Veterans hospitals charge less than $1.50 per tablet.) Yet despite 90 days of treatment with 50 mg of naltrexone per day—possibly costing more than $400.00—this is a small price to pay when compared with the amount of money a patient might spend simply on alcohol if he or she relapsed to drinking and subsequently resumed other more expensive treatments. Naltrexone is an adjunct to care and, as such, has an added cost. The provider—and in private settings, the patient—must consider carefully the value of possible enhancement of outcomes by approximately 50%, as measured by the two controlled studies on which the FDA based its approval of naltrexone for treating alcohol dependence. Our experience suggests that naltrexone augmentation of existing therapies reduces total family *and* individual patient health care costs.

Mental health professionals are often the closest and best-informed health care professionals working with alcoholic patients. Furthermore, clinicians hold a vested interest in teaching patients about the appropriate use of naltrexone as part of an overall program to overcome the serious and life-long disease of alcoholism.

Here are six specific clinical perspectives on the use of naltrexone in the treatment of alcoholism:

- Use naltrexone orally, 50 mg once a day, for the first 90 days of sobriety by adding it to the usual "90 by 90" recommendation. In other words, alcoholic patients should be advised to attend 90 AA meetings and take 90 doses of naltrexone during their first 90 days of recovery.

- Naltrexone should be considered for patients with a history of prior relapse to active alcoholism with a behavioral contract for 3-, 6-, 9-, or 12-month periods as part of their outpatient treatment.

- Use naltrexone once a day for short or long periods of acute risk of relapse (e.g., during a divorce; job change; or upon returning to a site where drinking was common in the past, such as a college reunion or an old neighborhood). It might be used once a day for 3 or 4 days—or several weeks or longer—with such high-risk experiences.

- Patients taking naltrexone who require an opiate analgesic should stop taking it 2 or 3 days before the expected use of the analgesic (such as for scheduled surgery or premenstrual cramps) and then return to it several days after the last dose of the opiate. This ensures that there is no remaining dependence that could precipitate opiate withdrawal.

- Patients who deny opiate dependence but for whom opiate dependence is a distinct possibility can be evaluated with a naloxone challenge before starting naltrexone. Naloxone, a short-acting opiate antagonist, can be given either intravenously or subcutaneously to detect the presence of opiate dependence. If the patient is dependent on the opiate, naloxone will cause an immediate withdrawal syndrome; if the patient is not dependent on opiates, the naloxone injection will produce no effect (Schuckit, 1995).

- When it is necessary to administer an analgesic to a patient who is taking naltrexone (in unscheduled or emergency situations), nonopiate analgesics can be used without interference by naltrexone, and opioid analgesics can be used as needed, probably at somewhat higher doses than would be required without naltrexone (often 1½ or 2 times the normal dose).

CONCLUSION

In early 1995, naltrexone (ReVia) was approved for the treatment of alcoholism. Studies conducted subsequently support the conclusion that ReVia reduces alcohol relapse when added to standard treatment for alcohol dependence. Clinicians responsible for the treatment of alcoholic patients should be aware of this new treatment and consider adding it to their therapeutic armamentarium. The addition of ReVia to any alcoholism treatment program should be expected to reduce the typical relapse rates experienced by that program. Ongoing studies may demonstrate efficacy in treating other forms of addiction, such as nicotine addiction, but it is too early to be certain.

REFERENCES

Cross, G. M., Morgan, C. W., Mooney, A. J. III, Martin, C. A., & Rafter, J. A. (1990). Alcoholism treatment: A 10-year follow-up study. *Alcoholism, Clinical Experimental Research, 14,* 169–173.

DuPont, R. L. (1995). Anxiety and addiction: A clinical perspective on comorbidity. *Bulletin of the Menninger Clinic, 59*(Suppl A), A53–A72.

DuPont, R. L., & Gold, M. S. (1995). Withdrawal and reward: Implications for detoxification and relapse prevention. *Psychiatric Annals, 25,* 663–668.

DuPont, R. L., & McGovern, J. P. (1994). *A Bridge to Recovery – An Introduction to 12-Step Programs.* Washington, DC: American Psychiatric Press.

Gold, M. S. (1994). Neurobiology of addiction and recovery: The brain, the drive for the drug, and the 12-step fellowship. *Journal Substance Abuse Treatment, 11*(2), 93–97.

Hodson, C. A., Davenport, A., Price, G., & Burden, H. W. (1993). Naltrexone treatment attenuates the inhibitory effect of nicotine treatment on serum LH in rats. *Life Sciences, 53,* 839–846.

Jaffe, J. H. (1990). Drug addiction and drug abuse. In A. G. Gilman, T. W. Rall, A. S. Nies, P. Taylor, (Eds.), *Goodman and Gilman's The Pharmacological Basis of Therapeutics* (8th ed., pp. 522–573). New York: Pergamon Press.

Johnson, C., & Gold, M. S. (1996). Nicotine addiction. *Journal of the Florida Medical Association, 83*(2), 102–106.

Mason, B. J., Ritvo, E. C., Morgan, R. O., Salvato, F. R., Goldberg, G., Welch, B., Mantero-Atienza, E. (1994). A double-blind, placebo-controlled pilot study to evaluate the efficacy and safety of oral nalmefene HCL for alcohol dependence. *Alcoholism, Clinical and Experimental Research, 18,* 1162–1167.

McMichael, C. K. (1995). Naltrexone: Another weapon against relapse approved—pharmacological strategy works better with psychotherapy. *Employee Assistance, April,* 18,20,21.

Miller, N. S., & Gold, M. S. (1991). *Drugs of Abuse: A Comprehensive Series for Clinicians. Volume II, Alcohol.* New York: Plenum Medical Book Co.

National Institute on Alcohol Abuse and Alcoholism. (1994). Economic issues in alcohol use and abuse. In *Eighth Special Report to the U.S. Congress on Alcohol and Health from the Secretary of Health and Human Services, September 1993* (NIH Publication No. 94-3699). Rockville, MD: U.S. Department of Health and Human Services, National Institutes of Health, National Institute on Alcohol Abuse and Alcoholism.

Nevo, I., & Hamon, M. (1995). Invited Review of 'Neurotransmitter and Neuromodulatory Mechanisms Involved in Alcohol Abuse and Alcoholism.' *Neurochemistry International, 26,* 305–336.

O'Malley, S. S., Croop, R. S., Labriola, D. F., & Volpicelli, J. R. (1995). Naltrexone in the treatment of alcohol dependence: A combined analysis of two trials. *Psychiatric Annals, 25,* 681–688.

O'Malley, S. S., Jaffe, A. J., Chang, G., Schottenfeld, R. S., Meyer, R. E., & Rounsaville, B. (1992). Naltrexone and coping skills therapy for alcohol dependence: A controlled study. *Archives of General Psychiatry, 49,* 881–887.

O'Malley, S. S., Jaffe, A. J., Sode, S., & Rounsaville, B. J. (1996). Experience of a 'slip' among alcoholics treated with naltrexone or placebo. *American Journal of Psychiatry, 153,* 281–283.

Rice, D. P., Kelman, S., Miller, L. S., & Dunmeyer, S. (1990). *The Economic Costs of Alcohol and Drug Abuse and Mental Illness: 1985.* Report submitted to the Office of Financing and Coverage Policy of the Alcohol, Drug Abuse, and Mental Health Administration, U.S. Department of Health and Human Services. San Francisco, CA: Institute for Health and Aging, University of California.

Schuckit, M. A. (1995). *Drug and Alcohol Abuse – A Clinical Guide to Diagnosis and Treatment.* (4th ed.). New York: Plenum Medical Book Co.

Swift, R. M., Whelihan, W., Kuznetsov, O., Buongiorno, G., Hsuing, H. (1994). Naltrexone-induced alterations in human ethanol intoxication. *American Journal of Psychiatry, 151,* 1463–1467.

Volpicelli, J. R., Alterman, A. I., Hayashida, M., & O'Brien, C. P. (1992). Naltrexone in the treatment of alcohol dependence. *Archives of General Psychiatry, 49,* 876–880.

Volpicelli, J. R., Davis, M. A., & Olgin, J. E. (1986). Naltrexone blocks the postshock increase of ethanol consumption. *Life Sciences,* 841–847.

Volpicelli, J. R., Watson, N. T., King, A. C., Sherman, C. E., & O'Brien, C. P. (1995). Effect of naltrexone on alcohol 'high' in alcoholics. *American Journal of Psychiatry, 152,* 613–615.

Wright, C., & Moore, R. D. (1989). Disulfiram treatment of alcoholism: Position paper of the American College of Physicians. *Annals of Internal Medicine, 111,* 943–945.

5

Inpatient Versus Outpatient Treatment of Alcoholism

Barbara W. Reeve, MD, MS

Dr. Reeve is a psychiatrist in private practice in Ellsworth, ME. She specializes in addiction medicine.

KEY POINTS

- This chapter provides a review of the current literature evaluating the efficacy of inpatient versus outpatient treatment.

- In general, the literature indicates that outpatient treatment, particularly intensive outpatient treatment, is at least as effective as inpatient treatment for alcohol dependence.

- For each type of treatment, some patients respond better. The goal is to use personal and clinical characteristics to match patients with the most favorable kind of treatment.

- To match individuals with inpatient or outpatient treatment, practitioners should use a hierarchical decision tree to assess (a) the presence of impending delirium tremens, other life-threatening conditions, and dangerousness to self and others; (b) severity of psychiatric symptoms; and (c) severity of family or employment factors.

- Severity of addiction does not consistently differentiate between patients who are likely to do better in outpatient or inpatient treatments.

- The single most meaningful variable for selecting between outpatient and inpatient treatments is the severity of psychiatric symptoms, as measured by the Addiction Severity Index.

INTRODUCTION

Professionals of all types who treat addictions are often chal-
lenged by the need to find the most effective treatment for the
resources available. For years, researchers have debated the
relative efficacy and the cost effectiveness of inpatient versus
outpatient treatment. However, the focus of the patient sometimes gets lost in that debate. Determining the most appropriate care can be especially difficult when many nonclinical
factors, such as benefit limits and managed care, are involved.
In a large study of insurance claims of patients receiving
recovery care, Holder and Blose (1991) found 70% to have at
least one inpatient or residential admission. They saw this as
a result of ". . .three key factors shaping the patterns of
alcoholism treatment: patient demand, the network of treatment providers, and health insurance coverage and restric-
tions" (Holder & Blose, 1991, p. 194).

During most of the 1970s and 1980s, inpatient treatment was
considered the gold standard. The availability of insurance
benefits made it possible for most insured patients to have 28
or 30 days of such treatment. However, in contrast to the
subjective impression of patients and addictions specialists
that inpatient treatment is more effective, the objective data
amassed from dozens of studies do not validate this belief.
Even though no clear advantage is apparent for one treatment
over another among large, heterogeneous groups of patients,
the literature does indicate that some clinical and demographic
elements can be used to match individual patients to treatment
modalities. This chapter reviews the current literature evaluating the relative effectiveness of inpatient and outpatient
treatment and identifies factors that can help match patients
with the most effective treatments.

COMPARING INPATIENT AND OUTPATIENT
TREATMENTS

In 1986, Miller and Hester reviewed a large number of uncontrolled studies and 15 controlled studies that compared inpatient with outpatient treatment for alcoholism. They concluded that ". . .no study to date has produced convincing evidence that treatment in residential settings is more effective than outpatient treatment" (Miller & Hester, 1986, p. 802). They also reviewed five studies comparing short inpatient stays (7–10 days) with longer ones (3–6 weeks). None of these studies showed "superior improvement for the longer-stay patients on any measure" (p. 799). These studies compared the overall effectiveness of various programs, but did not consider that different kinds of patients may benefit from different types or settings of treatment.

Miller and Hester (1986) also reviewed studies that attempted to predict treatment outcome in various settings based on patient attributes. Two patterns emerged: (a) patients with less severe addiction and more stable social situations before treatment had more favorable outcomes when in outpatient programs, and (b) more severe and less socially stable alcoholics do better in inpatient settings. They suggest, "When heterogeneous populations of alcoholics are averaged together, the consistent finding is comparable (or better) outcomes from outpatient as opposed to residential treatment" (p. 801).

In another comprehensive review of the literature, Annis (1986) evaluated studies that compared various treatment settings. She also concluded that neither inpatient detoxification nor inpatient rehabilitation is more effective than outpatient treatment when given to unselected groups of alcoholics seeking treatment.

Since the reviews by Miller and Hester and by Annis, a few more reports of controlled studies to compare inpatient with outpatient treatments have been published (Chapman & Huygens, 1988; Hayashida et al., 1989; McCrady et al., 1986; Walsh et al., 1991). In general, these studies have upheld the earlier conclusions, with the one possible exception of the study by Walsh and colleagues (1991). These researchers compared outcomes for 227 workers randomly assigned to one of three options: inpatient treatment (averaging 23 days) plus follow-up with Alcoholics Anonymous (AA) meetings, AA meetings alone, or a choice of either of these two or outpatient therapy (frequency not reported). During the 2-year follow-up period, no significant differences were found among the groups in job-related outcomes, including involuntary termination, warning notices, quality-of-job performance, and hours missed from work. However, those assigned to AA only or the "choice" option had much less success on drinking and drug use measures compared with hospitalization. Although these findings are notable, they are not surprising in that the very intensive treatment of the inpatient setting was compared with AA alone (although an invaluable adjunct to most treatment, not generally considered a treatment in itself). A more meaningful comparison would have been between inpatient and intensive outpatient treatment.

In another controlled study, McCrady and associates (1986) compared the effectiveness of inpatient treatment with that of partial hospital treatment. In this extension of the work begun by Longabaugh and colleagues (1983), 174 patients were randomly assigned to inpatient or partial treatment following a brief (6–7 days) inpatient detoxification. Follow-up at 12 months showed that the groups did not differ on drinking behavior measured as continuous abstinence and proportion of abstinent days. About one third of all patients were rehospitalized during the 12 months of follow-up, but no difference was found between the inpatient and partial hospital groups on this variable. Although over 30% of the original study group were not available for the 12-month follow-up, the researchers did not think that this affected the comparison between the two treatment groups.

In a third study, Chapman and Huygens (1988) assigned 113 male and female detoxified alcoholics to one of three study groups: 6-week inpatient, 6-week outpatient (twice per week), or a single confrontational interview. Follow-up at 6 and 18 months showed that "no treatment appeared to be consistently more effective than another" when compared on measures of abstinence, amount, and frequency of drinking and social factors, including employment and fights (Chapman &

Huygens, 1988, p. 76). One striking limitation of this study is that all patients received an inpatient detoxification lasting 2 weeks before assignment to a study group. It could be argued, therefore, that all subjects received a 2-week course of inpatient treatment.

A fourth study, by Hayashida and co-workers (1989), compared inpatient and outpatient detoxification. A total of 164 male veteran volunteers were randomized into the two treatment options; follow-up was conducted at 1 and 6 months. The dropout rate of the outpatients (28%) differed significantly from that of inpatients (5%). Because many of the dropouts in the outpatient group (8 of 24) occurred on Day 2 of the study, the authors speculated that some patients may have dropped out when they learned they did not get assigned to their preferred setting of inpatient treatment. No difference was found in the two groups regarding the acceptance of long-term rehabilitation following detoxification. At 1-month follow-up, the inpatient group had a better outcome on alcohol-related criteria, but this difference was not apparent by 6 months. The groups did not differ on other outcome measures, including work-related, legal, or psychiatric scales. However, the inpatient group showed a significantly higher rate of hospitalization for nonalcohol reasons. Because the subjects were randomized to either inpatient or outpatient treatment and because medical illness was not a deciding factor in assignment, this is an interesting finding. It is consistent with the findings of McLachlan and Stein (1982), who found that for those who were randomized to inpatient rehabilitation, the number of days spent in a hospital for medical reasons unrelated to addiction increased significantly in the year following treatment. Conversely, the number of hospital days was significantly lower for those treated as outpatients. These findings appear to support the notion that hospitalization for addictions treatment may encourage the sick role and lead to a greater use of the hospital for other conditions.

Overall, the literature upholds the position that outpatient treatment (especially intensive outpatient treatment) is at least as effective as inpatient treatment for alcohol dependence. In most of the studies reviewed, patients were not considered for randomization if their clinical condition (severe withdrawal or dangerousness) required hospitalization. In the comprehensive studies reviewed so far in this chapter, the heterogenous makeup of the study populations may have led to the finding that inpatient and outpatient treatments have comparable outcomes. It can be hypothesized that for each type of treatment, some kinds of patients do better, thus balancing out the overall comparisons. The goal, therefore, is to use personal and clinical characteristics to match patients with the treatment under which they are expected to do best.

MATCHING PATIENTS TO TREATMENT

Many researchers have attempted to delineate factors that make it possible to match patients with the most effective types of treatment. It is useful to focus on a few key studies with particular application for the mental health professional attempting to decide between inpatient and outpatient treatment for their patients.

Based on a comprehensive review of treatment studies, Emrick and Hansen (1983) reported a number of patient characteristics to be correlated with successful treatment outcome. These included "higher social class, employed, married, socially active, financially well situated, good work adjustment, good marital and family relationships, good social relationships, good residential adjustment, good 'general situation,' no or minimal pretreatment arrest history, good physical condition, higher intelligence, good psychological insight, at least moderate self-acceptance, good motivation, previous outpatient treatment, being diagnosed 'normal,' being cooperative during treatment, drinking none or a little during treatment, and having the spouse involved in treatment" (Emrick & Hansen, 1983, pp. 1079–1080).

In a retrospective study of 460 alcoholics, McLellan and

colleagues (McLellan, Luborsky, Woody, O'Brien, & Druley, 1983) found that severity of psychiatric symptoms was the most predictive of treatment outcome for patients attending one of six treatment programs that included a variety of inpatient and outpatient settings. Those with low psychiatric severity did well in any of the programs, and those with high severity did poorly, regardless of which program they attended. For those with mid-range psychiatric severity, the authors concluded, "While severe alcohol or drug use, and even medical or legal problems, may be dealt with effectively in our outpatient settings, middle-severity patients with family and employment problems seem to do better in inpatient treatment" (McLellan et al., 1983, p. 624). It is interesting to note that the severity of alcohol use did not correlate with outcome in any of the programs.

In a follow-up to the above study, the same group conducted one of the first prospective studies of its kind (McLellan, Woody et al., 1983). They compared outcomes for patients matched to one of six treatment programs with those who chose not to attend the program assigned by the matching criteria (referred to herein as "mismatched"). The subjects were male veterans treated in the Veterans Administration treatment network during 1978. A total of 179 alcohol-dependent subjects were administered the Addiction Severity Index (ASI) (U.S. Department of Health and Human Services, 1988) (Table 5.1), and severity scores were assigned for each of seven areas (psychiatric symptoms, alcohol use, drug use, legal, employment, family, and medical problems) (McLellan, Luborsky, O'Brien, & Woody, 1980; U.S. Department of Health and Human Services, 1988). All patients underwent a 5-day inpatient detoxification/stabilization program and were given their assignments based on the following matching scheme:

> Because in the prior study (McLellan, Luborsky et al., 1983) patients with low psychiatric severity did well in any setting, they were assigned to outpatient treatment unless they had a high employment severity. Patients with mid-range psychiat-

---

Table 5.1
ADDICTION SEVERITY INDEX

Because most of the more recent work in matching has
been done using the Addiction Severity Index (ASI), a
brief description is included here. The ASI is a structured interview tool that can be administered in about
45 minutes. Unlike many research tools, the ASI was
designed to be of use to the clinician as well as the
researcher. Many treatment programs use the ASI as the
basis for clinical assessment. For each of the seven
categories (medical, employment, alcohol, drug, legal,
family/social, and psychiatric) current, recent (past 30
days), and lifetime severity are assessed. The severity
rating — or need for treatment — is assigned by the interviewer following established guidelines for weighting
the objective and subjective data.

---

ric severity were assigned to inpatient treatment if either their
employment or family severity was high. Those with a high
psychiatric severity were all considered mismatched, as none
of the programs in the study were deemed appropriate.

During treatment, patients who attended the recommended
program (matched) were rated by staff as more motivated.
Moreover, they stayed in treatment longer with a higher proportion of favorable discharges compared with those who
were mismatched. At 6-month follow-up, matched patients
showed better outcome on 17 of 19 variables (eight of which
were statistically significant) when compared with those who
were mismatched.

IMPLICATIONS FOR ASSESSMENT AND TREATMENT

Although more research is needed to refine the definitions of characteristics for matching individual patients with treatment, some guidance can be drawn from what is known so far. To summarize:

- Research shows that when all types of patients are grouped together, no clear difference in effectiveness between inpatient and outpatient treatment can be found. This is especially apparent when comparing inpatient with intensive outpatient settings.

- Good medical practice dictates that patients with impending delirium tremens (DTs), other life-threatening medical conditions, or dangerousness to self or others need to be admitted to the hospital.

- Hospitalization longer than the length of time needed to stabilize medical or psychiatric conditions provides no additional advantage.

- Hospitalization may lead to a higher rate (and possible overuse) of hospitalization for medical conditions unrelated to the addiction.

- Social stability has been associated with successful outcome regardless of treatment type. Patients with a stable marriage, stable employment, and good social adjustment can be expected to do well in the less intensive settings.

- The severity of the addiction does not consistently differentiate between those who are likely to do well in inpatient treatment compared with outpatient treatment.

- The single most meaningful variable for selecting between treatment programs is the severity of psychiatric symptoms as measured by the ASI.

- Persons with low or medium psychiatric severity can be expected to do well in outpatient treatment unless employment or family factors present an insurmountable impediment to treatment compliance.

- Persons with high psychiatric severity do not do well in either inpatient or outpatient chemical dependency. Rather, they need a program specializing in the treatment of patients with dual diagnoses.

From this, we can derive a hierarchical decision tree (Figure 5.1) for assessing and referring patients to either inpatient or outpatient treatment. The first level of decision making is to assess the presence of impending DTs, other life-threatening medical conditions, or dangerousness to self or others. If any of these are present, the patient is best referred to inpatient treatment for stabilization.

Next, the level of psychiatric symptom severity must be assessed. In the studies by the McLellan group (McLellan, Luborsky et al.,1983; McLellan, Woody et al., 1983), this is not a diagnosis but an assessment by the interviewer based on patient report and interviewer observation regarding the current severity of psychiatric symptoms (such as depression, anxiety, hallucinations, and thoughts of suicide, among others). The ASI, the Global Assessment Scale (Endicott, Spitzer, Fleiss, & Cohen, 1976), a standardized clinical interview, or any other tool for assessing severity of psychiatric symptoms may be useful for this process. At this level of decision making, patients with high psychiatric severity should be referred to programs specializing in the treatment of dual diagnosis cases or with a strong psychiatric component.

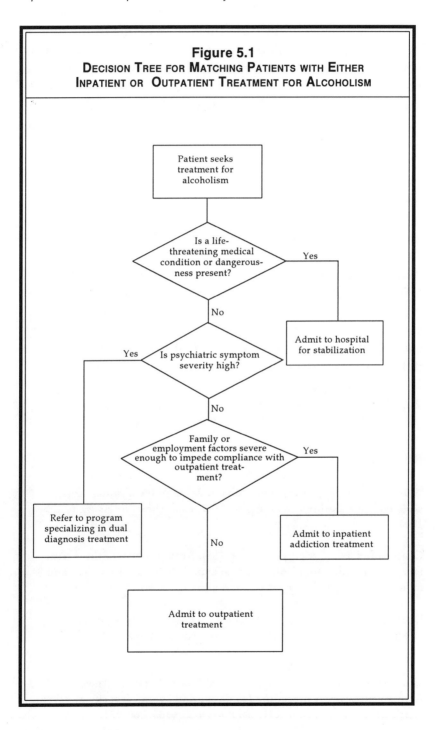

Figure 5.1
DECISION TREE FOR MATCHING PATIENTS WITH EITHER
INPATIENT OR OUTPATIENT TREATMENT FOR ALCOHOLISM

In a third level of decision making, patients in the low or middle range of psychiatric symptom severity are assessed for severity of employment and family factors. If these factors are so severe that they are expected to present significant impediments to compliance with an outpatient program, the patient should be referred for inpatient treatment; otherwise, he or she can be expected to do well in outpatient treatment.

SUMMARY

Well-controlled large studies of undifferentiated patient samples that compare the effectiveness of inpatient with outpatient treatment consistently find no significant difference in treatment effectiveness. Research supports the idea that some types of patients do better or worse in certain settings. Application of the current knowledge to clinical decision making can result in well-reasoned treatment decisions for both the patient and practitioner.

REFERENCES

Annis, H. M. (1986). Is inpatient rehabilitation of the alcoholic cost effective? Con position. *Advances in Alcohol and Substance Abuse, 5,* 175–190.

Chapman, P. H. L., & Huygens, I. (1988). An evaluation of three treatment programmes for alcoholism: An experimental study with 6- and 8-month follow-ups. *British Journal of Addiction, 83,* 67–81.

Emrick, C. D., & Hansen, J. (1983, October). Assertions regarding effectiveness of treatment for alcoholism: Fact or fantasy? *American Psychologist, 38,* 1078–1088.

Endicott, J., Spitzer, R. L., Fleiss, J. L., & Cohen, J. (1976). The Global Assessment Scale: A procedure for measuring overall severity of psychiatric disturbance. *Archives of General Psychiatry, 33,* 766–771.

Hayashida, M., Alterman, A. I., McLellan, A. T., O'Brien, C. P., Purtill, J. J., Volicelli, J. R., Raphaelson, A. H., & Hall, C. P. (1989). Comparative effectiveness and costs of inpatient and outpatient detoxification of patients with mild to moderate alcohol withdrawal syndrome. *New England Journal of Medicine, 320,* 358–365.

Holder, H. D., & Blose, J. O. (1991). Typical patterns and cost of alcoholism treatment across a variety of populations and providers. *Alcoholism, Clinical and Experimental Research, 15,* 190–195.

Longabaugh, R., McCrady, B., Fink, E., Stout, R., McAuley, T., Doyle, C., & McNeill, D. (1983). Cost effectiveness of alcoholism treatment in partial vs. inpatient settings: Six-month outcomes. *Journal of Studies on Alcohol, 44,* 1049–1071.

McCrady, B., Longabaugh, R., Fink, E., Stout, R., Beattie, M., & Ruggieri-Authelet, A. (1986). Cost effectiveness of alcoholism treatment in partial hospital versus inpatient settings after brief inpatient treatment: 12-month outcomes. *Journal of Consulting and Clinical Psychology, 54,* 708–713.

McLachlan, J. F. C., & Stein, R. L. (1982). Evaluation of a day clinic for alcoholics. *Journal of Studies on Alcohol, 43,* 261–272.

McLellan, A. T., Luborsky, L., O'Brien, C. P., & Woody, G. E. (1980). An improved evaluation instrument for substance abuse patients: The Addiction Severity Index. *Journal of Nervous and Mental Disease, 168,* 26–33.

McLellan, A. T., Luborsky, L., Woody, G. E., O'Brien, C. P., & Druley, K. A. (1983). Predicting response to alcohol and drug abuse treatments: Role of psychiatric severity. *Archives of General Psychiatry, 40,* 620–625.

McLellan, A. T., Woody, G. E., Luborsky, L., O'Brien, C. P., & Druley, K. A. (1983). Increased effectiveness of substance abuse treatment: A prospective study of patient-treatment 'matching.' *Journal of Nervous and Mental Disease, 171,* 597–605.

Miller, W. R., & Hester, R. K. (1986). Inpatient alcoholism treatment: Who benefits? *American Psychologist, 41,* 794–805.

U.S. Department of Health and Human Services. (1988). *Guide to the Addiction Severity Index: Background, administration, and field testing Results* (DHHS Publication No. ADM 88–1419). Rockville, MD: Author.

Walsh, D. C., Hingson, R. W., Merrigan, D. M., Levenson, S. M., Cupples, A., Heeren, T., Coffman, G. A., Becker, C. A., Barker, T. A., Hamilton, S. K., McGuire, T. G., & Kelly, C. A. (1991). A randomized trial of treatment options for alcohol-abusing workers. *New England Journal of Medicine, 325,* 775–782.

6

Marital and Family Therapy in the Treatment of Alcoholism

Timothy J. O'Farrell, PhD

Dr. O'Farrell is Associate Professor of Psychology in the Department of Psychiatry at Harvard Medical School, Boston, MA, where he directs the Harvard Families and Addiction Program and the Harvard Counseling for Alcoholics' Marriages (CALM) Project. He is also Associate Chief of the Psychology Service at the Veterans Medical Center in Brockton and West Roxbury, MA.

KEY POINTS

- Marital and family therapy is an effective treatment modality for alcoholism. Many alcoholics experience extensive marital and family problems, including separation, divorce, and child and spouse abuse. Moreover, marital and family conflicts often may precipitate excessive drinking and help to maintain an alcohol problem.

- Marital and family therapy interventions can be used effectively at different stages of the recovery process. The author offers strategies for tackling family problems associated with alcohol abuse at each stage, including initiating a change in behavior, stabilizing sobriety, dealing with drinking during treatment, maintaining long-term recovery, preventing relapse, and approaching marital and family issues after the client has achieved control.

- Once the alcoholic has decided to change his or her drinking behavior, marital and family therapy seeks to reduce or eliminate abusive drinking, support the alcoholic's efforts to change, and change marital and family patterns to provide an atmosphere more conducive to sobriety.

OVERVIEW

A 1974 report from the National Institute on Alcohol Abuse and Alcoholism (NIAAA) to the United States Congress called marital and family therapy in alcoholism treatment "one of the most outstanding current advances in the area of psychotherapy of alcoholism" (Keller, 1974, p. 116). Case reports and uncontrolled treatment studies that presented favorable results were the basis for this enthusiastic appraisal. NIAAA also recommended that controlled outcome studies be conducted to evaluate these promising treatment methods. In the 22 years since that report, considerable progress has been made in developing the rationale, clinical applications, and outcome research on marital and family therapy in the treatment of alcoholism.

This rationale has developed from several converging lines of research. Many alcoholics have extensive marital and family problems, and positive marital and family adjustment is associated with better treatment outcomes at follow-up. The literature describes reciprocal relationships between marital-family interactions and abusive drinking. Problem drinking leads to marital and family discord, including separation, divorce, and child and spouse abuse. At the same time, marital and family problems may stimulate excessive drinking, and family interactions often help to maintain alcohol problems once they have developed. Even when recovery from the alcohol problem has begun, marital and family conflicts often may precipitate renewed drinking by abstinent alcoholics. Marital and family therapy can help not only the alcoholic client but also other victims of alcoholism, such as family members.

The clinical applications of marital and family therapy in the treatment of alcoholism have grown considerably in the past 20 years. Formerly, marital and family therapy often was considered useful only for alcoholics with acknowledged serious marital and family problems. Currently, clinical guidelines suggest that marital and family therapy may be beneficial to couples and families with less serious problems who often are better able to work together to support the alcoholic's sobriety and to enrich the marital-family relationships that have been strained by alcoholism-related stressors. Even when marital-family factors do not play an important role in triggering or maintaining the abusive drinking, involving the spouse or family in treatment may support alternative nondrinking behaviors and strengthen the alcoholic client's ability to refrain from drinking while learning to deal with nonmarital factors.

Gone are the days when most treatment centers provided little or no marital or family involvement. Currently, the only justifiable reason for not including family members in the alcoholic client's treatment is refusal by the client or the family to consent to such contact. The standards of the Joint Commission on Accreditation of Healthcare Organizations for accrediting alcoholism treatment programs in the United States now require that the spouse or some other adult family member who lives with the alcoholic be included in at least the assessment process for all alcoholics who seek help.

Research accumulated over the past 20 years indicates that marital and family therapy interventions can be used effectively at different stages of the recovery process. Although many studies have been completed, the marital and family therapy methods that have shown the most promise in outcome research are not yet used widely by practitioners who treat alcoholics and their families.

INITIATING CHANGE

Four marital and family therapy approaches address the difficult and all-too-common case of the alcoholic who is not yet willing to stop drinking. Three of the approaches try to help family members motivate the uncooperative, denying alcoholic to stop drinking. Community Reinforcement Training for Families teaches the nonalcoholic family member (usually the wife) how to reduce physical abuse to herself or himself, encourage sobriety, encourage seeking professional treatment, and assist in treatment (Sisson & Azrin, 1986, 1993). The Johnson Institute "intervention" procedure involves three to four educational and rehearsal sessions to prepare family members (Johnson, 1973). During the intervention session, family members confront the alcoholic about the drinking and strongly encourage the alcohol abuser to enter an alcoholism treatment program (Johnson, 1973; Liepman, 1993). Unilateral family therapy helps the nonalcoholic spouse strengthen his or her coping capabilities, enhance family functioning, and facilitate greater sobriety on the part of the alcohol abuser (Thomas & Ager, 1993). This type of therapy provides a series of graded steps the spouse can use before confrontation. These steps may be successful in their own right or at least pave the way for a positive outcome to a "programmed confrontation" — similar to the Johnson approach and adapted for use with an individual spouse.

A fourth approach is a group program for wives of treatment-resistant alcoholics (Dittrich, 1993). This program helps the wives of alcoholics cope with their emotional distress and concentrate on their own motivations for change rather than trying to motivate the alcoholic to change. This approach borrows many concepts from Al-Anon, the most widely used source of support for family members troubled by a loved one's alcoholism. Al-Anon advocates that family members detach themselves from the alcoholic's drinking in a loving way, accept that they are powerless to control the alcoholic, and seek support from other Al-Anon program members (Al-Anon Family Groups, 1981).

STABILIZING SOBRIETY AND RELATIONSHIPS

Once the alcoholic has decided to change his or her drinking habits, marital and family therapy has two basic objectives to stabilize short-term change in the alcohol problem and in the alcoholic's marital-family relationships. The first goal is to reduce or eliminate abusive drinking and support the alcoholic's efforts to change. To this end, a high priority involves changing alcohol-related interactional patterns (e.g., nagging about past drinking but ignoring current sober behavior). One can encourage abstinent alcoholics and their spouses to engage in behaviors more pleasing to each other; however, if they continue focusing on past or potential future drinking, such arguments frequently lead to renewed drinking (Maisto, O'Farrell, Connors, McKay, & Pelcovits, 1988). They then feel more discouraged about their relationship and the drinking than before and are less likely to try pleasing each other again.

The second goal is to help alter general marital and family patterns, which provides an atmosphere more conducive to sobriety. This involves helping the couple repair the often extensive relationship damage incurred during many years of conflict over alcohol, as well as helping them find solutions to relationship difficulties that may not be related directly to the alcoholism. Finally, the couple must learn to confront and resolve relationship conflicts without the alcoholic partner resorting to drinking.

Alcohol-Focused Interventions:

After the alcoholic has decided to change, marital and family therapy with the spouse and other family members can support the alcoholic in adhering to this difficult and stressful decision. The first purpose of such treatment is to establish a clear and specific agreement between the alcohol abuser and family member(s) about the goal for the alcoholic's drinking and the role of each family member in achieving that goal. Behavioral contracting can be useful for this purpose. Specifying other behavioral changes needed in the alcoholic or the family requires a careful review of individual situations and conditions. Possible exposure to alcoholic beverages and alco-hol-related situations should be discussed. The spouse and family should decide whether they will drink alcoholic bever-ages in the alcoholic's presence, whether alcoholic beverages will be kept and served at home, if the couple will attend social gatherings involving alcohol, and how to deal with these situations. Particular persons, gatherings, or circumstances likely to be stressful should be identified. Couple and family interactions related to alcohol also must be addressed because arguments, tension, and negative feelings can precipitate more abusive drinking. Therapists need to discuss these patterns with the family and suggest specific procedures to be used in difficult situations.

Behavioral Contracting

Written behavioral contracts have a number of common elements that make them useful. The drinking behavior goal is made explicit. Specific behaviors that each spouse can incor-porate to help achieve this goal also are detailed. The contract provides alternative behaviors to negative interactions about drinking. Finally, the agreement decreases the nonalcoholic spouse's anxiety and need to control the alcoholic and his or her drinking.

Kivlahan and Shapiro (personal communication, May 18, 1984) ask alcoholics and their spouses to engage in what they call a *sobriety trust contract*. Each day at a specified time, the alcoholic initiates a brief discussion and reiterates the desire not to drink that day. The alcoholic then asks if the spouse has any questions or fears about possible drinking that day; the alcoholic answers the questions and attempts to reassure the spouse. Also, the spouse is not to mention past drinking or any future possible drinking beyond that day. Finally, the couple agrees to refrain from discussing drinking at any other time, to keep the daily trust discussion brief, and to end it with a positive statement.

Two examples illustrate other types of contracts used with alcoholic couples.

Case #1:

An alcoholic man, who recognized he had an alcohol problem and had abstained for 3 months (in the past year) was trying to engage in "social drinking." Occasionally, he would drink heavily for 3–5 days. Three serious binges had occurred in the past 6 weeks. Each binge ended after an intense fight in which he became verbally abusive; his wife threatened to terminate their marriage. At a conjoint session with the client's wife, the following agreement was negotiated: (a) the husband's goal was to abstain from drinking alcohol for a minimum of 6 months; (b) if he drank before then, he would start taking disulfiram (a drug that produces extreme nausea and sickness when the person taking it ingests alcohol) daily and continue taking the medication at least to the end of the 6-month period; (c) if the wife thought the husband had been drinking, she would remind him of their agreement and ask him to start disulfiram treatment; and (d) if the husband refused, the wife would leave their home until the husband had stopped drinking, arguing, or threatening her and started taking disulfiram. Two weeks later, the husband drank and then voluntarily started taking disulfiram. Both the client and his wife were pleased that their customary intense argument was not necessary to terminate the drinking.

Case #2:

A chronic alcoholic with serious liver cirrhosis reported progress in outpatient sessions but complained that his wife was unfairly accusing him of drinking. They also argued about financial and other problems. At approximately the same time, liver function tests showed elevated liver enzymes, most likely indicating recent drinking. Sessions with the couple established the following agreement: (a) each evening the husband would take a portable alcohol breath test called MOBAT (Sobell & Sobell, 1975) to verify he had not been drinking; (b) the wife would refrain from accusations about current drinking or complaints about past drinking; (c) the daily MOBAT review would continue until liver function test results were normal and there was no evidence of drinking for 2 consecutive months; and (d) the couple would continue in conjoint sessions about their other relationship problems. Only two isolated instances occurred in which the MOBAT indicated the husband had been drinking that day, and the couple's conflicts were resolved satisfactorily in later sessions.

Participation in Alcoholics Anonymous (AA) and Al-Anon self-help groups often is part of the behavioral contracts for those struggling with alcoholism. As with any other behavior that is part of a "sobriety contract," attendance at AA and Al-Anon meetings is reviewed at each therapy session.

A disulfiram contract is designed to maintain disulfiram ingestion and abstinence from alcohol and to decrease alcohol-related arguments and interactions between the alcoholic and the spouse. In the disulfiram contract, the alcoholic agrees to take disulfiram each day while the spouse observes. The spouse, in turn, agrees to positively reinforce the alcoholic for taking the disulfiram, to record the observation on a calendar provided by the therapist, and not to mention past drinking or any fears about future drinking.

Although disulfiram therapy is widely used, alcoholics in treatment have shown a tendency to discontinue the drug prematurely, thus diminishing its effectiveness. Before negotiating such a contract, the therapist should be sure that the alcoholic is willing and medically cleared to take disulfiram and that both the alcoholic and the spouse have been fully informed and educated about the effects of the drug. They should view the agreement as a cooperative method for rebuilding lost trust rather than as a coercive checking-up operation. O'Farrell and Bayog (1986) present details on how to implement the disulfiram contract and deal with common resistances to this procedure.

Miller (1972) used contingency contracting with an excessive drinker and his wife to produce reduced consumption and fewer arguments about drinking. The couple signed a contract that required the husband to limit his drinking to 1–3 drinks a day (with his wife before the evening meal) and the wife to refrain from negative verbal or nonverbal responses to her husband's drinking. Each partner agreed to pay the other $20 if he or she broke the agreement. They both received a few fines during the first few weeks of the contract, but the infractions rapidly diminished when each partner learned that the contract would, in fact, be enforced.

The alcohol abuser treated by Miller was employed and showed no medical damage from his excessive drinking; the negative impact of his drinking was confined to the marital relationship. These factors suggested an attempt to reduce rather than eliminate the drinking. Therapists must choose carefully in each individual case whether the goal of treatment should be moderation or total abstinence and should use available guidelines (Heather & Robertson, 1981; Miller & Caddy, 1977) prior to implementing such a behavioral contracting procedure.

Noel and McCrady (1993) used behavior modification procedures to decrease spouse behaviors that triggered or enabled abusive drinking with an alcoholic woman and her husband.

The couple identified behaviors by the husband that triggered drinking by the wife (e.g., drinking together after work, trying to stop her from drinking, and arguing with her about drinking). The wife reacted by criticizing her husband until he left her alone, at which point she would continue to drink. The husband unwittingly reinforced his wife's drinking by protecting her from the consequences of her drinking (e.g., helping her to bed when she was drunk and cleaning up after her when she drank).

Noel and McCrady helped the couple find mutually comfortable and agreeable methods to reverse the husband's behavior that inadvertently promoted his wife's drinking. The husband decided to give up drinking and worked hard to change his feelings that he must protect his wife from the negative consequences of her drinking. The therapists also taught the husband to provide positive reinforcers (e.g., going to movies) only when his wife had not been drinking.

Dealing with Drinking During Treatment

Drinking episodes often occur during marital and family therapy with alcoholics. This treatment modality works best if the therapist intervenes before the drinking goes on for too long. Asking the alcoholic to keep a daily record of urges to drink (and any drinking that occurs) and reviewing this record each session can help alert the therapist to the possible risk of a relapse. Between-session telephone calls to prompt completion of homework assignments also can alert the therapist to precursors of a drinking episode or to drinking already in progress. Once drinking has occurred, the therapist should try to get the client to stop drinking and see the couple as soon as possible to use the relapse as a learning experience. At the couple session, the therapist must be extremely active in defusing hostile or depressive reactions to the drinking; he or she should stress that drinking does not constitute total failure and that inconsistent progress is the rule rather than the exception. Also, the therapist should help the couple decide what they need to do to feel sure that the drinking is over and will not continue in the coming week (e.g., restarting disulfiram, attending AA and Al-Anon together, reinstituting a trust contract, or entering a detoxification ward). Finally, the therapist should try to help the couple identify what couple conflict (or other antecedent) led to the relapse and generate alternative solutions other than drinking for similar future situations.

Repeated drinking episodes can present a particularly difficult challenge. Each drinking episode should be used as a learning experience, and, depending on what is discovered, different strategies may be helpful. A careful analysis sometimes will show that the drinking is being precipitated by factors outside the marital relationship, such as work pressures or job-related drinking situations. Individual sessions with the alcoholic (to deal with the nonmarital precipitants) often can be useful. Another nonmarital factor that can lead to repeated drinking episodes is the alcoholic's ambivalence about whether to stop drinking or attempt to drink socially. Often, an individual session with the alcoholic helps the therapist establish the alcoholic's ambivalence as the basis for the repeated drinking and matter of factly lay out the choices facing the alcoholic about the drinking behavior.

At times, repeated drinking episodes are related (at least in part) to marital relationship issues. When the drinking has adaptive consequences for the relationship (e.g., facilitates sexual interaction or emotional communication for one or both spouses), the main strategy is to strengthen controls against drinking while working intensively with the couple to attain the same adaptive relationship consequences without the aid of alcohol. For other couples, repeated drinking episodes are a response to recurring, intense marital conflicts. The best approach for these couples is to devise specific methods tailored to their idiosyncratic needs that they can use to contain conflict and that the alcoholic can use to avoid drinking, strengthen nonmarital alcohol coping mechanisms (e.g., AA and disulfiram), and learn alternative communication and problem-solving skills.

Interventions to Improve Marital and Family Relationships:

Once the alcohol abuser has decided to change his or her drinking habits and has successfully begun to control or abstain from drinking, the therapist can focus on the alcoholic's marital and family relationships. Family members often experience resentment about past abusive drinking and fear and distrust about the possible return of abusive drinking in the future. The alcoholic often experiences guilt and a desire for recognition of current improved drinking behavior. These feelings experienced by the alcoholic and the family often lead to an atmosphere of tension and unhappiness in marital and family relationships.

The couple or family frequently has problems caused by drinking (e.g., bills, legal charges, and embarrassing incidents) that still need to be resolved. They often have a backlog of other unresolved marital and family problems that the drinking obscured. These long-standing problems may seem to increase as drinking declines, when, in fact, the problems simply are being recognized for the first time, now that alcohol cannot be used to excuse them.

Family members frequently lack the communication skills and mutual positive feelings needed to resolve these problems. As a result, many marriages and families are dissolved during the first year or two of the alcoholic's recovery. In other cases, marital and family conflicts trigger relapse and a return to abusive drinking by the alcoholic. Even in cases in which the alcoholic has a basically sound marriage and family life when he or she is not drinking, the initiation of sobriety can produce temporary tension and role readjustment as well as provide the opportunity for stabilizing and enriching the marriage and family. For these reasons, many alcoholics can benefit from assistance to improve their marital and family relationships once changes in their drinking habits have begun.

Two major goals of interventions focused on the alcoholic's marital-family relationship are to: (a) increase positive feeling, goodwill, and commitment to the relationship and (b) resolve conflicts, problems, and desires for change (O'Farrell, 1993a). The general sequence in teaching couples and families skills to increase positive interchanges and resolve conflicts and problems is therapist instruction and modeling, the couple practicing under a therapist's supervision, homework assignments, and review of homework with further practice.

Increasing Positive Interchanges

A series of procedures can increase a couple's awareness of benefits from the relationship and the frequency with which spouses notice, acknowledge, and initiate pleasing or caring behaviors on a daily basis. The therapist tells the couple that caring behaviors are "behaviors that show you care for the other person" and assigns homework called "Catch Your Partner Doing Something Nice" to assist couples in noticing the daily caring behaviors in the marriage. This assignment requires each spouse to record one caring behavior performed by the other each day on sheets provided by the therapist

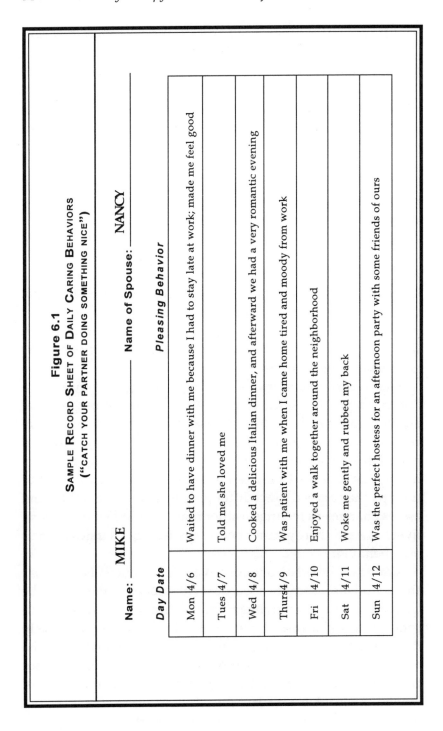

Figure 6.1

SAMPLE RECORD SHEET OF DAILY CARING BEHAVIORS
("CATCH YOUR PARTNER DOING SOMETHING NICE")

Name: **MIKE**   Name of Spouse: **NANCY**

Day Date	Pleasing Behavior
Mon 4/6	Waited to have dinner with me because I had to stay late at work; made me feel good
Tues 4/7	Told me she loved me
Wed 4/8	Cooked a delicious Italian dinner, and afterward we had a very romantic evening
Thurs 4/9	Was patient with me when I came home tired and moody from work
Fri 4/10	Enjoyed a walk together around the neighborhood
Sat 4/11	Woke me gently and rubbed my back
Sun 4/12	Was the perfect hostess for an afternoon party with some friends of ours

(Figure 6.1). The couple reads the caring behaviors recorded during the previous week at the subsequent session. Then, the therapist models acknowledging caring behaviors ("I liked it when you ____. It made me feel ____."), noting the importance of eye contact; a smile; a sincere, pleasant tone of voice; and only positive feelings. Each spouse then practices acknowledging caring behaviors from his or her daily list for the previous week.

After the couple practices the new behavior in the therapy session, the therapist assigns for homework a 2–5-minute daily communication session at home in which each partner acknowledges one pleasing behavior noticed that day. As couples begin to notice and acknowledge daily caring behaviors, each partner begins initiating more caring behaviors. Often, the weekly reports of daily caring behaviors show that one or both spouses are fulfilling requests for desired change voiced before the therapy. In addition, many couples report that the 2–5-minute communication sessions initiate more extensive conversations.

A final assignment involves each partner giving the other a "caring day" during the coming week by performing special acts to show caring for the spouse. The therapist should encourage each partner to take risks and to act lovingly toward his or her spouse rather than wait for the other to make the first move. The therapist may remind couples that at the start of therapy they agreed to act differently (e.g., more lovingly) and assess changes in feelings, rather than wait to feel more positively toward their partner before instituting changes in their own behavior.

Many families of alcoholics have discontinued or decreased shared leisure activities because in the past the alcoholic frequently sought enjoyment only in situations involving alcohol and embarrassed the family by drinking too much. Reversing this trend is important because participation by the couple and family in social and recreational activities is associated with positive alcoholism treatment outcome (Moos, Finney, & Cronkite, 1990).

Planning and engaging in shared rewarding activities can be initiated simply by asking each spouse to make a separate list of possible activities. Each activity must involve both partners (either by themselves, with their children, or with other adults) and can occur at or away from home. Before giving the couple a homework assignment of planning a shared rewarding activity, the therapist should model a shared rewarding activity that illustrates solutions to common pitfalls (e.g., waiting until the last minute so that necessary preparations cannot be made or getting sidetracked on trivial practical arrangements). Finally, the couple should not discuss problems or conflicts during their planned shared rewarding activity.

Core symbols, or symbols of special meaning, offer another means to enhance positive feelings and interactions in a relationship. A core symbol is any event, place, or object that carries special meaning for the relationship to both marital partners (Liberman, Wheeler, de Visser, Kuehnel, & Kuehnel, 1980); examples include a special song, their honeymoon, the place where the couple met, pictures, eating by candlelight, and wedding rings. Rituals and activities (e.g., going out for breakfast on Sunday morning) that go beyond recreational activities because of their special meaning to the couple also can become core symbols and represent an intimate shared time set aside for closeness. Therapists should introduce core symbols only after tension over drinking has decreased and the partners are beginning to experience some good will and positive feeling toward each other. After each partner provides one example of such a symbol, they are asked to list as many core symbols as possible for a homework assignment. In subsequent sessions, the couple chooses one or more core symbols to reexperience or reestablish in their day-to-day lives together. In relationships in which the search for core symbols not poisoned by alcohol proves fruitless, therapists should help the couple develop and enact new core symbols. Identifying and participating in such core symbols can help couples foster positive feelings that have been buried for years under many layers of hostility and disappointment. Renewed spiritual and religious practices are important for some couples.

Core symbols, planning recreational and leisure activities, and increasing positive behaviors can be applied to family therapy, which includes children and their parent(s). Family therapy sessions are particularly useful and indicated when an adolescent has an alcohol problem (Trepper, Piercy, Lewis, Volk, & Sprenkle, 1993) or when the alcoholic parent and his or her spouse have made some progress and the therapist wishes to include the children in the therapy. Using core symbols in family therapy sessions can be powerful because special activities and rituals forge strong family ties and traditions. Similarly, planning recreational and leisure activities for the whole family or selected members (e.g., father and son) can be rewarding. Increasing pleasing behavior often can lead to pronounced changes in the emotional tone of the family, especially when the therapist can encourage the entire family to participate.

Resolving Conflicts and Problems

Inadequate communication is a major problem for alcoholic couples (O'Farrell & Birchler, 1987). Indeed, an inability to resolve conflicts and problems can cause abusive drinking and severe marital and family tension to recur (Maisto et al., 1988). Training in communication skills often is begun by defining effective communication as "message intended (by speaker) equals message received (by listener)."

Therapists can use instructions, modeling, prompting, behavioral rehearsal, and feedback to teach couples and families how to communicate more effectively. The communication skills of listening and speaking and planned communication sessions are essential prerequisites for problem solving and negotiating desired behavioral changes. The training starts with nonproblem areas that are positive or neutral and moves to problem areas and charged issues only after each skill has been practiced on less problematic topics.

Communication sessions are planned, structured discussions in which spouses talk privately, face to face, without distractions, and with each spouse taking turns expressing his or her viewpoint without interruptions. Communication sessions can be introduced for 2-5 minutes daily when couples first practice acknowledging caring behaviors and in 10-15-minute sessions three to four times a week in later sessions when the concern is to practice a particular skill. The therapist discusses with the couple the time and place they plan to have their assigned communication practice sessions. The success of this plan is assessed at the next session, and any needed changes are suggested. Establishing a communication session as a method for discussing feelings, events, and problems can be helpful for many couples. The therapist encourages couples to ask each other for a communication session when they want to discuss an issue or problem and to keep in mind the ground rules of behavior that characterize such a session.

Listening skills help each spouse to feel understood and supported and slow down the couple's interactions to prevent quick escalation of aversive exchanges. The therapist instructs each spouse to repeat both the words and the feelings of the speaker's message and to verify if the message received was the message intended by his or her partner ("What I heard you say was. . . . Is that right?"). When the listener has understood the speaker's message, roles change and the first listener then speaks. Teaching a partner in an alcoholic marriage to communicate support and understanding by summarizing the spouse's message and verifying the accuracy of the received message before stating his or her own position is often a major accomplishment that must be achieved gradually. A partner's failure to separate understanding the spouse's position from agreeing with it often is an obstacle that must be overcome.

Speaking skills — expressing both positive and negative feelings directly — can be taught as an alternative to the blaming, hostile, and indirect responsibility-avoiding communication behaviors that characterize many marriages disrupted by alcoholism. The therapist tells the client that when he or she expresses feelings directly, there is a greater chance of being heard because the client (speaker) says these are his or her feelings and not some objective fact about the other person.

The speaker takes responsibility for his or her own feelings and does not blame the other person for how he or she feels. This reduces listener defensiveness and makes it easier for the listener to receive the intended message.

The therapist can present examples of differences between direct expressions of feelings and indirect and ineffective or hurtful expressions. The use of statements beginning with "I" rather than "you" is emphasized. After rationale and instructions have been presented, the therapist models correct and incorrect ways of expressing feelings and elicits the couple's reactions to these modeled scenes.

Next, the couple role plays a communication session in which they take turns being the speaker and the listener, with the speaker expressing feelings directly and the listener using the listening response. During this role-playing exercise, the therapist coaches the couple. Similar communication sessions, 10–15 minutes three to four times weekly, are assigned for homework. Subsequent therapy sessions involve more practice with role playing, both during the sessions and for homework. The topics on which the couple practices increase in difficulty each week.

After the couple has learned basic communication skills, they can learn skills to solve problems stemming from both external stressors (e.g., job and extended family) and relationship conflicts. The couple first lists a number of possible solutions. Then, while withholding judgment regarding the preferred solution, the couple considers positive and negative as well as short-term and long-term consequences of each solution. Finally, they rank the solutions from most to least preferred and agree to implement one or more of them. Problem-solving procedures help couples avoid polarizing and one partner pointing out the negative aspects of the other partner's solution.

Many alcoholics and their spouses need to learn positive methods to change their partner's behavior to replace the coercive strategies they used previously. Many changes that spouses desire from their partners can be achieved through the aforementioned caring behaviors, rewarding activities, and communication and problem-solving skills. However, deeper, emotion-laden conflicts that have caused considerable hostility and coercive interaction for years are more resistant to change. Learning to make positive specific requests and to negotiate and compromise can lead to sound behavior-change agreements to resolve such issues.

Positive specific requests are an alternative to the all-too-frequent practice of couples complaining in vague and unclear terms and trying to coerce, browbeat, and force the other partner to change. The couple is told that "each partner has to learn to state his or her desires in the form of: *positive* — what you want, not what you don't want; *specific* — what, where, and when; *requests* — not demands that use force and threats but rather requests that show possibility for negotiation and compromise." The therapist provides sample requests that do and do not meet these requirements. For homework, each partner lists at least five positive specific requests.

Negotiation and compromise come next. Spouses share their lists of requests, starting with the most specific and positive items. The therapist provides feedback on the requests presented, helps rewrite items as needed, and explains that negotiating and compromising can help couples reach an agreement in which each partner will do one thing requested by the other. After providing instructions and examples, the therapist coaches the couple while they have a communication session in which requests are made in a positive specific form, heard by each partner, and translated into a mutually satisfactory, realistic agreement for the upcoming week. Finally, the agreement is recorded on a homework sheet that the couple knows will be reviewed during the next session.

Agreements can be a major focus of a number of therapy sessions. Couples negotiate written behavior-change agreements for the forthcoming week, often with positive effects on their relationship. Figure 6.2 shows a typical example of a couple agreement. During the sessions, the therapist reviews unkept agreements briefly, provides feedback about what went wrong, and suggests changes needed in the coming week. After completing agreements under the therapist's supervision, the couple uses a communication session at home to negotiate an agreement on their own and brings it to the following session for review. A series of such assignments can provide a couple with the opportunity to develop behavior-change skills that they can use after the therapy ends. Good-faith agreements, in which each partner agrees to make his or her change independent of whether or not the spouse honors the agreement and without monetary (or other) rewards or punishments, are encouraged. This approach stresses the need for each spouse freely and unilaterally to make the changes needed to improve the marital relationship.

Communication, problem-solving, and behavior-change skills also apply to family therapy sessions involving an alcoholic and his or her children and spouse or an adolescent alcohol abuser and his or her parent(s). We relabel the communication sessions "family council meetings" or "family meetings" and emphasize strongly some additional ground rules that characterize such meetings. For example, one person speaks at a time, no interruptions are permitted, and a consensus must be reached to enact a decision. The latter guards against parents (or other subgroups) forcing their will on weaker family members. Behavioral family therapy with adolescents and parents can be extremely useful for families with alcohol problems because many adult alcoholics have severe problems with their adolescent offspring (Robin & Foster, 1989). Adolescent alcohol abusers frequently have troubled relationships with their parents (Trepper et al., 1993). Behavior-change agreements are also useful with children and their parents, but the behavior changes of the children may be more numerous than those of the parents. Often, reward-punishment contingencies are effective.

MAINTAINING LONG-TERM RECOVERY AND PREVENTING RELAPSE

After the change in the alcohol problem has been stable for 6

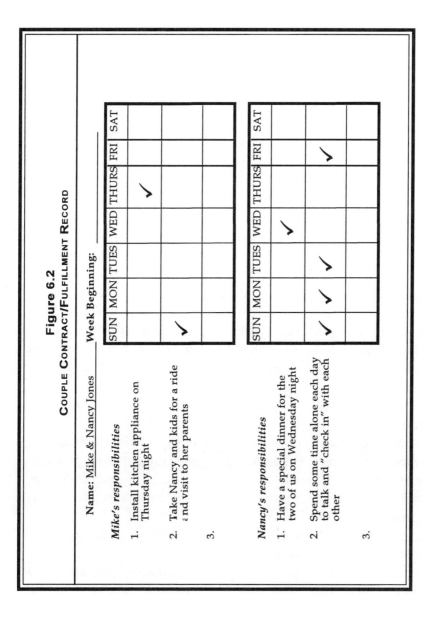

Figure 6.2

COUPLE CONTRACT/FULFILLMENT RECORD

Name: Mike & Nancy Jones   **Week Beginning:** _____

Mike's responsibilities

	SUN	MON	TUES	WED	THURS	FRI	SAT
1. Install kitchen appliance on Thursday night					✓		
2. Take Nancy and kids for a ride and visit to her parents	✓						
3.							

Nancy's responsibilities

	SUN	MON	TUES	WED	THURS	FRI	SAT
1. Have a special dinner for the two of us on Wednesday night				✓			
2. Spend some time alone each day to talk and "check in" with each other	✓	✓	✓			✓	
3.							

months, marital and family therapy has two goals in contributing to long-term maintenance of change: (a) to prevent relapse to abusive drinking and (b) deal with marital issues frequently encountered during long-term recovery.

Preventing Relapse:

Methods to ensure long-term maintenance of the changes in alcohol problems made through marital and family therapy are beginning to receive attention (McCrady, 1993; O'Farrell, 1993b). We use three general methods during the maintenance phase of treatment, defined somewhat arbitrarily as the phase that begins after at least 6 consecutive months of abstinence or consistent nonproblem drinking.

First, the therapist must plan maintenance before the termination of the active treatment phase. The previous marital and family therapy sessions are reviewed with the clients to determine which therapeutic interventions or behavior changes (e.g., disulfiram contract or communication sessions) have been most helpful. Then, a plan is developed to determine how the family can continue to engage in the desired new behaviors when needed (e.g., rehearsing how to cope with situations likely to interfere with the new behavior, rereading handouts from the therapy periodically, agreeing to periodic monitoring by the therapist).

A second method is to anticipate high-risk situations for relapse after treatment and to discuss and rehearse possible coping strategies that the alcoholic and other family members can use to prevent relapse when confronted with such situations.

A third method is to discuss and rehearse how to cope with a relapse when it occurs (Marlatt & Gordon, 1985). For example: allow a delay after the first drink, call the therapist and engage in realistic and rational thinking about the "slip." A specific couple-family relapse-episode plan, written and rehearsed before ending active treatment, can be particularly useful. Early intervention at the beginning of a relapse episode is essential and must be stressed. Often, spouses and family members wait until the drinking has reached dangerous levels again before acting.

We suggest continued contact with the couple and family via planned in-person and telephone follow-up sessions, at regular (and then gradually increasing) intervals, for 3–5 years after a stable pattern of recovery has been achieved. The therapist uses this ongoing contact to monitor progress, assess compliance with planned maintenance procedures, and evaluate the need for additional therapy. The therapist must take responsibility for scheduling and reminding the family of follow-up sessions and for placing agreed-on telephone calls so that continued contact can be maintained. The therapist tells clients that alcoholism is a chronic health problem that requires active, aggressive, ongoing monitoring to prevent or to quickly treat relapses for at least 5 years after an initial stable pattern of recovery. The follow-up contact also provides the opportunity to deal with marital and family issues that appear after a period of recovery.

Marital and Family Issues in Long-Term Recovery:

Many alcoholics continue to experience significant marital and family difficulties after a period of stable recovery. Although a variety of issues can present difficulties during long-term recovery, a number of concerns and life patterns predominate, including role readjustment when the alcoholic tries to regain important family roles lost through drinking, sex and intimacy, and parent-child relationships (especially communication and behavior management with adolescents).

During the recovery process, families seem particularly vulnerable to stresses created by critical transitions in the family life cycle (e.g., children leaving home), external life change events (e.g., job loss), or developmental changes in any of the family members (e.g., midlife crisis). These issues are by no means unique to alcoholic families. However, the therapist has two additional responsibilities when such issues are presented by alcoholic families during long-term recovery. First, the therapist must determine whether a relapse is imminent so that necessary preventive interventions can be instituted immediately. Second, the therapist must determine each family member's view of the relationship between the former alcohol problem and the current marital-family difficulties and carefully assess whether or not he or she shares the family member's view. This is important because family members often continue to attribute difficulties in their relationships to the previous alcohol problem rather than to their current life situation. Another frequent problem is that even though the alcohol problem is under control, the marriage is no longer viable. We label this "successful sobriety and the bankrupt marriage" and consider "breaking up without breaking out" a major accomplishment. Spouses may have grown apart or one may be unwilling to set aside the past hurts. Whatever the reason, facing the emptiness and inevitable dissolution of the marriage often precipitates a dangerous crisis. If there has been a strong tendency to blame the alcoholic for relationship problems, there is a strong push to want the alcoholic to drink again to provide the reason for the marital break-up. The therapist can try to help the couple confront separation and divorce without requiring the alcoholic to fail again and be the scapegoat for the break-up. If the couple can separate without the alcoholic drinking, the alcoholic's future relationship with his or her children may be preserved, and both spouses may be able to obtain a realistic assessment of the basis for their divorce.

SUMMARY

Marital and family therapy methods used at different stages of the alcoholism recovery process have shown promise in outcome research. Marital and family therapy strategies for initiating change and helping the family when the alcoholic is unwilling to seek help include three methods for encouraging reluctant alcoholics to stop drinking and to enter treatment.

Once the alcoholic has sought help, marital and family therapy can be used to promote sobriety, increase positive couple and family activities, and teach communication skills. Behavioral contracts provide social support for abstinence so that family members reinforce behaviors leading to abstinence and refrain from punishing attempts at sobriety. Building relationship cohesion and positive activities together provides a less stressful family environment, which reduces the risk of relapse. Teaching effective communication, problem-solving, and negotiation skills provides coping skills for dealing with marital and family issues and environmental stressors. After 6 months of sobriety, marital and family therapy can help prevent or minimize relapse and deal with marital and family issues experienced during the long and arduous process of continuing recovery.

REFERENCES

Al-Anon Family Groups. (1981). *This is Al-Anon*. New York: Author.

Dittrich, J. E. (1993). A group program for wives of treatment-resistant alcoholics. In Y. J. O'Farrell (Ed.), *Treating alcohol problems: Marital and family interventions* (pp. 78–114). New York: Guilford Press.

Heather, N., & Robertson, I. (1981). *Controlled drinking*. London, UK: Methuen.

Johnson, V. A. (1973). *I'll quit tomorrow*. New York: Harper & Row.

Keller, M., (Ed.). (1974). Trends in treatment of alcoholism. In *Second Special Report to the U.S. Congress on Alcohol and Health*. Washington, DC: Department of Health, Education, and Welfare.

Liberman, R. P., Wheeler, E. G., de Visser, L. A., Kuehnel, J., & Kuehnel, T. (1980). *Handbook of marital therapy: A positive approach to helping troubled relationships*. New York: Plenum Press.

Liepman, M. R. (1993). Using family member influence to motivate alcoholics to enter treatment: The Johnson Institute Intervention approach. In T. J. O'Farrell (Ed.), *Treating alcohol problems: Marital and family interventions* (pp. 54–77). New York: Guilford Press.

Maisto, S. A., O'Farrell, T. J., Connors, G. J., McKay, J., & Pelcovits, M. A. (1988). Alcoholics' attributions of factors affecting their relapse to drinking and reasons for terminating relapse events. *Addictive Behaviors, 13,* 79–82.

Marlatt, G. A., & Gordon, J. (1985). *Relapse prevention: Maintenance strategies in the treatment of addictive behaviors.* New York: Guilford Press.

McCrady, B. S. (1993). Relapse prevention: A couples therapy perspective. In T. J. O'Farrell (Ed.), *Treating alcohol problems: Marital and family interventions.* New York: Guilford Press.

Miller, P. M. (1972). The use of behavioral contracting in the treatment of alcoholism: A case report. *Behavior Therapy, 3,* 593–596.

Miller, W. R., & Caddy, G. R. (1977). Abstinence and controlled drinking in the treatment of problem drinkers. *Journal of Studies on Alcohol, 38,* 986–1003.

Moos, R. H., Finney, J. W., & Cronkite, R. C. (1990). *Alcoholism treatment: Context, process, and outcome.* New York: Oxford University Press.

Noel, N. E., & McCrady, B. S. (1993). Alcohol-focused spouse involvement with behavioral marital therapy. In T. J. O'Farrell (Ed.), *Treating alcohol problems: Marital and family interventions* (pp. 210–235). New York: Guilford Press.

O'Farrell, T. J. (1993a). A behavioral marital therapy couples group program for alcoholics and their spouses. In T. J. O'Farrell (Ed.), *Treating alcohol problems: Marital and family interventions* (pp. 170–209). New York: Guilford Press.

O'Farrell, T. J. (1993b). Couples relapse prevention sessions after a behavioral marital therapy couples group program. In T. J. O'Farrell (Ed.), *Treating alcohol problems: Marital and family interventions* (pp. 305–326). New York: Guilford Press.

O'Farrell, T. J., & Bayog, R. D. (1986). Antabuse contracts for married alcoholics and their spouses: A method to insure Antabuse taking and decrease conflict about alcohol. *Journal of Substance Abuse Treatment, 3,* 1–8.

O'Farrell, T. J., & Birchler, G. R. (1987). Marital relationships of alcoholic, conflicted, and nonconflicted couples. *Journal of Marital and Family Therapy, 13,* 259–274.

Robin, A., & Foster, S. L. (1989). *Negotiating parent-adolescent conflict: A behavioral-family systems approach.* New York: Guilford Press.

Sisson, R. W., & Azrin, N. H. (1993). Community Reinforcement Training for families: A method to get alcoholics into treatment. In T. J. O'Farrell (Ed.), *Treating alcohol problems: Marital and family interventions* (pp. 32–53). New York: Guilford Press.

Sisson, R. W., & Azrin, H. H. (1986). Family-member involvement to initiate and promote treatment of problem drinkers. *Journal of Behavioral Therapy and Experimental Psychiatry, 17,* 15–21.

Sobell, M. B., & Sobell, L. C. (1975). A brief technical report on the MOBAT: An inexpensive portable test for determining blood alcohol concentration. *Journal of Applied Behavioral Analysis, 8,* 117–120.

Thomas, E. J., & Ager, R. D. (1993). Unilateral family therapy with spouses of uncooperative alcohol abusers. In T. J. O'Farrell (Ed.), *Treating alcohol problems: Marital and family interventions* (pp. 3–33). New York: Guilford Press.

Trepper, T. S., Piercy, F. F., Lewis, R. A., Volk, R. J., & Sprenkle, D. H. (1993). Family therapy for adolescent alcohol abuse. In T. J. O'Farrell (Ed.), *Treating alcohol problems: Marital and family interventions* (pp. 261–278). New York: Guilford Press.

FOR FURTHER READING

The Hatherleigh guide to marriage and family therapy. (1996). New York: Hatherleigh Press.

7

Trends in Hallucinogenic Drug Use: LSD, "Ecstasy," and the Rave Phenomenon

Mark S. Gold, MD, FCP, FAPA

Dr. Gold is Professor, Departments of Neuroscience, Psychiatry, Community Health, and Family Medicine, University of Florida Brain Institute, Gainesville, FL.

KEY POINTS

- Hallucinogenic drugs were popular in the 1960s and 1970s in the United States. After a decline in use during the 1980s, recent years have seen a revival in the use of lysergic acid diethylamide (LSD) and 3, 4-methylenedioxymethamphetamine (MDMA), especially among adolescents and young adults.

- LSD and MDMA, the latter of which is more commonly referred to as "Ecstasy," tend to be used at parties, dances, or "raves," all-night parties packed with participants who, fueled on hallucinogenic drugs, dance frenetically—almost to the point of exhaustion—to pulsating music.

- The effects of LSD and Ecstasy are both physiologic and psychological; care of a patient in a toxic state resulting from intake of either of these drugs must address both kinds of effects. However, the majority of adverse reactions are mostly psychiatric in nature; attention in this area often is the most critical.

- Prolonged and habitual use of hallucinogens and marijuana can be as devastating and harmful as alcoholism or narcotic addictions. Fatalities have been reported in association with the use of LSD or Ecstasy. Prevention is essential. If prevention fails, prompt diagnosis and intensive treatment approaches are indicated.

INTRODUCTION

Over time, society finds that the questions never change, only the answers do. After the great increase in the use of psychedelic drugs in the 1970s, the question of the 1980s was, "Have we made headway in decreasing hallucinogenic drug use?" As of 1990, the answer was *yes*, with a decrease of approximately 10%. However, as time has passed, our 1970s and 1980s population has aged. Today, we face a newer, younger group of users of hallucinogens. Reversing a trend that began in 1985, marijuana use has increased every year and now has begun again to alarm national policy leaders. The most recent data from the University of Michigan (UM) survey (National Institute on Drug Abuse [NIDA], 1996) showed that at least 5% of all current high school seniors smoke marijuana at least once daily.

These increases are part of an apparent resurgence in drugs previously associated with the 1960s. Lysergic acid diethylamide (LSD) use among 8th graders has increased and use before graduation among high school seniors in the class of 1995 was estimated at greater than 10%. So, in the 1990s, our questions return with unsettling answers. In the 1980s, statistics indicated a decline in the use of LSD; however, now there is renewed interest in the drug among teenagers. Each generation has given us its unique cultural imprint, and the drug use culture has its own unique patterns as well.

In assessing the current epidemic in marijuana use, we now have to consider "Ecstasy" or "X" (3, 4-methylenedioxymethamphetamine [MDMA]), a synthetic amphetamine derivative, and LSD as the drugs of choice of American adolescents and at parties known as "raves" (described below). Although they are entirely different drugs, Ecstasy and LSD are grouped together in this chapter because of the association of their use. Both drugs technically qualify as stimulants by pharmacologic effect—profoundly altering time, space, thinking, perceptions, emotions, and sense of self. Ecstasy and LSD are primarily used for the brain rewarding effects, high or excitement and hallucinogenic effects of distorted visual and auditory perceptions. In addition, it is not uncommon for these drugs to be combined with alcohol and marijuana.

THE RAVE PHENOMENON

The concept of using alcohol or other drugs dates back to the Roman orgy; the rave is our modern expression. In the 1920s, the Charleston was the hit of the speakeasies that served liquor during Prohibition. The late 1930s saw the association of jazz music with "reefer." The rave is this generation's newest contribution along these lines.

Raves are all-night dance parties packed with participants fueled on Ecstasy, LSD, marijuana, and other hallucinogenic drugs. The rave occurrence began in Great Britain as an underground event with a cloak of mystique in finding such an event. To discover its location, there was a string of ever-changing phone numbers, a trail of curious flyers, or other clues found at the local record store. Today, the events are much more commercial, with steep entrance fees. Raves might be held at an old building, in an empty apartment, or a rented warehouse.

The music at a rave is unique: a trend toward "pulse," often referred to as "techno," with electronic instrumentation. Music is played by a disk jockey; it is never live. A mechanical beat blends one song into the next, producing a continual flow of music and beat that leads to nonstop dancing by the participants (Millman & Beeder, 1994).

Fashion plays a significant role at a rave as well. Common items include oversized floppy hats; brightly colored, oversized skirts; oversized shirts; and baggy, low-riding shorts or jeans. Combat boots are worn for shoes.

Drinks are sold at a rave: they usually are combinations of juice drinks and vitamins, possibly to counter the exhaustive effect of Ecstasy. Drinks and drinking have been actively promoted after deaths and medical emergencies were reported and attributed to hyperpyrexia and dehydration. In animals MDMA's toxic effects, including neurotoxicity, are most readily observed in states of increased core body temperature. Mineral water has been replaced by "smart drinks," which might contain lecithin, a precursor to serotonin, in the hope of increasing or prolonging the effect of the drug. Serotonin replacement has become important to counteract the widespread understanding that MDMA can cause serotonergic neurotoxicity. The "rave" or "X" culture has confused these findings. It is generally believed that Ecstasy can cause a decrease in the spinal fluid, again serving to convince users to drink and drink smart. The availability of smart drinks at raves in England and the absence of either soft drinks or water have led to dehydration and heatstroke. Participants perspire greatly from the heavy clothing, large crowds, and intense activity. Ecstasy and amphetamine-related drugs may raise the body's temperature, thereby causing heatstroke or fatigue (Miller & Gold, 1994).

EPIDEMIOLOGY AND PREVENTION OF SUBSTANCE ABUSE

According to a recent, comprehensive report by the Robert Wood Johnson Foundation (1993), substance abuse is the number-one health problem in the United States. Each year, $238 billion is spent on substance abuse and more deaths and disabilities result from substance abuse than from any other preventable cause. Of the 2 million deaths from substance abuse in the United States each year, one in four is attributable to use of alcohol, illicit drugs, or tobacco; 100,000 people die from abuse of alcohol, 19,000 from illicit drug use and related acquired immunodeficiency syndrome (AIDS), and 400,000 from use of tobacco products. The report indicated a direct link between substance abuse and crime, with one half to two thirds of homicides and serious crimes involving substance abuse and nearly one half of men arrested for homicide and assault testing positive for an illegal drug.

Educational and preventive efforts have been successful in reducing occasional drug use, with significant decreases reported since the drug use epidemic peaked in 1985 (Table 7.1). With these marked decreases, many experts in the United States thought that the drug problem had been tamed. To the contrary, the number of addicts and problem users has remained relatively constant: as reported by the Senate, the estimated number of cocaine addicts stands at 2 million. The most recent user data supports this conclusion; recent cocaine use decreased dramatically from 1985 to 1992 but thereafter has not changed and is slowly increasing among high school seniors. However, the use of marijuana, LSD, and other drugs (including Ecstasy) is increasing dramatically among school-age children (Johnson, Gold, & Gleaton, 1996).

Table 7.1
USE OF ALCOHOL AND DRUGS
IN THE UNITED STATES, 1985–1992
(WITHIN PAST 30 DAYS)

	1985 (000,000)	1992 (000,000)	% Change
Alcohol	113	98	-13
Nicotine	60	54	-10
Marijuana	18	9	-50
Cocaine	6	1.3	-79

After years of lying dormant, LSD (as well as hallucinogens in general) appears to be making a comeback. Gold, Schuchard, and Gleaton (1993) recently presented data from their annual, nationwide survey of 522,328 junior and senior high school students from schools across the United States. This anonymous, drug-use prevalence questionnaire was administered to all students in these schools and grades, and results from the previous 2 years were compared. Hallucinogen use has increased significantly ($p<0.01$ chi-square), from 4.9% to 5.3%. Annual hallucinogen use was 2.4% for 8th graders and 7.2% for 12th graders (Figure 7.1). These data are consistent with a report from the National Institute on Drug Abuse (NIDA, 1993): the percentage of high school seniors reporting cocaine use in the past year decreased from 7.9% in 1988 to 3.1% in 1992, whereas the use of LSD increased from 4.8% to 5.6% (NIDA, 1993). In addition, the law enforcement seizures associated with LSD use were the third highest among illegal drugs, with more than 500,000 LSD dosage units confiscated by the Drug Enforcement Agency in 1990 (National Narcotics Intelligence Consumers Committee [NNICC], 1991).

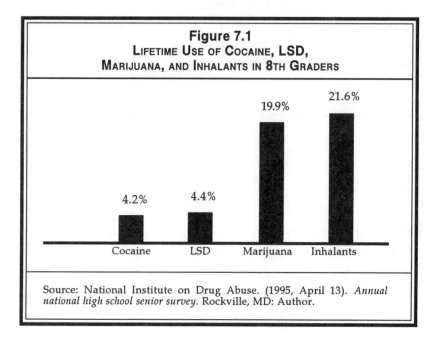

Figure 7.1
LIFETIME USE OF COCAINE, LSD, MARIJUANA, AND INHALANTS IN 8TH GRADERS

Source: National Institute on Drug Abuse. (1995, April 13). *Annual national high school senior survey*. Rockville, MD: Author.

Data from this high school senior survey suggest that many adolescents believe that cocaine is more dangerous than LSD; only 36.4% of high school seniors reported that there is "great risk" associated with LSD experimentation compared with 52.0% for cocaine. The NIDA high school senior survey (NIDA, 1995) also indicated an increased acceptance of LSD use among seniors; disapproval of LSD experimentation fell from 91.6% in 1987 to 81.1% in 1995. In a survey conducted by Johnson and colleagues (1996), adolescents appeared to believe that LSD is "spiritually uplifting," and 63.6% of high school seniors believed that trying LSD a few times is not harmful. The perception of danger, integral to successful cocaine education and decreased cocaine use (Gold, 1991), does not appear to have been applied to LSD.

The significance of antidrug attitudes can be seen in the dramatic decline in cocaine use by high school seniors in the United States from 1985 to 1991. In 1985, the NIDA high school survey indicated that 13.1% of 12th graders had used cocaine within the past year (NIDA, 1985); by 1992, this number had declined to 3.1% (NIDA, 1992). During the same period, the percentage of students disapproving of adults trying cocaine increased from 79.3% to 93%.

Data from the 1994–1995 PRIDE survey of 198,241 students strongly suggested a resurgent use of hallucinogenic and other illicit drugs (Johnson et al., 1996). Comparing the UM/ NIDA 1994 to 1995 surveys has shown annual hallucinogen use increased significantly (p<0.05) from 2.1% to 2.4% (6th–8th grade), 6.6% to 7.7% (9th–12th grade), 8.8% to 9.7% (12th grade). The PRIDE data demonstrates a significant increase in hallucinogenic drug use at all grade levels surveyed. These data are consistent with the 1995 UM/NIDA data (NIDA, 1995). UM/NIDA data demonstrate that illicit drug use in general has been increasing, for example use of any illicit drug among 12th grade students has risen from 31% to 35.8% between 1993-1994 (p < 0.001). UM/NIDA data support findings of marked increases in hallucinogen use. They report increases in 8th, 10th, and 12th grade students, with 11.4% of 12th graders reporting use. The increasing use of so-called rave or club drugs in several major cities has been reported by the Executive Office of the President. These drugs frequently include Rohypnol (Roofies), MDMA, LSD, psilocybin, and another hallucinogen called Nexus. The 1995 PRIDE data confirm these early reports and also show that this is the first year that the trend of decreasing cocaine use has reversed.

These data confirm a 3-year increasing trend in illicit drug use lead by a resurgence in 1960s drugs and attitudes. The lessons of the cocaine epidemic, with resultant decreases in cocaine use, appear to have an independent course from those of LSD, marijuana, and Ecstasy. The toxic effects of LSD have been forgotten, and LSD is increasingly viewed as less dangerous than drugs with much lower toxicities. Romanticization of the 1960s, with the revival of 1960s music (even Woodstock), has contributed to the notion that marijuana and other drugs are not as dangerous; as a result, drug use has been, and still is, increasing.

Treatment services are the missing link in our society, where increasing social stigma, prohibition, and drug education/prevention have had marked effects on most groups of users, with the exception of regular and heavy users. According to the Robert Wood Johnson Foundation report, 6%–23% of all employees are affected by chemical dependency, but only 0.3% of employees seek treatment for their problems in any given year. Fortunately, education and prevention services are continually improving and now clearly demonstrate efficacy and cost benefits.

LYSERGIC ACID DIETHYLAMIDE (LSD)

In 1938, LSD was produced from *ergot,* a fungus naturally present on the rye plant. It was researched as an analgesic, for which it was found to be ineffective. The active drug, lysergic acid diethylamide, was an obscure part of research until 1943, when it was accidentally ingested by its creator, a Swiss chemist, Dr. Albert Hoffmann, who synthesized the compound from lysergic acid. Dr. Hoffman reported its effect as "a stream of fantastic images." In his laboratory journal, he wrote:

> I sank in a kind of drunkenness which was not unpleasant and which was characterized by extreme activity of imagination .... There surged upon me an uninterrupted stream of fantastic images of extraordinary plasticity and vividness and accompanied by an intense, kaleidoscope-like play of colors. This condition gradually passed off after about 2 hours (Gold, 1993).

Following the discovery of LSD, it was used primarily for further research and was evaluated by many different governmental agencies and researchers throughout the United States. Over the next 30 years, LSD was tested as a treatment for various mental disorders, including alcoholism. It was hoped that with its effect on self-image, it would possibly enhance a person's ability for self-evaluation and produce change. The Central Intelligence Agency investigated the drug as a possible method of manipulating beliefs, especially those of very strong-willed persons.

In the early 1960s, Dr. Timothy Leary, Assistant Professor of Psychology at Harvard University, experimented personally and professionally with LSD and introduced it to the world, encouraging its use as "mind expanding." Dr. Leary, who was well respected and had published widely, was impressed by the drug's ability to alter perception in a powerful manner. Convinced that the drug could expand consciousness, Dr. Leary told thousands of fans at a 1967 rock concert in San Francisco to "turn on, tune in, and drop out." By the 1960s, LSD had become a part of our everyday language, with the term *acid* being used at rock concerts and on college campuses. The publicity surrounding Dr. Leary shocked academia in the United States and helped change attitudes about the drug.

Use of LSD reached a peak in the late 1960s, at which time a steady decline in usage began. The decline was caused by several factors:

- The using population had come to know the unpredictability of the drug.

- Strange behavior and even deaths were reported (Aghajanian, 1994). Unpleasant mental states, panic, and other negative reactions related to LSD became known as a "bad trip."

- Subsequent reports of permanent damage and possible chromosomal damage emerged.

Effects on the Brain:

LSD is a synthetic drug that is relatively easy to manufacture. The standard psychologically effective dose of LSD is rather low, usually 50–100 μg. The low dose is extensively metabolized and distributed into the total body mass. The drug is extremely well absorbed orally. Although the toxic dose of LSD is unknown, the full hallucinogenic effect is achieved at 400 μg. Reports of massive quantities taken with little long-lasting effect remain anecdotal.

The major effect of LSD is caused by its high affinity for both 5-hydroxytryptamine (serotonin) receptors (5-HT$_{2A}$ and 5-HT$_{2C}$). Its effects last from 8 to 24 hours. Sympathetic stimulation with increased heart rate, increased respiration, and some cholinergic effects have been reported as well. The psychopharmacology of LSD explains the high correlation of its interaction with the 5-HT$_2$ receptors and its resultant hallucinogenicity. Furthermore, LSD has marked effects on the so-called 5-HT$_{1A}$, or presynaptic, autoreceptors in the raphe nuclei and elsewhere (Aghajanian, 1994).

Other Effects:

The most notable effect of LSD is its profound alteration of perception: objects move, their edges distort, and colors become more vivid or change. Many persons take LSD seeking these effects. Some writers believe that LSD can expand their creativity and lend new ideas; some musicians believe that LSD can add new form to their works. However, after stopping LSD use, such artists report creating very little or absolutely nothing of value. Distortion of time, space, and body image occurs, possibly leading to serious accidents. Spatial awareness is altered and distances misperceived (Bowers & Freedman, 1966). For example, an LSD user may perceive that he or she can swim in a pool with no water or "fly" off a balcony. LSD users experience difficulty in concentrating, and their thinking is unclear. Impaired judgment may lead to high-risk sexual behavior; LSD use is associated with disinhibition, and contracting AIDS or other serious sexually transmitted diseases is possible. Mood swings may range from an intense focus on thoughts or music to withdrawn dysphoria. Memory is impaired both during and following LSD usage.

One of the effects most often noted by LSD users is a feeling of self-loss that is described best as depersonalization. Derealization, a state in which a person has difficulty in distinguishing whether he or she is in a dream or experiencing reality, may occur as well. Both states may cause fear, panic, and anxiety. A common, and often sought, effect of LSD is the concept of *synesthesia* (a mixing of the senses). Colors may be "heard," sounds "seen," and inert objects "smelled." These hallucinations usually are recognized as being not real.

LSD can produce rapid and dramatic alterations in mood and emotion. Moods may change with great rapidity and unpredictability. The beginning of a "trip" may be intensely euphoric, whereas the end may be frightening and sad. LSD "trippers" are familiar with the phenomenon of a "bad trip" (Cohen, 1960). Each event of LSD use is unpredictable, possibly related to different surroundings, moods, and preusage states of mind. A person who has used LSD previously without obvious adverse effects may experience at another time a loss of self-identity, paranoia, suspiciousness, anxiety, panic, and the possibility of toxic psychosis (Bowers, 1972). These disturbances may persist past the drug's psychoactive phase as a posthallucinogen perceptual disorder (PHPD), a complex of chronic problems (anxiety, panic, distortions) that continues for days — even weeks — later. LSD users also have described "flashbacks." These visual effects, similar to LSD tripping, may occur without explanation days, weeks, or months after LSD use. Such flashbacks are usually perceived as unpleasant or frightening.

Smith and Seymour (1994) have identified the adverse effects of psychedelic drugs as "largely psychological" and classified them as either *acute* or *chronic* aftereffects. Acute effects include anxiety, loss of control, changes in cognition, and poor judgment. Five chronic reactions to LSD have been reported: (a) prolonged psychotic reactions; (b) depression sufficiently severe as to be life-threatening; (c) flashbacks; (d) exacerbations of preexisting psychiatric illness; and (e) hallucinogen persisting perception disorder (flashbacks), which is listed in the fourth edition of the *Diagnostic and Statistical Manual of Mental Disorders* (DSM-IV) (American Psychiatric Association, 1994). New onset or worsening of LSD flachback syndrome have been reported in two cases with prior history of abuse of LSD (Markel, Lee, Holmes, & Domino, 1994).

Persons who have used LSD have begun to show long-term effects, including permanent changes in personality, loss of judgment, and prolonged psychotic changes. Smith and Seymour (1994) have described such changes as similar to schizophrenic reactions, which have been noted most often in persons with preexisting psychological difficulties (Aghajanian, 1994). PHPD is best described as a continuation of "tripping-like" effects. With this disorder, persons experience a vision akin to posttraumatic stress disorder: "trails" with moving objects, persistent smells, or a "haze" around their environment. The association of PHPD with alcohol and marijuana use may worsen or precipitate these symptoms.

Lowering the unit dose of LSD administered as part of current LSD use, has been the apparent response of LSD sellers to the 1960s reputation that LSD earned. According to some experts, LSD has been reduced to the point that it is one fifth as potent and thus less likely to produce a profound toxic psychosis. Users in 1996 report low dose use of LSD associated with some but not all of the psychedelic effects typically reported by users.

ECSTASY (MDMA)

MDMA, more commonly known as "Ecstasy," is a recreational drug that is gaining popularity worldwide. Although this drug was thought to be safe by recreational users, it has been reported to cause cardiovascular-related deaths, hyperthermia, disseminated intravascular coagulation, convulsions, rhabdomyolysis, renal failure, and cerebral infarction associated with MDMA abuse (Hanyu, Ikeguchi, Imai, Imai, & Yoshida, 1995). MDMA made its appearance in the late 1960s. It remained an occasionally used drug for years, only to emerge in the past 10 years as "Ecstasy," which is used most often by college students as a "social" stimulant. Research confirmed the serious effects of MDMA on the brains of laboratory animals, leading to its being placed on schedule I of the Controlled Substance Act in 1985.

Ecstasy is readily available at high school and college parties, concerts, and raves. Use of Ecstasy at college and at raves is a phenomenon of primarily white, ethnically diverse teenagers. Ecstasy is generally expensive, with a common price of $20.00 a tablet. This expense has led to a search for similar but alternatively cheaper substitutes, such as methamphetamine (Desoxyn) ($2.00–$3.00/tablet), phencyclidine (PCP), or psilocybin. The use of some obscure and poorly made "designer drugs" has resulted in permanent neurologic damage (American Council for Drug Education, 1994).

Ecstasy frequently is used by adolescents who do not smoke cigarettes or drink and have no previous association with the drug culture. Its party appeal makes it more acceptable to affluent youth, who are not attracted to the mainstream drug culture. Most adolescents do not know what Ecstasy is or why it is a dangerous drug.

Effects on the Brain:

A synthetic-substituted phenethylamine similar to mescaline, MDMA is a short-acting drug (usually lasting 2–4 hours), which was invented and patented by Merck & Company in 1914. Like LSD, MDMA is hallucinogenic, but it produces fewer perceptual distortions than does LSD. Thought disturbances occur less frequently with MDMA, and there are fewer reports of depersonalization or profound emotional instability.

Ecstasy usually is taken in oral doses of 100–150 mg. The

drug's effect begins with a rush and plateaus over the next 2–4 hours. Although the overall length of action is short, it usually results in a residual stage or hangover, lasting a day or longer. Gold (1993) has described MDMA more like a hybrid of mescaline plus amphetamine. It is a serotonin reuptake blocker specific to the 5-HT sites. Furthermore, it causes the release of an excess of serotonin, which probably is responsible for the drug's effect (Bowers & Freedman, 1966). MDMA is addicting in humans and is believed to be addicting on the basis of animal models such as conditioned place preference. The Delta opioid antagonist Naltrindole has recently been demonstrated to block MDMA's enhancement of bar pressing for rewarding brain stimulation (Reid, Hubbell, Tsai, Fishkin, & Amendola, 1996). These and other data suggest that dopamine may be modulated by endogenous opioid systems and MDMA response may be demonstrated to be modified by novel interventions in the future.

Initially claimed to be safer than alcohol, MDMA's recognized adverse side effects include trismus, anorexia and nausea, hyperthermia, and tachycardia with hypotension. The pharmacologic effects of the drug are compounded by physical exertion, and its popular use in America and Britain as a 'dance drug' has shown it to be dangerous, sometimes with fatal consequences. Concern over MDMA use has emerged from research findings with monkeys. Researchers at the National Institutes of Health (McCann et al., 1993) found that at full dose, MDMA reduces serotonin levels in the brain by 90%, with long-lasting effects measurable up to 18 months. The results show clear neurotoxic effects, as do cumulative findings. Neurotoxicity has been studied by a number of investigators (Gold & Gleaton, 1994; Schecter, 1991). In addition to the central neurotoxic effects, three cases of jaundice after ingestion of Ecstasy have been reported prompting physicians to warn that the ingestion of 'ecstasy' should be considered when investigating unexplained jaundice in younger patients (Dykhuizen, Brunt, Atkinson, Simpson, & Smith, 1995).

Other toxic consequences of use are now being discovered.

For example, two cases of aplastic anaemia following exposure to Ecstasy have been recently reported. In both cases, the aplastic anaemia resolved spontaneously 7-9 weeks after presentation. Because MDMA may have been the cause of the bone marrow suppression in these two cases, close hematological monitoring of young adults presenting with toxicity from MDMA and a detailed history of exposure to illicit drugs in all new patients presenting with aplastic anaemia are recommended (Marsh et al., 1994). Recently changes in eating behavior have been reported with loss of appetite and weight loss and chocolate craving (Schifano & Magni, 1994).

Other Effects:

Ecstasy is an amphetamine-like drug with stimulant effects; it can keep users awake and stimulated for hours. Indeed, users become talkative and describe feelings of warmth, empathy, and understanding. Most users experience a need to move about and a sense of energy (hence, it is the ideal drug for dancing). Advocates of the drug report losing inhibitions and experiencing feelings of closeness. Barriers to social interaction, they maintain, are quickly lost; conversation seems more intimate and meaningful. In addition, understanding of oneself and others seems enhanced.

The effects of acute intoxication include sleeplessness, loss of appetite, jaw clenching, and teeth grinding. Both male and female users report changes in sexual performance (e.g., the inability to become aroused or, for men, the inability to maintain an erection). Clinical experiences and research outcomes demonstrate that female Ecstasy users experience greater negative effects from the drug than do male users (Gold & Gleaton, 1994). This finding has been correlated with data showing that female users experience more significant decreases in dopamine. Other effects include headaches, nausea, anxiety, and paranoia. In addition, users note a hangover the next day, with lethargy, mental confusion, and appetite loss. In England, heatstroke, associated with taking the drug in a hot, crowded setting with continuous dancing, is a problem (Millman & Beeder, 1994).

The effects of long-term use of MDMA include confusion, loss of hygiene, fatigue, memory distortions, and sleep disturbances. Other enduring effects are exhaustion, depression, and fatigue. Although the adverse psychological reactions associated with Ecstasy are not as severe as those with LSD, they do cause distress and include panic, psychotic reactions, delusions, and rage-filled reactions. Table 7.2 categorizes the effects of MDMA.

TREATMENT

Acute Phase:

MDMA is a drug of abuse that combines the effects of amphetamine and LSD. Adverse effects including anxiety, panic, insomnia, paranoia, depression, and cognitive changes have been reported.

The toxicology of LSD and MDMA is dramatic and based on both psychological and physiologic effects. Both drugs exhibit some primary medical effects caused by their sympathomimetic actions, but the majority of adverse reactions are mostly psychological in nature (Smith, 1967). These effects may complicate underlying medical conditions, thereby aggravating hypertension, cardiovascular disease, thyroid conditions, diabetes mellitus, asthma or emphysema, and seizure disorders.

Overdose with MDMA presents like an amphetamine overdose and is characterized by tachycardia, arrhythmias, hypertension, hyperthermia, stroke, intervascular coagulation, rhabdomyolysis, and death. Acute medical care is necessary in a hospital setting.

Immediate care of a person in a toxic state must address both physical and psychological symptoms. Body temperature should be quickly assessed, and cooling measures should be considered. The presentation of MDMA overdose with increased heart rate, hyperthermia, and confusion could well

Table 7.2
THE EFFECTS OF MDMA USE

Subjective Effects

Altered time perception
Increased social interactions
Decreased defensiveness
Changes in visual perception
Increased awareness of emotions
Decreased aggression
Speech changes
Decreased obsessiveness
Decreased impulsivity

Adverse Effects

Decreased desire and ability to perform mental or physical tasks
Decreased appetite
Trismus (lockjaw)
Bruxism (clenching of the teeth)
Decreased libido
Inability to complete the sexual response cycle
Increased restlessness
Increased anxiety
Depressed mood
Nystagmus
Motor tics
Headaches

Short-Term Effects

Decreased sleep
Decreased appetite
Increased sensitivity to emotions
Decreased desire and ability to perform mental or physical tasks
Increased ability to interact with others
Fatigue
Decreased aggression
Decreased fear
Depressed mood
Decreased obsessiveness
Altered perception of time
Decreased anxiety
Decreased libido

Source: Gold, M. S., & Gleaton, T. J. (1994, May 20). 49th Annual Meeting of the Society of Biological Psychiatry, Philadelphia.

be misdiagnosed as ordinary heatstroke. Supportive measures include intravenous fluids as well as monitoring pulse and blood pressure. With less severe presentations, cooling may be provided by an air-conditioned environment; fluid replacement needs can be met with an electrolyte-balanced fluid such as Gatorade. Temperature and age play important roles in the neurotoxicity, especially the serotonergic toxicity, of MDMA. The effect was not produced by temperature alone, but increased temperature increased MDMA's neurotoxicity (Broening, Bowyer, & Slikker, 1995).

In severe cases, patients are disoriented and may be garrulous and panicky. Delusions and hallucinations occur. The stimulation of these drug effects may result in enough emotional and physical energy that the person attempts to act out on these thought distortions. The power of hallucinogens to produce totally believable hallucinations, both auditory and visual, is strong. Psychological effects also may affect a person's ego strength and self-concept, leading to outright panic. In addition, patients experience fear from the loss of control. This condition should not be underestimated because suicidal ideation can and does occur; accordingly, treatment should protect patients from harming themselves or others, especially because inadvertent harm may occur during a period of poor judgment. Physical restraint is rarely necessary; most of the adverse behavior requires another person to be present to provide reality support and reinforcement that the condition will not be permanent.

Psychological treatment varies. At the height of hallucinogen use in the 1970s, the recognition and lay treatment of adverse reactions at rock concerts brought the medical profession an understanding of "talking down" a bad trip. This experience revealed that many toxic reactions could be best supported with fewer medications and more human support. In general, support involves placing the person in a quiet, soothing, nonstimulating environment, with another person always present. "Talking down" relates to letting the person know that the hallucinations and delusions are not real and bringing the person back to discussing reality. Allowing the patient to walk about or pace may be useful.

If panic and emotionality persist despite these efforts, the use of medications is indicated. Alprazolam (Xanax), 2–4 mg administered either intramuscularly or orally, has proved the most useful medication for treating hallucinogenic reactions. Other benzodiazepines, such as lorazepam (Ativan) or diazepam (Valium) may be useful for extreme panic, agitation, and anxiety. Severe confusion may actually require short-term inpatient care.

Chronic Phase:

Prolonged and habitual use of hallucinogens and marijuana can be as devastating and harmful as alcoholism or narcotic addiction. Treatment approaches should be no less intensive. Recognition is the first step to help, and psychiatrists, counselors, teachers, and families should become alert to repeated intoxications. The user should be confronted with the situation, most preferably in an intervention format with family, friends, and peers present to corroborate evidence of the problem and to confront denial. After a person recognizes the problem and is willing to accept help, recovery can begin.

Treatment efforts are multifocal. Individual counseling is useful for addressing the major problem but tends to be useful only later in the recovery process — *after* the patient is able to demonstrate some capacity for abstinence and participation in peer–support–oriented recovery. The value of the 12-step meeting process for recovery is well documented as the treatment of choice for addiction recovery. Hallucinogen-addicted persons may well find themselves comfortable with Narcotics Anonymous; with freedom from all mind-altering chemicals, they may find other 12-step programs acceptable as well. Clinicians must recognize persistence of the disease and resistance to treatment; patients may attempt to minimize their problem as well as claim that "those meetings" and therapy are unnecessary. In the end, acceptance of the problem as a lifetime disease and commitment to a long-term recovery process facilitates both realistic treatment goals and positive outcomes.

REFERENCES

Aghajanian, G. K. (1994). Serotonin and the action of LSD in the brain. *Psychiatric Annals, 24,* 137-141.

American Council for Drug Education. (1994). *Flashback: Bad news for bored teens.* Rockville, MD: Author.

American Psychiatric Association. (1994). *Diagnostic and statistical manual of mental disorders* (4th ed.). Washington, DC: Author.

Bowers, M. D., Jr. (1972). Acute psychosis induced by psychotomimetic drug abuse. *Archives of General Psychiatry, 27,* 437–442.

Bowers, M. D., Jr., & Freedman, D. X. (1966). 'Psychedelic' experiences in acute psychoses. *Archives of General Psychiatry, 15,* 240–248.

Broening, H. W., Bowyer, J. F., & Slikker, W. (1995). Age-dependent sensitivity of rats to the long-term effects of the serotonergic neurotoxicant 3, 4-Methylenedioxymethamphetamine (MDMA) correlates with the magnitude of the MDMA-induced thermal response. *Journal of Pharmacology and Experimental Therapeutics, 275,* 325-222.

Cohen, S. (1960). Lysergic acid diethylamide: Side effects and complications. *Journal of Nervous and Mental Disease, 130,* 30-40.

Dykhuizen, R. S., Brunt, P. W., Atkinson, P., Simpson, J. G., & Smith, C. C. (1995). Ecstasy induced hepatitis mimicking viral hepatitis. *Gut, 36,* 939-941.

Gold, M. S. (1993, November). LSD: A brief profile. In *Hallucinogens, LSD, and raves*. Proceedings of the Symposium of the National Press Club, Washington, DC.

Gold, M. S. (1991). Prevention, education, and drug therapy in cocaine abuse and dependence. *Biological Psychiatry, 2*, 60–62.

Gold, M. S., & Gleaton, T. J. (1994, May 20). 49th Annual Meeting of the Society of Biological Psychiatry, Philadelphia.

Gold, M. S., Schuchard, K., & Gleaton, T. (1993, May). *LSD in the USA: Déjà vu again*. 48th Annual Meeting of the Society of Biological Psychiatry, San Francisco.

Hanyu, S., Ikeguchi, K., Imai, H., Imai, N., & Yoshida, M. (1995). Cerebral infarction associated with 3, 4-Methlenedioxymethamphetamine ("Ecstasy") abuse. *European Neurology, 35*, 173.

Johnson, C. R., Gold, M. S., & Gleaton, T. J. (1996). Hallucinogen and other illicit drug uses increases in the USA. *Biological Psychiatry, 39*, 628.

Markel, H., Lee, A., Holmes, R. D., & Domino, E. F. (1994). LSD flashback syndrome exacerbated by selective serotonin reuptake inhibitor antidepressants in adolescents. *Journal of Pediatrics, 125*, 817-819.

Marsh, J. C., Abboudi, Z. H., Gibson, F. M., Scopes, J., Daly, S., O'Shaunnessy, D. F., Baugan, A. S. J. (1994). Aplastic anaemia following exposure to 3, 4-Methlenedioxymethamphetamine ("Ecstasy"). *British Journal of Haematology, 88*, 281-285.

McCann, U. D., et al. (1993). Evidence for serotonin neurotoxicity in recreational MDMA ('Ecstasy') users: A controlled study (Abstract). *Society of Neuroscience, 19*, 1169.

Miller, N. S., & Gold, M. S. (1994). LSD and Ecstasy: Pharmacology, phenomenology, and treatment. *Psychiatric Annals, 24*, 131–133.

Millman, R. B., & Beeder, A. B. (1994). The new psychedelic culture: LSD, ecstasy, "rave" parties and The Grateful Dead. *Psychiatric Annals, 24*, 148-150.

National Institute on Drug Abuse. (1985). *Annual national high school senior survey*. Rockville, MD: Author.

National Institute on Drug Abuse. (1992). *Annual national high school senior survey.* Rockville, MD: Author.

National Institute on Drug Abuse. (1993). *Annual national high school senior survey.* Rockville, MD: Author.

National Institute on Drug Abuse. (1995). *Annual national high school senior survey.* Rockville, MD: Author.

National Institute on Drug Abuse. (1996). *Annual national high school senior survey.* Rockville, MD: Author.

National Narcotics Intelligence Consumers Committee [NNICC]. (1991). *The NNICC Report 1990: The supply of illicit drugs to the United States.* Washington, DC: Drug Enforcement Agency.

Reid, L. D., Hubbell, C. L., Tsai, J., Fishkin, M. D., & Amendola, C. A. (1996). Naltrindole, a delta-Opioid antagonist, blocks MDMA's ability to enhance pressing for rewarding brain stimulation. *Pharmacology, Biochemistry and Behavior, 53,* 477-480.

The Robert Wood Johnson Foundation. (1993). *The Robert Wood Johnson report.* Boston, MA: Brandeis University.

Schecter, M. D. (1991). Effect of MDMA neurotoxicity upon its conditioned place preference and discrimination. *Pharmacology, Biochemistry and Behavior, 38,* 539-544.

Schifano, F., & Magni, G. (1994). MDMA ('Ecstasy') abuse: Psychopathological features and craving for chocolate. *Biological Psychiatry, 36,* 736-767.

Smith, D. E. (1967). Editor's note. *Journal of Psychedelic Drugs, 1,* 1–5.

Smith, D. E, & Seymour, R. B. (1994). LSD: History and toxicity. *Psychiatric Annals, 24,* 145–147.

FOR FURTHER READING

DuPont, R. L., & Verebey, K. (1994). The role of the laboratory in the diagnosis of LSD and ecstasy psychosis. *Psychiatric Annals, 24,* 142-144.

Fischman, M. W. (1993, November). Hallucinogens, LSD, and raves. In *Hallucinogens, LSD, and raves.* Proceedings of the Symposium of the National Press Club, Washington, DC.

8

Caffeine and Anxiety Disorder

Malcolm Lader, MD, PhD, DSc, FRCPsych

Dr. Lader is Professor of Clinical Psychopharmacology, Institute of Psychiatry, London, UK.

KEY POINTS

- Caffeine is the most widely consumed psychotropic substance in the world. Accordingly, it is essential that substance abuse counselors understand the nature and side effects of this drug.

- Caffeine affects many parts of the body; in particular, it stimulates the central nervous system, resulting in both physical and emotional changes. It produces withdrawal effects such as headaches, nausea, vomiting, yawning, drowsiness, and disinclination to concentrate on work.

- The symptoms of generalized anxiety disorder (GAD) may be confused with the effects of caffeine intake. Careful analysis must be performed to determine whether GAD or excessive caf-

feine consumption must be treated.

- Clients with GAD or panic disorder may have a higher sensitivity to caffeine than normal persons. Such clients must be assessed for their history of caffeine intake.

- Three criteria for caffeine intoxication are: recent caffeine intake; psychological, behavioral, and physical symptoms that are presumed to be indicative of caffeine intake; and symptoms due to physical or mental disorders.

- The author provides strategies for clients to minimize their urges to consume caffeine, such as asking family and friends for help, avoiding caffeine-ingesting cues, and maintaining an accurate caffeine intake diary.

INTRODUCTION

Humankind has used psychotropic substances to stimulate, sedate, or induce novel experiences since the dawn of history. These compounds were extracted from naturally occurring preparations usually found in plants, but occasionally in animals. Such substances are still widely used; caffeine and alcohol top the list.

As with all biologically active compounds, problems can arise, chiefly in the form of undesired results. Side effects or idiosyncratic responses may result from excessive concentrations of the active material, unforeseen impurities (particularly liable to occur with plant material), an above-average sensitivity in a part of the population, or a qualitative difference in the biochemical make-up of a few susceptible persons.

Caffeine is the most widely consumed psychotropic substance in the world; it is primarily found in coffee, tea, cocoa, and soft drinks. Although caffeine can bring enjoyment to almost all who use it in moderation, it may cause health problems when taken in excess or by unduly susceptible persons. This chapter reviews the background of caffeine use, its pharmacology and health aspects, and the implications for health practitioners (with particular respect to anxiety and anxiety disorders). Finally, I will provide some points regarding management of clients with caffeine problems.

PHARMACOKINETICS

Caffeine is readily absorbed through all routes of administration; following oral ingestion, its absorption is 99% complete after 45 minutes (Bonati et al., 1982); maximal plasma concentrations are attained within 1–2 hours. Caffeine is distributed throughout the body, crosses the placenta, and is excreted into mother's milk (Tyrala & Dodson, 1979). It is transported across the blood-brain barrier by carrier-mediated mechanisms, secreted into saliva, and excreted in the urine.

The mean plasma elimination half-life of caffeine is 4 hours. In other words, it takes approximately 4 hours to eliminate half the concentration of caffeine; but this time may be increased quite substantially in late pregnancy (Knutti, Rothweiler, & Schlatter, 1982). The oral contraceptive pill and drugs that compete with liver enzymes, such as cimetidine (Tagamet), also prolong the half-life. Conversely, the half-life is decreased in smokers and in patients taking drugs that induce liver enzymes.

PHARMACOLOGY

Caffeine has several effects on the central nervous system (CNS). It stimulates contraction of the heart and the blood vessels in the brain. It significantly reduces cerebral blood flow and is a constituent of some migraine treatments.

Caffeine has a marked and well-known diuretic effect, caused in part by an increase in renal blood flow. It probably stimulates gastric secretion and may exacerbate peptic ulcers. Effects on respiration are minimal. Caffeine also increases the rate at which heat is given off by a person at rest (basal metabolic rate). Normal amounts of caffeine have negligible neuroendocrine effects, but caffeine does increase skeletal muscle tension and tremor.

PSYCHOPHARMACOLOGY

Caffeine is generally regarded as a CNS stimulant (Lader & Bruce, 1989). Behavioral studies in humans mainly have involved psychomotor and cognitive measures. Hand steadiness decreases fairly consistently with increased caffeine use. However, reaction-time tests are inconsistent; shortening, prolongation, and "no effect" of caffeine have all also been reported. Effects on the simple tapping rate and cognitive function have also been inconsistent. Attempts to reconcile these various findings have been made; the most convincing theory is that caffeine has a nonspecific arousal effect. The effect on psychomotor and cognitive performance depends on whether increased arousal impairs or facilitates performance (Humphreys & Revelle, 1984).

Another question concerns whether caffeine can improve performance above baseline levels or whether it simply alleviates deficits caused by fatigue, particularly in monotonous, repetitive tasks. Basically, the evidence suggests that caffeine does improve baseline performance, although its effects are particularly noticeable in tasks of sustained attention (Frewer & Lader, 1991).

The effects of caffeine on mood have been extensively researched (e.g., Gilbert, 1976; Roach & Griffiths, 1987). Those who have consumed caffeine rate themselves more alert and physically active, clearer in mind, and full of energy and ideas. However, caffeine also increases feelings of anxiety and tension and may instigate anger and hostility.

The effects of caffeine on children are important because soft drinks contain substantial quantities. Children seem no more and no less sensitive to caffeine than adults. Claims that caffeine results in disruptive classroom behavior generally have not been supported although some children seem to be affected adversely by this substance (Baer, 1987; Rapoport, Berg, Ismond, Zahn, & Neims, 1984).

USE OF CAFFEINE

Before reviewing the adverse effects of caffeine, it is important to put its use into perspective. The actual amount of caffeine per drink varies with the method of preparation and the size of the cup. Highest concentrations are found in percolated coffee, with amounts of 150 mg or even 200 mg/150-mL cup recorded. Lower amounts (60–100 mg/cup) are found in instant coffee. Caffeine levels in tea vary greatly according to the type of leaf and length of brewing, but generally range between 40 and 60 mg /200-mL cup. Hot chocolate drinks average approximately 20 mg/cup (plus variable amounts of theobromine, a bitter substance closely related to caffeine), and cola drinks average 40 mg/360-mL can or bottle. Foods containing caffeine include ice cream and chocolate. The caffeine content of a small chocolate bar is approximately 20 mg.

Estimates of caffeine consumption in the United States suggest a daily intake of approximately 180 mg/70 kg for the total adult population (Barone & Roberts, 1984). However, this includes consumers as well as nonconsumers. Among habitual consumers, caffeine intake averages 280 mg/70 kg for adults and can easily be double this amount for inveterate coffee drinkers. Assuming an average of 80 mg/cup, this equates to an average of 4 cups of coffee per day. Caffeine intake in the United Kingdom is nearly double this amount, reflecting the apparently inexhaustible supply of strong tea. On a mg/kg basis, children ingest 25%–50% of the adult amount.

Caffeine consumption tends to rise during early adulthood, peaks in middle age, and then declines somewhat. Some surveys have shown a small but consistently higher level of intake for women than men in most age groups. This is consistent with the results of the Framingham Heart Study, in which the mean coffee intake was 3 cups a day for 2500 women and 2.8 cups a day for 1992 men.

PSYCHOPATHOLOGY

Anxiety:

High caffeine consumption can lead to the clinical picture of "caffeinism," or caffeine intoxication, which closely resembles that of generalized anxiety disorder (GAD). The fourth edition of the *Diagnostic and Statistical Manual of Mental Disorders* (DSM-IV) of the American Psychiatric Association (1994) expounds the essential features of the disorder (Table 8.1).

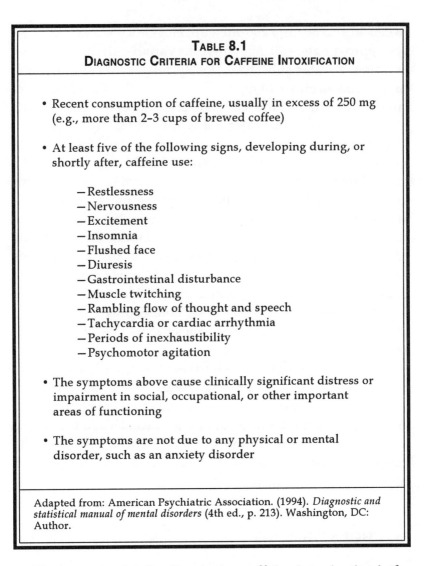

TABLE **8.1**
DIAGNOSTIC CRITERIA FOR CAFFEINE INTOXIFICATION

• Recent consumption of caffeine, usually in excess of 250 mg (e.g., more than 2-3 cups of brewed coffee)

• At least five of the following signs, developing during, or shortly after, caffeine use:

— Restlessness
— Nervousness
— Excitement
— Insomnia
— Flushed face
— Diuresis
— Gastrointestinal disturbance
— Muscle twitching
— Rambling flow of thought and speech
— Tachycardia or cardiac arrhythmia
— Periods of inexhaustibility
— Psychomotor agitation

• The symptoms above cause clinically significant distress or impairment in social, occupational, or other important areas of functioning

• The symptoms are not due to any physical or mental disorder, such as an anxiety disorder

Adapted from: American Psychiatric Association. (1994). *Diagnostic and statistical manual of mental disorders* (4th ed., p. 213). Washington, DC: Author.

The first criterion for diagnosing caffeine intoxication is the *recency criterion*, which concerns the recent consumption of caffeine, usually in excess of 250 mg. This implies that the ensuing symptom pattern is a consequence of *acute* toxicity. However, the clinical problem relates to consequences of *chronic* excessive caffeine intake (Greden, 1974). Many studies, as well as personal experience, attest to the chronic anxiety disorder associated with high caffeine intake.

The second criterion comprises a list of symptoms presumed to be indicative of the effects of caffeine. Some of these are psychological effects, such as nervousness; some are behavioral, such as restlessness and periods of inexhaustibility; others are physical, particularly diuresis and gastrointestinal disturbance. All, however, can occur in anxiety disorder and some may occur in mania.

The third criterion requires the most careful examination: the condition defined is an acute one. The presence of another mental disorder, such as an anxiety disorder, must be excluded. This would be easy on the temporal course alone, but most anxiety disorders are chronic or sometimes recurrent. The clinical problem is to distinguish between chronic caffeine intoxication and anxiety disorder. Confronted by an anxious client, how can one be sure that excessive caffeine use is not the cause?

Obviously, the first step is to undertake a careful inquiry of caffeine intake in the examination of all such persons. Questioning should cover such topics as consumption rates of coffee, tea, cocoa, and soft drinks, as well as the type of preparation. Even a few cups per day of strong, percolated coffee could provide an excessive caffeine load. Sometimes the daily symptom pattern of anxiety can be related to caffeine intake.

In any client who has a medium-to-high caffeine intake with an apparent anxiety disorder, an attempt should be made to decrease caffeine consumption. Because the effects of caffeine so closely mimic the symptoms of GAD, it is difficult and often impossible to distinguish between them. More important, in many GAD clients, caffeine usage worsens the condition. In one study, 24 consecutive referrals to an anxiety clinic were instructed to abstain from caffeine for 1 week prior to an investigation involving a caffeine challenge (Bruce & Lader, 1989). Of the 24 patients, 6 improved substantially, 5 required no further treatment, and 1 needed only a small dose of anxiolytic (antianxiety medication). All patients met the criteria for GAD or panic disorder.

The clinical implications are clear: excessive caffeine intake must be excluded before definitively diagnosing an anxiety disorder. Beyond this, it is important to evaluate the possible contribution of caffeine to the symptomatology of every anxious client.

Caffeine Sensitivity:

Several studies suggest that anxious clients may be supersensitive to the effects of caffeine (Boulenger & Uhde, 1982). Investigators recently compared the administration of 250 mg and 500 mg of caffeine with placebo in 12 GAD patients, 12 patients with panic disorder, and 12 normal subjects (Bruce, Scott, Shine, & Lader, 1992). Patients with GAD were more responsive than the normal controls with respect to various psychological and psychophysiologic measures as well as to self-ratings of anxiety and sweating. Although sample sizes were small, this study demonstrates the abnormal responsivity of anxious persons to caffeine.

If anxiety is aggravated by caffeine, why do clients fail to detect this and spontaneously decrease their caffeine intake? Some evidence suggests that this does indeed occur to some extent. Boulenger, Uhde, Wolff, and Post (1984) reported a negative correlation between caffeine consumption and self-reported anxiety in anxious, panicky persons, but observed no such correlation in nonanxious controls. They asserted that anxious patients did indeed voluntarily avoid caffeine. Another survey suggested that more than half of anxious patients were aware that caffeine made their anxiety symptoms worse (Breier, Charney, & Heninger, 1986).

There is also a belief that some persons have a very marked sensitivity to caffeine and respond not with anxiety symptoms but with dizziness, weakness, tremors, headache, nausea, or vomiting. No systematic research has been performed on these sufferers, and it is not clear whether or not this response is idiosyncratic.

Panic Disorder:

Several studies have examined the effects of caffeine in those suffering with panic disorder. Studies have demonstrated that the administration of 500 mg (or more) of caffeine can cause panic attacks in normal persons. Caffeine challenges were given to a group of patients with panic disorder, and the responses on a wide range of measures were compared with those in normal controls (Charney, Heninger, & Jalow, 1985). Increased sensitivity was found with respect to diastolic blood pressure and self-reporting of nervousness, anxiousness, fearfulness, the feeling of being mellow and happy, tremor, nausea, restlessness, and palpitation. However, in a study by Bruce and co-workers (1992), panic disorder patients differed from controls only with respect to brainwave activity and fatigue. Furthermore, they were less reactive than GAD patients with respect to several variables, both physiologic and subjective.

These studies and those addressing GAD suggest that those with panic disorder and GAD are more sensitive to caffeine than controls with respect to physiologic reactivity. In turn, such persons may be more aware of these physiologic changes, which may in turn provoke additional anxiety or panic. At this time, the field lacks studies that evaluate the therapeutic effects of reducing caffeine intake in those with panic disorder. Meanwhile, the evidence is sufficiently strong to warrant the same type of advice in diagnosis and management of panic disorder as that given earlier for GAD.

Insomnia:

Sleep disturbances are amenable to precise evaluation using routine sleep laboratory techniques. Various studies have consistently reported disruptive effects of caffeine on sleep. For example, Karacan and colleagues (1976) administered caffeine, 77, 177, and 322 mg/70 kg, to subjects 30 minutes before bedtime. Sleep-onset latency was prolonged and total sleep duration shortened in a dose-dependent manner. Subjective reports parallel these monitored effects of physiologic activity during sleep: a longer time was needed to fall asleep, and sleep was shorter and had a poorer quality. Caffeine also prolongs the time taken to fall asleep again after waking during the night.

One study compared 18 women who did not drink coffee with 38 who drank at least 5 cups a day (Goldstein, Kaizer, & Whitby, 1969). Placebo drinks were substituted on some days; habitual consumers reported more sleepiness than did abstainers on placebo days. The sleepiness was relieved by caffeine. But even habitual consumers slept more soundly on placebo nights than caffeine nights, suggesting some disturbance in sleep in these habitual caffeine consumers.

In contrast to these fairly consistent findings, questionnaire studies have yielded conflicting results. Adults tend not to associate caffeine intake with quality of sleep. Persons with insomnia tend not to drink fewer caffeine-containing beverages than sound sleepers. However, more detailed evaluations have suggested that caffeine consumption in the 4 hours prior to sleep is associated with prolonged sleep latency (Hicks, Hicks, Reyes, & Cheers, 1983).

Overall, there seems to be little doubt that caffeine disrupts sleep although there is marked interindividual variation; some insomniacs are unaware of, or deny, the link to caffeine. A caffeine history is essential in evaluating a client who presents with insomnia, and caffeine curtailment is an important part of counseling such clients.

Other Conditions:

In contrast to possible decreased caffeine intake with anxiety, depressed clients may increase their caffeine use, presumably to alleviate the lethargy and lack of motivation, attention, and concentration (Neil, Himmelhoch, Mallinger, Mallinger, & Israel, 1978). However, there is some evidence from both animal and human studies that indicates caffeine may decrease aggression.

Psychiatric inpatients are notoriously heavy consumers of caffeine drinks. Unlimited access often is permitted by the institutions in the belief that caffeine helps to counteract the boredom of ward life. In addition, caffeine may lessen the sedative effects of some antipsychotic and antidepressant medications (Greden, Procter, & Victor, 1981). However, suspicions have been voiced that the excessive use of caffeine may exacerbate some psychopathologic disorders. Several studies have substituted decaffeinated coffee for regular coffee in psychiatric hospitals. Some improvements in behavior were noted; but, in general, the effects were minimal.

In psychogeriatric wards, urinary incontinence is a standard problem. The frequency of incontinence can be reduced by substituting decaffeinated coffee, thereby obviating the diuretic effect. Some hospitals recommend the use of decaffeinated coffee routinely for incontinent patients.

Caffeine has been used to treat hyperkinetic children although most investigators have found it of little or no use. Caffeine may prolong the duration of the fit with electroconvulsive therapy. It has also been tried unsuccessfully in a range of psychopathologic conditions.

CAFFEINE WITHDRAWAL

The discontinuation of caffeine in habitual consumers causes a documented sequence of withdrawal symptoms. A severe headache may ensue approximately 18 hours after the last intake of caffeine, peaking 6 hours later. Other symptoms include nausea, vomiting, yawning, nasal discharge, drowsiness, and a disinclination to concentrate on work (Dreisbach & Pfeiffer, 1943). Tiredness is the most consistent effect of caffeine withdrawal. The headache observed on withdrawal explains the common practice by pharmaceutical manufacturers of including caffeine in headache remedies.

Tolerance can occur with habitual caffeine use particularly with respect to the diuretic effects. However, tolerance is often incomplete and varies with each client. Certainly, there is a common belief that caffeinated beverages maintain their mild stimulant effects, even on lifetime use.

The question of whether caffeine is addictive and can be abused is occasionally raised. Griffiths and Woodson (1988) concluded that caffeine can act as a "reinforcer" but only to a minor extent. Within a social context, no evidence suggests that caffeine produces problems indicative of a significant abuse potential.

TOXIC EFFECTS

Caffeine is generally a safe drug. It would be difficult to take a fatal overdose because gastric irritation and vomiting would develop before much drug had been absorbed (McGee, 1980). However, occasional cases have been reported in which the diuretic and emetic (vomitory) effects led to electrolyte imbalances.

OTHER PATHOLOGIC EFFECTS

The ingestion of caffeine equivalent to 1–3 cups of coffee produces acute rises in blood pressure of 5–15 mm Hg systolic and 5–10 mm Hg diastolic. The heart rate, however, hardly changes; if anything, it slows slightly. Such changes interact with other factors, such as cigarette smoking, psychosocial stress, and personality-related predispositions. More worrisome, studies have consistently shown that chronic caffeine use is associated with persistent hypertensive effects. It seems that regular consumption of coffee, tea, or soft drinks may well result in sustained hypertensive effects in some, perhaps many, habitual users (Shirlow, Berry, & Stokes, 1988). Epidemiologic evidence is controversial, but the involvement of caffeine use in the pathogenesis or maintenance of cardiovascular disease remains a possibility.

The relationship between caffeine ingestion and tumor growth remains contentious and unresolved. By and large, evidence is not compelling except, perhaps, for colonic cancer, where a weak but positive and fairly consistent association has been described.

At high doses, caffeine has teratogenic effects in animals, capable of producing a range of birth defects. However, the much lower doses ingested by humans suggest that caffeine is unlikely to be a teratogen in man; epidemiologic evidence is consistent with this view.

MANAGEMENT OF CAFFEINE CONSUMPTION

For both psychopathologic and somatic problems stemming from above-average caffeine use, the evidence reviewed suggests the need to establish safe levels of caffeine intake and to devise simple, but effective, methods of helping clients reduce their caffeine usage. The general consensus is that 10 caffeinated beverages per day, approximately 600 mg caffeine daily, is excessive. Accordingly, three to five beverages per day might be regarded as the recommended upper limit, depending on the type of drink — such as tea versus coffee, percolated coffee versus instant coffee. More stringent limits or even abstinence might be appropriate in particular high-risk groups such as those who are anxious, panicky, or insomniac, or those with cardiovascular disorder or urinary incontinence.

Surprisingly few studies have addressed the issue of how to reduce caffeine intake (James, Stirling, & Hampton, 1985). The usual technique is to institute a program of self-monitoring by educating the client to identify caffeinated drinks and then to record intake. Self-reported intake correlates to a useful extent with bodily concentrations (James, Bruce, Lader, & Scott, 1989). Additional useful information can be recorded, such as the usual situations for caffeine use, smoking, and alcohol consumption. Next, targets are set to reduce consumption gradually, with a defined time course and endpoint. For example, reducing from 20 cups of coffee per day to 5 might be accomplished over 3–6 weeks. A series of hints can be given to aid this process (Table 8.2). As with all drug withdrawal schedules, follow-up is essential (Foxx, 1982), "booster" withdrawal courses may be necessary, and success rates are high in motivated individuals.

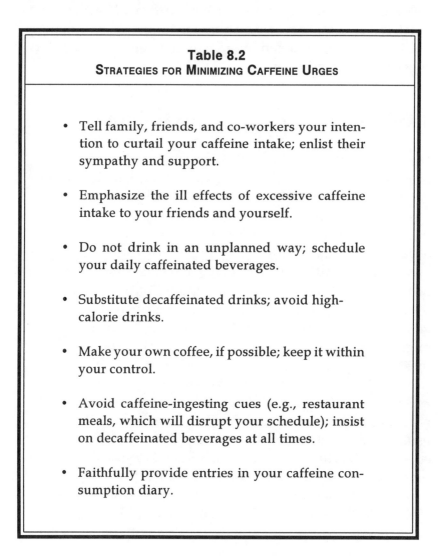

Table 8.2
STRATEGIES FOR MINIMIZING CAFFEINE URGES

• Tell family, friends, and co-workers your intention to curtail your caffeine intake; enlist their sympathy and support.

• Emphasize the ill effects of excessive caffeine intake to your friends and yourself.

• Do not drink in an unplanned way; schedule your daily caffeinated beverages.

• Substitute decaffeinated drinks; avoid high-calorie drinks.

• Make your own coffee, if possible; keep it within your control.

• Avoid caffeine-ingesting cues (e.g., restaurant meals, which will disrupt your schedule); insist on decaffeinated beverages at all times.

• Faithfully provide entries in your caffeine consumption diary.

REFERENCES

American Psychiatric Association. (1994). *Diagnostic and statistical manual of mental disorders.* (4th ed.). Washington, DC: Author.

Baer, R. A. (1987). Effects of caffeine on classroom behavior, sustained attention, and a memory task in preschool children. *Journal of Applied Behavior Analysis, 20,* 225-234.

Barone, J. J., & Roberts, H. (1984). Human consumption of caffeine. In P. B. Dews (Ed.), *Caffeine: Perspectives from recent research* (pp. 59-73). Berlin: Springer-Verlag.

Bonati, M., Latini, R., Galletti, F., Young, J. F., Tognoni, G., & Carattini, S. (1982). Caffeine disposition after oral doses. *Clinical Pharmacology and Therapeutics, 32,* 98-106.

Boulenger, J. P., & Uhde, T. W. (1982). Caffeine consumption and anxiety: Preliminary results of a survey comparing patients with anxiety disorders and normal controls. *Psychopharmacology Bulletin, 18,* 53-57.

Boulenger, J. P., Uhde, T. W., Wolff, E. A., & Post, R. M. (1984). Increased sensitivity to caffeine in patients with panic disorders. *Archives of General Psychiatry, 41,* 1067-1071.

Breier, A., Charney, D. S., & Heninger, G. R. (1986). Agoraphobia with panic attacks: Development, diagnostic stability, and course of illness. *Archives of General Psychiatry, 43,* 1029-1036.

Bruce, M. S., & Lader, M. (1989). Caffeine abstention in the management of anxiety disorders. *Psychological Medicine, 19,* 211-214.

Bruce, M., Scott, N., Shine, P., & Lader, M. (1992). Anxiogenic effects of caffeine in patients with generalized anxiety disorder. *Archives of General Psychiatry, 49,* 867-869.

Charney, D. S., Heninger, G. R., & Jalow, P. I. (1985). Increased anxiogenic effects of caffeine in panic disorders. *Archives of General Psychiatry, 42,* 233-243.

Dreisbach, R. H., & Pfeiffer, C. (1943). Caffeine withdrawal headache. *Journal of Laboratory and Clinical Medicine, 28,* 1212-1219.

Foxx, R. M. (1982). Behavioral treatment of caffeinism: A 40-month follow-up. *Behavior Therapy, 5,* 23–24.

Frewer, L. J., & Lader, M. (1991). The effects of caffeine on two computerized tests of attention and vigilance. *Human Psychopharmacology, 6,* 119–128.

Gilbert, R. M. (1976). Caffeine as a drug of abuse. In R. J. Gibbins, Y. Israel, H. Kalant, R. E. Popham, W. Schmidt, & R. G. Smart (Eds.), *Research advances in alcohol and drug problems.* (Vol. 3, pp. 49-176). New York: Wiley.

Goldstein, A., Kaizer, S., Whitby, O. (1969). Psychotropic effects of caffeine in man, IV: Quantitative and qualitative differences associated with habituation to coffee. *Clinical Pharmacology and Therapeutics, 10,* 489–497.

Greden, J. F. (1974). Anxiety or caffeinism: A diagnostic dilemma. *American Journal of Psychiatry, 131,* 1089–1092.

Greden, J. F., Procter, A., & Victor, B. (1981). Caffeinism associated with greater use of other psychotropic agents. *Comprehensive Psychiatry, 22,* 565–571.

Griffiths, R. R., & Woodson, P. P. (1988). Reinforcing properties of caffeine: Studies in humans and laboratory animals. *Pharmacology, Biochemistry and Behavior, 29,* 419–427.

Hicks, R. A., Hicks, G. J., Reyes, J. R., & Cheers, Y. (1983). Daily caffeine use and the sleep of college students. *Bulletin of Psychonom Soc., 21,* 24–25.

Humphreys, M. S., & Revelle, W. (1984). Personality, motivation, and performance: A theory of the relationship between individual differences and information processing. *Psychological Review, 91,* 153–184.

James, J. E., Bruce, M. S., Lader, M. H., & Scott, N. R. (1989). Self-report reliability and symptomatology of habitual caffeine consumption. *British Journal of Clinical Pharmacology, 27,* 507–514.

James, J. E., Stirling, K. P., & Hampton, B. A. M. (1985). Caffeine fading: Behavioural treatment of caffeine abuse. *Behavior Therapy, 16,* 15–27.

Karacan, I., Thornby, J. I., Anch, A. M., Booth, G. H., Williams, R. L., & Salis, P. J. (1976). Dose-related sleep disturbances induced by coffee and caffeine. *Clinical Pharmacology and Therapeutics, 20,* 682–689.

Knutti, R., Rothweiler, H., & Schlatter, C. (1982). The effect of pregnancy on the pharmacokinetics of caffeine. *Archives of Toxicology, 5*(suppl), 187–192.

Lader, M. H., & Bruce, M. S. (1989). The human psychopharmacology of the methylxanthines. In I. Hindmarch & P. D. Stonier (Eds.), *Human psychopharmacology: Measures and methods* (pp. 179-200). Chichester, UK: Wiley.

McGee, M. B. (1980). Caffeine poisoning in a 19-year-old female. *Journal of Forensic Science, 25,* 29–32.

Neil, J. F., Himmelhoch, J. M., Mallinger, A. G., Mallinger, J., & Israel, H. (1978). Caffeinism complicating hypersomnic depressive syndromes. *Comprehensive Psychiatry, 19,* 377–385.

Rapoport, J. L., Berg, C. J., Ismond, D. R., Zahn, T. P., & Neims, A. (1984). Behavioral effects of caffeine in children: Relationship between dietary choice and effects of caffeine challenge. *Archives of General Psychiatry, 41,* 1073-1079.

Roach, J. D., & Griffiths, R. R. (1987). Interactions of diazepam and caffeine: Behavioral and subjective dose effects in humans. *Pharmacology, Biochemistry, and Behavior, 26,* 801-812.

Shirlow, M. J., Berry, G., & Stokes, G. (1988). Caffeine consumption and blood pressure: An epidemiological study. *International Journal of Epidemiology, 17,* 90-97.

Tyrala, E. A., & Dodson, W. E. (1979). Caffeine secretion into breast milk. *Archives of Disease in Childhood, 54,* 787–800.

9

Cognitive-Behavioral Group and Family Treatment of Cocaine Addiction

Paul Richard Smokowski, MSW, and John S. Wodarski, PhD

Mr. Smokowski is a student in the Doctoral Program in Social Welfare at the University of Wisconsin School of Social Work, Madison, WI. Dr. Wodarski is the Janet B. Wattles Research Professor and Director of the Doctoral Program and Research Center at the State University of New York at Buffalo School of Social Work, Buffalo, NY.

KEY POINTS

- In the 1980s, drug abuse trends in the United States showed a sharp increase in high-dosage cocaine use. Although cocaine was once viewed as an upper-class, highly educated person's drug of choice, cocaine use has significantly increased in unskilled, less educated workers; minorities; women; and adolescents.

- This chapter outlines current research developments in cocaine dependency treatment models that are based on relapse prevention and cognitive-behavioral techniques. Models discussed include adaptation and social learning, and operant and classic conditioning.

- Cognitive-behavioral treatment programs have had encouraging success in both retaining users in treatment and achieving initial cocaine abstinence.

- Group work is an integral treatment modality for substance use disorders. The group serves as a therapeutic, supportive network that can replace the addict's former drug-promoting interpersonal relationships.

- Integration of the family is an invaluable tool in the treatment of cocaine addiction. Initial indications recommend using caution when planning this intervention for chaotic or impoverished families.

INTRODUCTION

The widespread use of cocaine within the past two decades has cut across all levels of American society, causing public health workers to declare it a problem of epidemic proportions (Gropper, 1991; Nunes-Dinis & Barth, 1993). In the 1980s, drug-abuse trends in the United States showed a sharp increase in high-dosage cocaine use, which became exacerbated with the introduction of intensely euphoric and highly addictive "crack" cocaine (Rawson, Obert, McCann, Smith, & Ling, 1990).

Since then, our public health and social service systems have been confronted with a wide array of crises, including cocaine-related emergency room admissions quadrupling from 1986 to 1989, an upsurge in cases of syphilis due to the sexual promiscuity often associated with dealing and using cocaine, increased drug-related crime and violence, overcrowding of prisons, a fear of the spread of acquired immunodeficiency syndrome (AIDS) through the reuse of infected syringes, and the tragic and costly debut of cocaine-addicted "crack babies" born to substance-abusing parents (Gfroerer & Brodsky, 1993; Koppelman & Jones, 1989).

Although cocaine was once assessed as a drug used by upper-class, highly educated, working persons, the demographic characteristics of cocaine users have changed dramatically. Since the mid-1980s, significant increases in cocaine use by unskilled, less educated, lower-income persons; minorities; women; and adolescents have been documented (Means et al., 1989; Semlitz & Gold, 1986). This phenomenon may be attributed to a combination of factors, including decreased cost combined with increased availability.

TREATMENT OVERVIEW

In response to the cocaine crisis, a diverse array of treatment modalities have been developed and implemented. Little consensus, however, exists on the effectiveness of treatment outcomes for cocaine abuse. A range of outpatient interventions has been reported, with success rates between 30% and 90% for cocaine abusers who remain in treatment (Gawin & Ellinwood, 1988). Yet, keeping persons with addictions in treatment is a major problem, and relapse is a common occurrence. Wells, Peterson, Gainey, Hawkins, and Catalano (1994, p. 2) stated that "no controlled treatment outcome study has shown superiority of treatment over no treatment, and no treatment program has been shown to be superior to any other." Results of their group intervention comparison study, for example, found that patients in both relapse prevention and 12-step groups reduced cocaine and marijuana use posttreatment. However, treatment attendance seemed to be the most significant aspect of improvement because there were no differential treatment effects over time (Wells et al., 1994).

To date, no pharmacologic agent has been found to be effective for treating cocaine dependence (Nunes-Dinis & Barth, 1993; Rawson et al., 1990). Instead, a movement has developed to form outpatient cocaine dependency treatment models, which are based on relapse prevention and cognitive-behavioral techniques (Magura, 1994). This chapter outlines current research developments in cocaine treatment models using these strategies. The etiologies of addiction are discussed from a behavioral perspective, and specific cognitive-behavioral intervention techniques are outlined, with a special emphasis on group and family treatment of cocaine addiction.

COGNITIVE-BEHAVIORAL ETIOLOGIES OF ADDICTION

The lack of a pharmacologic agent to treat cocaine addiction has led researchers to propose "neurobehavioral" (Rawson et al., 1990) and "biopsychosocial" (Nunes-Dinis & Barth, 1993; Wallace, 1991) theories of cocaine use and treatment. These theories acknowledge the chemical and physiologic sides of addiction but base treatment paradigms heavily on psychological and environmental explanations of abuse.

Operant Conditioning:

Skinner's (1953) classic work on operant conditioning contends that a stimulus, serving as a positive reinforcer, will cause the environmental response (or operant) that directly preceded it to recur. Put simply, this means behavior that is rewarded will probably be repeated. Within this framework, the euphoric "high," or numbing and distancing effects of cocaine, acts as a strong positive reinforcer for cocaine use. The operant actions of drug administration, as well as the environmental cues associated with cocaine use, become paired with, and reinforced by, all the positive feelings cocaine use produces. The positive association further prompts the increased frequency of cocaine-seeking behavior.

The application of this rationale to crack cocaine is particularly poignant. Because inhaled cocaine takes effect in 20–60 minutes, injected cocaine in 5 minutes, and smoked crack cocaine immediately (Weddington, 1993), the euphoria cocaine brings becomes a strong positive reinforcer; this is the case not only because of the feelings it engenders, but also because of the haste of the reinforcement. Compared with the immediate positive reinforcement of cocaine use, the negative reinforcements of cocaine toxicity, withdrawal, and aftereffects are quite distant in time, which decreases their power as conditioning stimuli.

The operant conditioning concept of negative reinforcement is also functionalized by the abuser's continued use of cocaine. As craving, withdrawal, and dysphoria (negative environmental stimuli) set in, users finds they can escape from this punishment by consuming more cocaine. In this way, the addiction cycle is fed, and the positive reinforcement of cocaine use is further strengthened.

Solomon (1980) addressed this connection by developing the opponent-process model of conditioning. This model described conceptualized sets of opposite, or opponent, processes playing antagonistic roles within the conditioning response. The strength and frequency of an initial positive reinforcer are proportional to the power and haste of the onset of the opponent process (Peele, 1985). Specifically in terms of addiction, this paradigm predicts that more severe withdrawal and toxicity accompany heavier and more frequent drug use, with the user initially seeking the reinforcing "high" and subsequently scrambling to avoid the torments of withdrawal and craving.

Physiologic tolerance adds another dimension to this process. As cocaine tolerance develops, higher doses of the drug are needed to achieve the same euphoric effects. Not only does this add to the amount used, it also establishes an intermittent reinforcement schedule. The user, still seeking the reinforcing euphoria, sometimes receives this feeling and sometimes does not. This may cause the drug-seeking behavior to increase in dosage as well as in frequency. However, if tolerance extinguishes the positive reinforcement effects of cocaine use, it may also be a precipitating factor for the user to enter treatment (Wallace, 1991).

Classic Conditioning:

The classic conditioning model developed by Pavlov (1927) contributes several significant concepts to the addiction process. Pavlov's experiments showed that an unconditioned neutral stimulus repeatedly paired with a strong positive reinforcer becomes "conditioned" so the previously neutral stimulus presented on its own can elicit the learned response.

The pairing of environmental stimuli with drug-taking behavior has critical implications for both the maintenance of addiction and treatment (Carroll, Rounsaville, & Keller, 1991; Koppelman, & Jones, 1989). Furthermore, an idiosyncratic generalization within the user's learning processes may occur; as a result, previously neutral environmental stimuli may become associated with drug-taking behavior. For instance,

Carroll and associates (1991) described a recovering addict who was overcome with intense cocaine craving when she passed a car on the road that was the same color as her previous drug dealer's car. In this way, conditioned craving and exposure to drug-taking, environmental cues can often lead to relapse.

Wallace (1991) described how classic conditioning can be operationalized for both tolerance and withdrawal. In conditioned tolerance, the body reacts to environmental drug-taking cues by physiologically triggering processes to anticipate and attenuate the drug's effects. This attempt at homeostasis requires the user to take more of the drug for the same effect or to habituate to use at a certain dosage. This habituation, or conditioned tolerance, depends on the environmental cues. Thus, in a new environment without the conditioned cues, the body's conditioned tolerance may not become functionalized, causing the user's habitual dose now to become an overdose.

Conditioned withdrawal is yet another learning possibility. Environmental cues (pipes, needles, etc.) may come to initiate craving *and* to elicit withdrawal responses. This, being unpleasant, may then lead to further drug use to escape the punishment capacities of withdrawal.

Adaptation and Social Learning:

Bandura (1977) formulated a branch of conditioning literature called the *social learning theory*. This framework emphasized the social, emotional, environmental, and psychological aspects of drug use by hypothesizing that deficits in coping mechanisms and social skills leave persons vulnerable to the temptation of using drugs as a way to regulate internal and external states. Substance use becomes a method to handle stress and a way to deal with unwanted emotional and psychological states.

This theory is noteworthy because of its broadening of the behavioral etiologies to include motivations, emotions, and social processes. It adds further complexity to the levels and factors leading to cocaine use.

COGNITIVE-BEHAVIORAL TREATMENT OF COCAINE ADDICTION

Effective treatments of cocaine addiction are still in their infancy and require further development. In general, standard types of treatments of addiction are not as effective for battling cocaine as they may be for other types of drugs (Weddington, 1993). The length of time a patient is in treatment and program completion have been reported to be better predictors of outcome than other patient characteristics or program types (Rawson et al., 1990). Nunes-Dinis and Barth (1993, p. 613) reported that "1-year abstinence rates for cocaine users who stayed in treatment for at least 3 months were about 43%, whether treated residentially or with other modalities." These facts highlight two significant struggles in treating cocaine addiction: getting users into treatment and retaining them there.

Multicomponent behavioral treatment programs have had encouraging initial success in both retaining users in treatment and achieving initial cocaine abstinence (Higgins, Budney, Bickel, Hughes, Foerg, & Badger, 1993; Higgins et al., 1991; Washton, Gold, & Potash, 1986). The approach by Washton and associates (1986) combined cognitive-behavioral techniques, psychoeducation, family involvement, self-help groups, and urine testing. Of 127 patients, 65% completed a 6- to 12-month program, and 75% of these patients remained abstinent at 1- to 2-year follow-up. Higgins and colleagues (1991) reported superior retention and initial abstinence rates for behavioral treatment using a contingency management and community reinforcement approach over both 12-step and drug-abuse counseling based on a disease model for addiction and recovery (Higgins et al., 1993). In the second study (Higgins et al., 1993), 58% of the 19 patients who received behavioral treatment completed 24 weeks of treatment, and 68% of these patients achieved 8 continuous weeks of cocaine abstinence, whereas only 11% of the 19 patients who received counseling completed 24 weeks of counseling and only 11% of these patients achieved 8 continuous weeks of abstinence.

These preliminary indications of efficacy, coupled with the behavioral framework's empiric grounding, support further development of treatment paradigms using this modality. With this in mind, our discussion now turns to specific conceptual aspects of the cognitive-behavioral approach and then concludes with the application of these concepts within group and family therapy.

Contingency Management:

Considering cocaine use as an operant behavior reinforced by the chemical effects of the drug, the logical behavioral treatment response is either to remove the positive reinforcement of taking the drug or to make alternative nondrug reinforcers available to reinforce abstinence over drug use.

The first approach is being addressed by the pharmacologic search for a cocaine antagonist. However, a variety of pharmacologic agents have been tested with only a modicum of success and little satisfactory replication of results (Rawson et al., 1990). Behaviorally, the objective of removing the positive reinforcement is difficult to obtain. If the drug's action cannot be curtailed, the drug must be eradicated from the environment to terminate its reinforcing qualities. Unlike in laboratory animal studies, where the drug can simply be withheld, this is extremely difficult in many human situations; numerous national, state, and local drug enforcement agencies can attest to this fact.

On a smaller scale, the second approach has been attempted in behavioral treatment in two ways. Anker and Crowley (1982) performed a study on negative contingency management. They attempted to overshadow the positive effects of drug use by setting up a strong negative reinforcement schedule, where positive tests for drug use were met with a negative contingency, such as a letter detailing cocaine use being sent to the user's employer. The problem with this attempt was the fact that only 48% of users approached were willing to participate. Of the users who did, 80% maintained abstinence for 3 months of their contract. However, once the contract expired and the negative contingency was withdrawn, approximately half relapsed.

Higgins, Budney, and Bickel (1994, p. 89) described a different approach. Their treatment entailed "rearranging the drug user's environment so that (a) drug use and abstinence are readily detected, (b) drug abstinence is positively reinforced, (c) drug use results in the immediate loss of reinforcement, and (d) the density of reinforcement derived from nondrug sources is increased to compete with the reinforcing effects of drugs." In this paradigm, contingency contracts called for positive rewards, such as specified amounts of money to purchase recreational items (including ski-lift passes and gift certificates to restaurants) within the community. This reinforcement was withdrawn when a participant tested positive for cocaine use. In addition, non–drug-using friends or significant others were integrated into the treatment for support in enacting the contingency contracts. Preliminary evaluations of this treatment indicated it was acceptable to patients, retained them in treatment, and rendered clinically significant levels of initial abstinence (as compared with 12-step and standard counseling groups).

This empirical evidence on the superior results of positive over negative contingency contracts confirms the observation noted elsewhere (Mattaini, 1991; O'Brien & Childress, 1991) that few patients agree to participate in studies or treatments that involve discomfort.

Extinction:

Classic extinction or "cue-exposure" techniques are attempts to disassociate the conditioned response (cocaine craving) from the unconditioned environmental stimuli (seeing a pipe, vial, or drug dealer). This is accomplished by repeatedly exposing the user to environmental drug-associated cues without reinforcement. For instance, therapists have addicts repeatedly handle cocaine paraphernalia, watch videotaped drug-taking situations, or read drug-related books to break the conditioned association between the cue and the memory, anticipation, and physiologic craving for cocaine use (Koppelman & Jones, 1989).

O'Brien and Childress (1991) have reported successful reduction in the responses of conditioned craving and conditioned withdrawal after repeated presentations of drug-related stimuli. However, they also found conditioned physiologic responses to be persistent (significant responses continued after 28 days of treatment). Furthermore, to what extent extinction in the therapeutic community generalizes to the user's natural environment is always questionable. The extinction process depends on the context within which it is accomplished, thus showing poor generalization, especially when compared with the wide generalization that accompanies the original conditioning (Tobena et al., 1993). This context, or state-dependent learning, causes users to continue to be vulnerable to relapse long after detoxification and treatment. It has also prompted researchers to recommend strengthening extinction strategies as much as possible, specifically by performing extinction exercises and training in a context as close to the original conditioning one as possible (Bouton & Swartzentruber, 1991).

Extinction protocols alone are rarely powerful enough to counter the conditioning completely. To maximize the treatment potential, extinction must be coupled with the establishment of alternative reinforcement schedules that reward prosocial (drug-free) behavior. This is the necessary marriage of extinction strategies to contingency management techniques. Although extinction protocols are enacted, contingency contracts are set. At first, contingency contracts call for simplistic, achievable goals so patients can gain a sense of success. Then, as treatment progresses, more sophisticated alternative reinforcement schedules can be designed. It is crucial for extinction procedures and contingency contracts to complement each other, with each one working to maximize the other's chance of success. Methods of facilitating this within the settings of group and family therapy are described in the next section.

COGNITIVE-BEHAVIORAL GROUP AND FAMILY THERAPY

Group Work:

Group work has been an important modality in substance-abuse treatment and is an integral contributor to multicomponent treatment paradigms (Arzin, Donahue, Besalel, Kogan, & Acierna, 1995; Falkowski, 1991; Rawson et al., 1990; Wells et al., 1994). The group environment can serve as a forum for the dissemination of information about cocaine dependence, effects, relapse, and abstinence. Perhaps most important, the group serves as a therapeutic, supportive network that can replace the addict's former drug-promoting interpersonal relationships (Spitz, 1987).

The alternative reinforcement schedules sought through contingency contracts reverberate through a group in several significant ways. In a supportive group, members often will reinforce the abstinence of others while alternatively confronting other members (negative reinforcement) about relapses, "slips," or the overuse of denial. In this way, group members become therapeutic agents and reinforce prosocial efforts for each other. Members who are firmly on the road to recovery can provide role models for newer recruits, and isolation, which may have previously led to drug use, can be avoided. This socialization becomes one source of alternative reinforcement.

Using Reward Structures

Group reward structures can also be an effective tool in group work (Wodarski & Feit, 1994). The positive contingency contract for recreational reinforcers to be given on negative urinalysis is an example of an individual reward structure

(Higgins, Budney, & Bickel, 1994). However, this system can be a powerful motivator within a group, supplemented even further by cooperative reward structures. For instance, a group may decide to attend a particular sports event after 4 consecutive weeks of cocaine abstinence. This goal not only places pressure on more vulnerable members not to relapse, but it also motivates more capable (less vulnerable) group members to assist the more vulnerable ones. This sets up a system in which there are several levels of positive reinforcement supporting abstinence (the sports event, interpersonal encouragement, and meeting individual needs for affiliation) as well as several levels of negative reinforcement for relapse (not going to the sports event, group frustration, and interpersonal rejection).

Wodarski and Feit (1994) outlined six principles to increase the success of group reward structures:

1.   Appropriate behavior must be reinforced.

2.   Reinforcers must be available to all members, but not too easily available.

3.   Reinforcers should be delivered close in time to the occurrence of the behavior they reinforce.

4.   Reinforcers must be consistent in their application.

5.   Reinforcers must be appropriate to the chosen behavior change.

6.   There must be a pattern of consistent reinforcement by significant others in a person's environment.

Group contingency contracts can add a powerful tool to the group worker's repertoire.

Enhancing Extinction

The process of extinction may also be strengthened by adding it to a group's agenda. Not only can the presentation of environmental cues occur within the group, but the group has greater resources than individual settings for mobilizing support to handle the reactions of craving. Considering the wide generalization of unconditioned environmental stimuli, not all group members will be triggered by the same stimulus. This creates the opportunity for members who are not affected to notice the effects of craving more objectively and to offer support and advice to the group members who are affected.

To achieve extinction more completely, the group setting represents an environment that can more aptly stimulate the user's "real-world" setting in which the conditioning occurred. With a variety of different persons present and access to superior resources for reenactment and behavioral rehearsals, the group offers an array of therapeutic opportunities. Role-playing situations can be constructed to re-create the conditioning context, which can then be methodically and painstakingly deconstructed to disassociate the environmental cues from the operant reinforcement of the drug. Similarly, enactments can also be created to place the user in a threatening relapse scenario so he or she might test or rehearse different methods of coping with the situation. The fact that all of these methods can be used with the support and problem-solving advice of fellow group members makes the group a powerful force to strengthen the user's psychological, emotional, and interpersonal skills.

Mobilizing the Sociometric Network

One final group attribute that can be used for therapeutic effect is mobilizing the group's sociometric network (Hale, 1981) to form "buddy systems." This entails group members' choosing partners or subgroupings with whom to affiliate. "Buddies" perform gradual extinction by taking turns escorting each other into actual environmental situations. The buddy who has progressed further in the recovery process thus becomes a control and a "stabilizing presence" for the other:

interpersonal bonding occurs, and this close pairing may endure even beyond the therapeutic setting (Wallace, 1991).

Integrating the Family:

Abortive Efforts

Incorporating components of the family into treatment paradigms has been widely recommended in the cocaine-abuse literature (Nunes-Dinis & Barth, 1993; Rawson et al., 1990). In addition, having family members participate in treatment has been reported to be a robust predictor of abstinence (Higgins Budney, & Bickel, 1994; Higgins, Budney, Bickel, & Badger, 1994; Weddington, 1993).

Behavioral family interventions for substance abuse, whether implemented alone or in a multicomponent package, have specifically gained clinical favor (Spitz & Spitz, 1987). Their main goals are to achieve rapid abstinence; to identify stimuli that perpetuate drug-taking behavior; and subsequently to supplant dysfunctional behavior patterns with new, more adaptive patterns. Tools for achieving these goals are similar to the strategies available to group workers: contingency contracts, cognitive restructuring, alternative reinforcement schedules, various types of skills training, and behavioral rehearsals.

Compared with fellow group members, family members may be in better positions to facilitate and reinforce treatment goals because of their proximity to the user and because they often are aware of the user's psychological and emotional triggers. This makes them an invaluable source of information for therapists in structuring extinction protocols. Furthermore, family participation may aid in the extinction process if members are willing to support the user to overcome conditioned behavior within the conditioning context. Family members may help the user through dangerous relapse situations by offering assistance within environments where drugs are readily available. This is a necessity for many users who are discharged from treatment to return home to neighborhoods that are infested with drugs. Other family members often have experienced the same environments but have developed coping strategies to help them avoid taking drugs. These strategies can be used to help build the user's behavioral repertoire and to act as a support to prevent relapse.

In forming and implementing contingency contracts, consistency is needed across environments. Reinforcement schedules that are discarded as soon as the patient leaves the therapeutic community quickly lose their potency and are ultimately doomed to failure. However, family members provide critical support for the user's recovery by consistently reinforcing new, adaptive behaviors. For instance, in the studies of Higgins and associates (Higgins, Budney, & Bickel, 1994; Higgins, Budney, Bickel, & Badger, 1994) the user chose certain drug-free significant others (spouses, parents, friends, etc.) to support his or her treatment. The significant others underwent relationship enhancement counseling with the user and implemented contingency contracts that were linked to periodic drug testing. Urinalysis results were immediately conveyed to significant others. A negative result was reinforced by the significant other, who performed whatever rewarding contingency was in the contract (for instance, having a romantic dinner or attending a recreational event). A positive result was given no rewarding reinforcement, but the significant others offered the user supportive suggestions and encouragement to retain abstinence. Participants liked this method, and the participation of significant others has become one of the treatment model's strongest predictors of positive treatment outcome.

Potential Dangers

Other reports in the literature on families of cocaine abusers are not as auspicious. In a sample of 95 cocaine abusers, Kang and colleagues (1991) found an inverse relationship between psychological impairment and family cohesion. In another study of 100 inpatient crack users, Boyd and Mieczkowski (1990) reported that 22% of users were initiated to crack smoking through a family member, 21% through a girlfriend, and 50% through a boyfriend. When asked who might help them overcome their addiction, 60% of women and 70% of men in the sample identified a female family member.

These findings have implications for therapists. Integration of significant others into cocaine treatment can be an important tool for supporting recovery; however, initial indications recommend using caution when planning this intervention for chaotic or impoverished family environments. Such families may require therapeutic assistance before the user's reintegration into the family environment. If, for instance, the user's addiction originated within the family, or extended family, contact with drug-related family members or friends will have to be addressed in treatment so the postdischarge support system does not promote drug relapse rather than abstinence. Therapists must work with the user to differentiate persons who can truly support recovery from persons who cannot. Once found, these nurturing persons can greatly enhance the treatment process.

REFERENCES

Anker, A. L., & Crowley, T. Y. (1982). Use of contingency in specialty clinics for cocaine abuse. In L. S. Harris (Ed.), *Problems of drug dependence* (pp. 452–459). Kensington, MD: National Institute on Drug Abuse.

Arzin, N., Donahue, B., Besalel, V., Kogan, E., & Acierna, R. (1995). Youth and drug abuse treatment: A controlled outcome study. *Journal of Child and Adolescent Substance Abuse, 3*(3), 1-16.

Bandura, A. (1977). *Social learning theory.* Englewood Cliffs, NJ: Prentice-Hall.

Bouton, M. E., & Swartzentruber, D. (1991). Sources of relapse after extinction in Pavlovian and instrumental learning. *Clinical Psychology Review, 11,* 123-140.

Boyd, C. J., & Mieczkowski, T. (1990). Drug use, health, family, and social support in 'crack' cocaine users. *Addictive Behaviors, 15*, 481–485.

Carroll, K. M., Rounsaville, B. J., & Keller, D. S. (1991). Relapse prevention strategies for the treatment of cocaine abuse. *American Journal of Alcohol Abuse, 17*, 249–265.

Falkowski, W. (1981). Group psychotherapy for alcoholics and drug addicts. In B. Glass (Ed.), *The international handbook of addiction behavior.* New York: Routledge.

Gawin, F. H., & Ellinwood, E. H. (1988). Cocaine and other stimulants: Actions, abuse, and treatment. *New England Journal of Medicine, 318*, 1173–1182.

Gfroerer, J. S., & Brodsky, M. D. (1993). Frequent cocaine users and their use of treatment. *American Journal of Public Health, 83*, 1149–1154.

Gropper, M. (1991). The many faces of cocaine use: The importance of psychosocial assessment in diagnosing and treating cocaine abuse. *Social Work in Health Care, 16*, 97–112.

Hale, A. E. (1981). *Conducting clinical sociometric explorations: A manual for psychodramatists and sociodramatists.* Roanoke, VA: Royal Publishing.

Higgins, S. T., Budney, A. J., & Bickel, W. K. (1994). Applying behavioral concepts and principles to the treatment of cocaine dependence. *Drug and Alcohol Dependence, 34*, 87–97.

Higgins, S. T., Budney, A. J., Bickel, W. K., & Badger, G. J. (1994). Participation of significant others in outpatient behavioral treatment predicts greater cocaine abstinence. *American Journal of Drug and Alcohol Abuse, 20*, 47–56.

Higgins, S. T., Budney, A. J., Bickel, W. K., Hughes, J. R., Foerg, F., & Badger, G. (1993). Achieving cocaine abstinence with a behavioral approach. *American Journal of Psychiatry, 150*, 763–769.

Higgins, S. T., Delaney, D. D., Budney, A. J., Bickel, W. K., Hughes, J. R., Foerg, F., & Fenwick, J. W. (1991). A behavioral approach to achieving initial cocaine abstinence. *American Journal of Psychiatry, 148*, 1218–1224.

Kang, S., Leinman, P. H., Todd, T., Kemp, J., & Lopton, D. S. (1991). Familial and individual functioning in a sample of adult cocaine abusers. *Journal of Drug Issues, 21,* 579–592.

Koppelman, J., & Jones, J. M. (1989). Crack: It's destroying fragile low-income families. *Public Welfare,* Fall, 13–15.

Magura, S. (1994). Social workers should be more involved in substance abuse treatment. *Health and Social Work, 19,* 3–5.

Mattaini, M. A. (1991). Choosing weapons for the war on 'crack': An operant analysis. *Research on Social Work Practice, 1,* 188–213.

Means, L. B., Small, M., Capone, D. M., Capone, T. J., Condren, R., Peterson, M., & Hayward, B. (1989). Client demographics and outcome in outpatient cocaine treatment. *International Journal of the Addictions, 24,* 765–783.

Nunes-Dinis, M., & Barth, R. P. (1993). Cocaine treatment and outcome. *Social Work, 38,* 611–617.

O'Brien, C. P., & Childress, A. R. (1991). Behavior therapy of drug dependence. In B. Glass (Ed.), *The international handbook of addiction behavior.* New York: Routledge.

Pavlov, I. P. (1927). *Conditioned reflexes* (G. V. Anrep, Trans.). London, UK: Oxford University Press.

Peele, S. (1985). *The meaning of addiction: Compulsive experience and its interpretation.* Lexington, MA: Lexington Books.

Rawson, R. A., Obert, J. L., McCann, M. J., Smith, D. P., & Ling, W. (1990). Neurobehavioral treatment for cocaine dependency. *Journal of Psychoactive Drugs, 22,* 159–171.

Semlitz, L., & Gold, M. S. (1986). Adolescent drug use: Diagnosis, treatment, and prevention. *Substance Abuse, 9,* 455–473.

Skinner, B. F. (1953). *Science and human behavior.* New York: Macmillan.

Solomon, R. L. (1980). The opponent process theory of acquired motivation: The cost of pleasure and the benefits of pain. *American Psychologist, 35,* 691–712.

Spitz, H. I. (1987). Cocaine abuse: Therapeutic group approaches. In H. I. Spitz & J. S. Rosecan (Eds.), *Cocaine abuse: New directions in treatment and research*. New York: Brunner/Mazel.

Spitz, H. I., & Spitz, S. T. (1987). Family therapy of cocaine abuse. In H. I. Spitz & J. S. Rosecan (Eds.), *Cocaine abuse: New directions in treatment and research*. New York: Brunner/Mazel.

Tobena, A., Fernandez-Teruel, A., Escoriheula, R. M., Nunez, J. F., Zapata, A., Ferre, F., & Sanchez, R. (1993). Limits of habituation and extinction: Implications for relapse prevention programs in addiction. *Drug and Alcohol Dependence, 3,* 209–217.

Wallace, B. C. (1991). *Crack cocaine.* New York: Brunner/Mazel.

Washton, A. M., Gold, M. S., & Potash, A. C. (1986). *Treatment outcomes in cocaine abusers.* (Research Monograph no. 67). Rockville, MD: National Institute on Drug Abuse.

Weddington, W. W. (1993). Cocaine diagnosis and treatment. *Psychiatric Clinics of North America, 16,* 87–95.

Wells, E. A., Peterson, P. L., Gainey, R. R., Hawkins, J. D., & Catalano, R. F. (1994). Outpatient treatment for cocaine abuse: A controlled comparison of relapse prevention and 12-step approaches. *American Journal of Drug and Alcohol Abuse, 20,* 1–17.

Wodarski, J. S., & Feit, M. D. (1994). Applications of reward structures in social group work. *Social Work With Groups, 17,* 123–142.

10

Motivational Enhancement in the Treatment of Addictions

Emil Chiauzzi, PhD

Dr. Chiauzzi is Director of the Addictions Treatment Program at the Deaconess Waltham Hospital in Waltham, MA.

KEY POINTS

- Each year, nearly 250 million prescriptions are taken incompletely or not at all. Among a broad range of medical treatments, most estimates of noncompliance range from 30%–60%.

- Denial and resistance are prevalent among patients with addictions. Resistance to psychotherapy is also common. Delivering a treatment is not enough; *reception* is critical.

- It is important to distinguish compliance from motivation. *Compliance* means adherence to a prescribed regimen. *Motivation* implies a combination of patient characteristics, clinician characteristics, the manner of treatment delivery, and elements of illness or condition.

- Noncompliance is not necessar-

ily a negative development. Resistance may represent internal forces that oppose change, often in the interest of self-protection; it should be a subject explored in — rather than an obstacle to — treatment.

- The author presents three motivational enhancement models to improve the efficacy of medical interventions: the patient-centered care model, the treatment adherence model, and motivational enhancement therapy.

- The risk of noncompliance is reduced if clinicians attend to four steps: orient the patient to treatment, address not only the content but the process of treatment, educate in an objective manner, and intervene with resistance as a component of treatment.

INTRODUCTION: THE SCOPE OF THE
NONCOMPLIANCE PROBLEM

The level of advancement in medical and psychological science is matched only by the level of resistance (also referred to herein as "noncompliance" or "lack of motivation") in patients receiving the potential benefits of these advancements. Among a broad range of medical treatments, most estimates of noncompliance range from 30%–60% (Meichenbaum & Turk, 1987). Noncompliance encompasses the entire range of an intervention, from not honoring an appointment to not following a regimen. Each year, nearly 250 million prescriptions are taken incompletely or not at all (Buckalew & Sallis, 1986). Noncompliance also occurs when patients do not tell the clinician (Stark, 1992) about alternative treatments they are receiving outside the clinician's area of expertise. One in four Americans uses "unconventional" therapies (chiropractic, acupuncture, self-help groups), but only 30% of these patients inform their doctors of the treatments (Eisenberg et al., 1993). Meichenbaum and Turk (1987) suggested that these trends apply to a broad range of diseases, because many patients with cancer, epilepsy, migraine, and diabetes fail to self-administer medication correctly.

Resistance to psychotherapy is equally distressing and is most evident in follow-up and drop-out rates. Even worse are the facts that: at least one third of patients offered psychotherapeutic treatment refuse it (Garfield, 1980); 41% of patients referred for group therapy never attend a session (Klein & Carroll, 1986); between 30% and 60% of patients drop out of mental health clinic treatment (Pekarkik, 1983); and almost two thirds of patients receiving private psychotherapy (often considered the most motivated patients) leave treatment before the tenth session (Garfield, 1986).

Denial and resistance are quite prevalent among patients with addictions. Approximately 50% of applicants for methadone treatment do not make it through orientation, and 52%–75% of alcoholic patients receiving outpatient therapy fail to continue after four sessions. Moreover, between 23% and 39%

of alcoholic patients leave inpatient detoxification programs prematurely (Baekland & Lundwall, 1975). Overall, the attrition rate within the first month of treatment is more than 50% (Stark, 1992). Despite the recognized importance of aftercare, less than 50% of patients completing inpatient addiction treatment comply with aftercare recommendations (Siegel, Alexander, & Lin, 1984; Walker, Donovan, Kivlahan, & O'Leary, 1983).

These statistics are indeed troubling. Good intentions, clinical skill, and empiric efficacy mean little when treatment regimens are not followed. Treatment resistance is likely one of the factors underlying the dreaded "one third rule" for alcoholic persons — by age 65, one third are dead or in poor condition, one third are abstinent or drinking less, and one third are still trying to stop drinking (Seligman, 1993). Delivering a treatment is not enough — *reception* of treatment is the critical element.

This chapter will explore the factors in treatment resistance and noncompliance and review a variety of motivational enhancement strategies. In the following discussion, the reader should note that *compliance* and *motivation* are not identical concepts. The patient who is apparently noncompliant is not necessarily unmotivated; there may be other factors that explain this behavior. Likewise, the patient who is apparently compliant may be presenting a good impression without making meaningful changes. The clinician who can distinguish these concepts increases the likelihood of significant change.

FACTORS IN RESISTANCE

Meichenbaum and Turk (1987) delineated four major factors in patient resistance: patient variables, relationship variables, illness and symptom variables, and treatment variables. Patient variables include individual characteristics, the patient's perception of the illness, social supports, expectations about treatment, and personal resources.

Patient variables have profound effects on the ways in

which patients and clinicians perceive presenting problems. Within medicine, patients are more likely to focus on the psychosocial aspects of their complaints, whereas physicians attend to symptoms (Allshouse, 1993). Medical patients experience "illnesses," which encompass psychological and social dimensions as well as physical discomforts. Physicians focus on "diseases," which fall in the biomedical realm. As a result, symptoms, rather than patients' *experiences* of illness, are stressed.

In addition, the "disease" approach assumes a passive patient stance, whereas the "illness" approach suggests a more active, dynamic interaction between patient and clinician. As in hospital care, traditional treatment of addictions encourages passivity—acceptance of a set of philosophic beliefs. Patients who agree with these beliefs are considered "good" or "motivated," whereas patients who challenge suggestions are deemed to be "in denial" or "unmotivated." In his review of motivation in alcoholic clients, Miller (1985) stated, "A client tends to be judged as motivated if he or she accepts the therapist's view of the problem (including the need for help and the diagnosis), is distressed, and complies with treatment prescriptions." The traditional perspective on motivation ignores the culturally based beliefs, perceptions about treatment, and need for involvement in clinical decision making that many patients seek. Psychosocial stressors, mental disorders, and past motivational history may also affect the motivational presentation.

Motivation is affected by a second factor—relationship variables. These variables relate to the quality of communication, rapport, and patient-clinician attitudes and behaviors. "Motivation" should not be considered a personality trait (implying that the patient is completely to blame for negative outcomes) but an interactional phenomenon (implying dual responsibility). Health care professionals who develop unilateral treatment goals, confront clients too forcefully, or lack empathy increase the risk of treatment resistance. Negotiated, individualized treatment goals are essential for effective medical and addiction treatments (Allshouse, 1993; Miller, 1985). Good communication should not be confused with simple satisfaction with the practitioner. For example, one study found that compliance with a drug regimen correlated negatively with patient satisfaction but positively with an understanding of the treatment (Wartman, Morlock, Malitz, & Palm, 1983).

Illness and symptom variables are a third factor in patient compliance (Meichenbaum & Turk, 1987). Treatments for illnesses with symptoms that are easily recognized and relieved are more likely to be followed. Patients are less likely to comply with treatments when they are preventive or the illnesses lack distressing symptoms (Meichenbaum & Turk, 1987). This conclusion is especially relevant to the treatment of addictions, most of which occurs after the effects of the substance have been eliminated.

Treatment variables represent the fourth major factor in noncompliance (Meichenbaum & Turk, 1987). These variables include the characteristics of the treatment setting, continuity and timing of care, complexity of the treatment regimen, and treatment side effects. Despite the potential usefulness of a treatment regimen of daily Alcoholics Anonymous (AA) meetings, individual counseling, aftercare groups, psychiatric care (when indicated), and Al-Anon (for family members), recovering patients may feel overwhelmed with the costs and time associated with these multiple involvements. They may also dislike the "side effects" — changes in social involvements, increased family expectations, emotional uncovering, and time constraints.

COMPLIANCE VERSUS MOTIVATION

The previous findings clearly indicate a need to distinguish compliance from motivation. *Compliance* represents adherence to a prescribed regimen, which may result from unilateral goals developed by the clinician. Compliance may not lead to unfavorable outcomes with relatively direct interventions; for example, prescribing an antibiotic for an infection. However, the danger of noncompliance increases as the intervention affects psychological, social, or lifestyle dimensions; for example, nutritional plans for treating obesity. Ironically, a patient's apparent compliance may not necessarily indicate a favorable outcome, because many persons are concerned with being "perfect patients" and may not divulge negative treatment effects. In addition, the patient who merely follows orders may not be equipped to engage in independent problem solving when other problems arise. The active and involved patient will be more likely to learn methods to prevent relapse.

Motivation implies a combination of factors — patient characteristics, clinician characteristics, the manner of treatment delivery, and elements of the illness or condition. What appears to be a lack of motivation in the patient may actually result from difficulties in recognizing symptoms, a lack of information, a poor understanding of treatment recommendations, or barriers to receiving treatment (such as a lack of proximity to the treatment site or a lack of child care).

Noncompliance should not necessarily be considered a negative development. Resistance in the form of noncompliance may represent internal forces that oppose change and should be a subject, rather than an obstacle, in treatment (Zweben, 1989). Such opposition may actually reflect a self-protective tendency; for example, in an alcoholic person who self-medicates to mask a negative affect arising from past sexual abuse. Apparent resistance to treatment may not even indicate disagreement, because addiction-related cognitive deficits may interfere with the comprehension or learning of new skills (McCrady, 1987). Areas of noncompliance may suggest avenues for further exploration, not a therapeutic impasse.

Furthermore, motivation should not be considered a static phenomenon. Goals and motives change as problem behaviors are identified and addressed. These changes are best illustrated by the "stage of change" model proposed by Prochaska, Norcross, and DiClemente (1994). They evaluated 15 problem behaviors (including various addictions) and found that only 20% of persons with these problems were prepared for active change at any given time. They also noted that more than 90% of treatment programs focus on this minority, so it is no surprise that only 10% of alcoholic persons seek help.

Prochaska and colleagues (1994) defined five distinct stages of change: (a) *precontemplation,* in which the addicted person has no recognition of a problem; (b) *contemplation,* which represents recognition of the problem but an uncertainty about taking action; (c) *preparation,* in which the person resolves to make a change and develops a plan; (d) *action,* which is the interventional phase; and (e) *maintenance,* in which the change endures through relapse prevention strategies. At each stage, treatment goals and interventions vary. This model suggests that action-oriented approaches are appropriate during the action stage but may be premature and ineffective during earlier stages. The patient may appear "unmotivated" but may simply require a different approach; for example, convincing feedback that there is a problem (precontemplation) or a discussion of "pros and cons" of changing behavior (preparation). Matching the intervention to the stage increases the likelihood of compliance and, therefore, motivation.

MOTIVATIONAL ENHANCEMENT MODELS

Despite the well-documented high relapse rates in the addiction field, there has been relatively little discussion of motivational enhancement in the literature. As a result, this chapter will draw upon two treatment models that have addressed ways to improve the effectiveness of medical interventions — the patient-centered care model and the treatment adherence model. The final model, motivational enhancement therapy, specifically addresses the treatment of addiction.

These models promote an understanding and sensitivity about the factors underlying motivation by assuming collaboration between the clinician and the patient. They encourage the establishment of treatment styles, interventions, and environments that improve a patient's readiness to change. Most important, they assist the clinician in developing hypotheses and strategies when the patient is seemingly resistant.

Picker/Commonwealth Patient-Centered Care Model:

The Picker/Commonwealth Program for Patient-Centered Care is located at the Beth Israel Hospital in Boston, Massachusetts, and is devoted to ways in which the quality of care in hospitals can be improved by adopting a collaborative approach with patients (Gerteis, Edgman-Levitan, Daley, & Delbanco, 1993). Although these investigators are not primarily concerned with improving motivation, their observations about the treatment process have strong implications for the degree of motivation that the patient may display.

Seven primary dimensions of patient-centered care have been defined: (a) respect for patients' values, preferences, and expressed needs; (b) coordination and integration of care; (c) information, communication, and education; (d) physical comfort; (e) emotional support and alleviation of fear and anxiety; (f) involvement of family and friends; and (g) transition and continuity. Based on these dimensions, the investigators believe that medical treatment will be most effective when it: involves the patient in decision making and enhances autonomy and dignity; promotes communication among treatment-team members and among support services; provides education about the clinical status, progress, prognosis, and self-management related to the illness; reduces pain and provides a comfortable and accessible treatment environment; addresses apprehensiveness about the effects of the illness on the patient and others; involves, supports, and educates family members and friends; and delineates aftercare recommendations and plans. The nature of the treatment of addictions (and medical care in general) increasingly emphasizes personal responsibility, prevention, and efficient care delivery. Thus, the previous interventions enhance the possibility of a consensus and cooperation among the clinician, patient, and family members. The latter factor should not be underestimated; one study of coronary primary prevention found that patients with "low support" averaged a compliance rate of 70%, whereas patients with "high support" averaged a compliance rate of 96% (Doherty, Schrott, Metcalf, & Iasiello-Vailas, 1983).

Treatment Adherence Model:

Meichenbaum and Turk (1987) have developed a set of behavioral techniques based upon the disease, patient, treatment, and relationship variables previously mentioned. What appears to be a lack of motivation actually follows behavioral principles, because such behavior is influenced by its antecedents as well as by positive and negative consequences. Effective management of contingencies increases the likelihood of "motivation" and can be implemented through self-monitoring, explicit goal setting, corrective feedback, and behavioral contracting. Training patients to maximize reinforcement from themselves or others can also enhance motivation.

According to Meichenbaum and Turk (1987), treatment compliance ("adherence") should not be interpreted as an obstacle within the patient but as a complex interplay of a variety of factors. To maximize motivation, the clinician must assess noncompliant behavior through self-report, behavioral measures (such as records of attendance or medications taken), biochemical measures (to detect whether the drug was taken), and clinical outcome. They do not regard noncompliance as necessarily counterproductive, because refusal to take a medication with negative side effects may be self-protective.

Motivational Enhancement Therapy:

Motivational enhancement therapy (MET) (Miller & Rollnick, 1991; Miller, Zweben, DiClemente, & Rychtarik, 1994) is a treatment technique for alcoholism based upon the stages-of-change model previously described. The "confrontation-of-denial" approach of traditional treatment of alcoholism heavily emphasizes the label of "alcoholic," relies on the disease concept, treats resistance as a trait requiring confrontation, and attempts to convince the patient of these philosophies. In contrast, MET does not use labeling as a crucial element; it emphasizes personal choice, focuses on objective assessment, and views resistance as an interpersonal behavior pattern subject to influence by the therapist. Rather than directly confronting patient resistance, this approach encourages the exploration of patient perceptions without promoting a "right way" of viewing alcoholism; patient responsibility as opposed to "powerlessness"; objective feedback in the form of alcoholism questionnaires, laboratory tests, neuropsychological tests, and comparison of the patient's drinking habits to those of population norms; alternate strategies from the patient and social support network; and "matching" interventions to the stage of change.

The basic principles of MET include the following factors: expression of empathy through reflective listening; development of discrepancy through discussion of the biopsychosocial consequences of drinking; avoidance of argumentation, which may actually increase resistance; "rolling" with resistance by reframing patient perceptions and inviting new ways of problem solving; and supporting self-efficacy by encouraging hopeful strategies for change (Miller et al., 1994). In short, MET is a "soft sell" method that evokes, rather than directs, solutions.

STRATEGIES OF MOTIVATIONAL ENHANCEMENT

It is interesting that these three models achieve similar conclusions despite highlighting different clinical populations in diverse settings. Essentially, the risk of resistance or noncompliance is reduced if the clinician attends to four major steps: (a) orient the patient to treatment; (b) address not only the content but the process of treatment; (c) provide education in an objective and interactive manner; and (d) intervene with resistance as a component of, not an obstacle to, treatment. The following sections will review a variety of strategies for these four areas.

Treatment Orientation:

Understanding Resistance

One of the clinician's first goals is to recognize that ambivalence is an essential feature of the process of change in addictions (Miller & Rollnick, 1991; Shaffer, 1992). For many patients, addiction is perceived at least as a known quantity and at best as a protective mechanism. The addictive lifestyle is a full-time job and requires massive alterations for abstinence to be maintained; ambivalence should be expected.

In addition, most patients bring their own model of addiction to treatment. The goal is to gain access to this model rather than to convert the patient to the therapist's clinical model. As Shaffer (1992) reported, patients may view addiction as a disease, an excessive habit, a punishment, a biologic dilemma, a stress management tool, a personal weakness, or an average functioning compared with that of their reference group. The clinician who understands the patient's "theory" of addiction will likely gain a rich source of information about which, if any, therapeutic interventions will be successful.

Individualizing Treatment

All of the approaches previously mentioned emphasize the need for individualized treatment and a sense of control over the treatment process. When the number of choices is reduced or the patient perceives that he or she is receiving a "cookbook" treatment, the patient may resist due to a sense of limited freedom. Offering a menu of alternatives (e.g., 12-step groups, psychotherapy, addiction counseling, or inpatient treatment) with a discussion of potential consequences of each alternative may increase a patient's commitment to treatment (Miller & Rollnick, 1991; Newman, 1994). Treatment selection may also be matched based upon psychosocial stressors, medical problems, the level of care needed (inpatient, outpatient, residential, or partial hospitalization), or the abused substance (Miller, 1989). Even if the patient selects a treatment unsuccessfully, the likelihood exists for increased urgency for change and more information about the relapse process.

Negotiating Treatment Goals

The initial points of contention in setting goals usually revolve around the abstinence goal and 12-step approaches. Abstinence is the most practical goal because there are various contraindications to moderation (health risks, a history of dangerous behavior, and a lack of social support for moderation) and because the history of addicted patients usually indicates a low probability of success with this approach. The patient should be encouraged to attempt a trial of abstinence to experience potential positive physical, psychological, and social effects. Drug substitution also can be discouraged by using a goal of complete abstinence.

Furthermore, many patients are resistant to 12-step meetings. Such resistance should not be accepted too readily, because it may represent a lack of understanding of the culture, process, and language of self-help meetings. Even concerns about the "higher power" concept can be overcome by focusing on the practical advantages of self-help meetings: they offer a "ready-made" support group, they disseminate information about recovery, and they reduce the potential for trial and error by allowing contact with successful recovering members. In cases of extreme philosophic conflict, alternatives, such as rational recovery, can be presented.

Handling High-Risk Groups

A study of treatment dropouts in an outpatient alcoholism treatment facility indicated that patients most likely to require treatment (young, female, unskilled, and less educated persons) were more likely to leave treatment prematurely (Mammo & Weinbaum, 1993). This study yielded two other major findings. Self-referred patients, often considered the most motivated group, were the most likely to drop out. Court-mandated patients were the most likely to complete treatment.

These results suggest the need for more intensive motivational strategies with groups possessing fewer resources. In addition, self-referral does not guarantee motivation; patients may seek treatment impulsively or for vague reasons. As a result, such patients may require more intensive motivational intervention if the initial determination to change behavior appears to be waning.

Process Issues:

Exhibiting Empathy

An empathic therapeutic approach conveys a sense of acceptance, tolerance, and understanding. Miller and Rollnick (1991) suggested five strategies to enhance an empathic style: (a) ask open-ended questions; (b) listen reflectively; (c) provide affirmation of the patient using compliments and other forms of appreciation; (d) summarize key points; and (e) elicit self-motivational statements — allow the patient to state the reasons for change. These strategies avoid a tendency to "lead the witness" and will help build intrinsic motivation ("owning" the problem). Newman (1994) recommended the Socratic method, a technique in which the therapist leads the patient toward a self-motivated conclusion by asking a series of thought-provoking questions.

Structuring Treatment

The structure of treatment can have a dramatic effect on compliance. Meichenbaum and Turk (1987) suggested that appointments are more likely to be kept when a specific time is given, reminders are included, a short referral time is used, and reasons for missed appointments are discussed. Treating the patient as a passive receptacle of such information is not recommended. In psychiatry, estimates of missed appointments run as high as 60% of scheduled sessions (Sparr, Moffitt, & Ward, 1993). It is important to provide a clear rationale for the referral through a discussion of key questions that may be addressed in treatment. Continuity of care is essential; patients who perceive a lack of communication or flow of paperwork among professionals may become skeptical of the quality of care provided. Practical matters should be confronted early — treatment should be geographically accessible and fit into the patient's schedule.

Improving Communication

Effective motivational enhancement is based upon a collaborative stance by the patient and the therapist. Communication about nontechnical, patient-centered issues has a positive impact on patient satisfaction and health outcomes (Daley, 1993). The most important determinant of therapeutic outcome is the quality of patient participation in treatment (Orlinsky, Grawe, & Parks, 1994). Addicted patients frequently have preconceived notions of the causes, consequences, and treatments of their addictions. No matter how misguided their beliefs may be, it is critical to allow patients to participate in hypothesizing the possible factors in addiction. Differences between therapists and patients can then be approached as alternative hypotheses, rather than mutually exclusive opinions. Furthermore, treatment can be framed as a mutual search for confirming evidence of these hypotheses.

Patient Education:

Overcoming Neuropsychological Deficits

During the early stages of recovery, patients experience deficits in abstract reasoning, learning new material, problem solving, short-term memory, and visuospatial abilities (McCrady, 1987). Repetition, concrete presentation, personally relevant content, and prefaces/summaries of each session all enhance retention and comprehension (Chiauzzi, 1991). Daley (1987) suggested that patients keep a "sobriety journal" to prevent themselves from forgetting newly learned material.

Considering Psychoeducational Issues

There are numerous benefits of patient education. In addition to increasing knowledge, effective educational strategies decrease the rate of rehospitalization and improve adherence to medical regimens (Ellers, 1993). Education should be directed at three primary areas: the treatment process, case conceptualization, and treatment interventions.

Many patients approach treatment with little more than perceptions gleaned from their friends or the mass media. In this day of talk shows, personal testimonials of recovery, made-for-television movies, and self-help literature, many people still have little understanding of the treatment of addictions. They seek immediate relief with minimal effort in a short amount of time. Some patients wonder only half jokingly whether the therapist possesses a "magic wand" or "magic pill." Therapists who do not assess their patients' knowledge about treatment run the risk of future noncompliance when these expectations are not met. Clinicians should discuss the role of patients during the therapeutic process, the expected length and stages of treatment, and the need for periodic progress reports (Newman, 1994). Educating patients about treatment assists in the assessment of patient readiness and casts patients as active consumers.

Sharing the case conceptualization with the patient is another effective educational approach (Newman, 1994). Integrating historic information about biopsychosocial risk factors, addictive patterns, negative consequences, and psychosocial stressors permits the patient to view problems more objectively and to collaborate with the therapist. The patient can also learn to attend to, prioritize, and interpret information.

Information related to treatment interventions should be presented concretely, evenly, and with the use of various media. For instance, relaxation techniques may be presented in writing, on audiotape, or orally. The patient's comprehension, skill level, and ability to evaluate his or her performance should be assessed. For example, many alcoholic patients are encouraged to attend AA meetings, seek a sponsor, and participate in the proceedings. However, these suggestions assume a level of social skill that a newly recovering alcoholic person may not possess. Unfortunately, many therapists interpret noncompliance with suggestions such as a lack of motivation, rather than a lack of social skills.

Social Support

The best treatment plan can be undermined if the patient's social-support system does not reinforce the efforts of the clinician. The patient's perceptions of addiction and treatment seldom occur in a vacuum. Treatment gains will more likely be maintained if a parallel educational process occurs with friends and family members. Several messages should be emphasized:

- Collaboration offers the best chance of success

- Supportive persons may offer feedback or set limits that increase patient motivation

- The patient, significant other, and therapist have mutually interlocking roles in problem resolution

- Recovery involves stages of growth, which may be potentially threatening to a relationship

Early sobriety requires concrete life changes, but later stages often involve reassessment of past and present relationships. Active involvement and mutual growth of significant others minimize the disruption caused by these changes.

Behavioral Interventions:

Enhancing Commitment to Change

Commitment to change is enhanced if the patient makes a public declaration that is specific in the frequency and duration of the targeted behavior (Meichenbaum & Turk, 1987). Behavioral contracting provides the best method for specifying the terms of a patient's commitment to change. Contracts should include a detailed description of the target behavior (e.g., attendance at AA meetings), the frequency (e.g., three times per week), and possible reinforcements (e.g., coffee with a friend afterward). Written contracts add a sense of formality. Most important, the negotiation process leading to an agreement communicates flexibility, problem solving, and reinforcements that compete with substance use.

Feedback

Miller and colleagues (1994) recommended avoiding the following feedback approaches: arguing, judging, "scare tactics," logical persuasion, analyzing reasons for resistance, confronting patients with authority, and sarcasm. Instead, these authors recommended that therapists should elicit "self-motivational" statements from patients. In addition to empathic listening, reframing and summarizing are useful. Reframing is accomplished by restating patient comments with a new perspective. For instance, patients may regard drinking as a reward or stress reduction method. Reframing may suggest that these goals are acceptable, but there are healthy alternatives. Summarizing repeats key points in such a manner that the patient can draw a larger conclusion. For instance, the alcoholic patient who has randomly admitted a variety of negative consequences of drinking throughout a treatment session may realize the extent of his or her alcoholism as the therapist reviews them in a succinct manner.

Objectivity is a cardinal rule of motivational feedback. Addicted patients often are ready to debate when emotional appeals, dogma, guilt, legalistic logic, or scare tactics are used. Forcing acceptance of labels ("alcoholic" or "addict") or engaging in philosophic arguments is often fruitless. Instead, therapists who rely on the patient's intrinsic motives and repeat objective information with empathy (in the patient's "language") are less likely to encounter resistance. For instance, data collected from psychological testing, alcoholism questionnaires, laboratory tests, or cognitive tasks create a discrepancy with the patient's perception of addiction (Miller et al., 1994). This feedback is not forced but presented as information that must be taken seriously. Once the patient becomes aware of an inconsistency, contemplation of change may begin.

'Devil's Advocate'

Resistance or noncompliance should be predicted as a possible outcome. Engaging the patient not only reviews potential obstacles to change and affirms the difficulty of change, but also provides the patient with an opportunity to defend the need for change. Delineation of pros and cons of change is useful, and patients should be encouraged to "do their homework" to accept fully the direction of treatment.

Mnemonics

Two of the models described in this chapter can be summarized with mnemonics. Each one encapsulates the essential points for the clinician to emphasize in treatment.

Learn:

The Picker/Commonwealth group (Allshouse, 1993) suggested these steps for enhancing treatment:

- Listening with empathy

- Explaining your perceptions of the problem

- Acknowledging differences and similarities between the patient's and clinician's perceptions of the problem

- Recommending treatment

- Negotiating agreement

Frames:

Miller and Rollnick (1991) suggested the following components of effective motivational enhancement:

- Feedback from structured and objective assessments

- Responsibility for making changes

- Advice by the clinician for the patient to make a behavioral change

- Menu of treatment alternatives

- Empathy

- Self-efficacy

SUMMARY

This chapter has reviewed the factors, models, and techniques associated with the enhancement of motivation for addicted patients. Clues for enhancing motivation can be found in all areas of health care, because all disciplines have grappled with patient resistance. This chapter has advocated the conceptualization of motivation as an interpersonal phenomenon that is subject to assessment and intervention. Individualized orientation, psychoeducation, and appropriate treatment structuring not only enhance motivation but also improve outcomes.

REFERENCES

Allshouse, K. D. (1993). Treating patients as individuals. In M. Gerteis, S. Edgman-Levitan, J. Daley, & T. L. Delbanco (Eds.), *Through the patient's eyes: Understanding and promoting patient-centered care* (pp. 19–44). San Francisco: Jossey-Bass.

Baekland, F., & Lundwall, L. (1975). Dropping out of treatment: A critical review. *Psychological Bulletin, 82,* 738–783.

Buckalew, L. W., & Sallis, R. E. (1986). Patient compliance and medication perception. *Journal of Clinical Psychology, 42,* 49–53.

Chiauzzi, E. J. (1991). *Preventing relapse in the addictions: A biopsychosocial approach.* Needham, MA: Allyn & Bacon.

Daley, D. (1987). Relapse prevention with substance abusers: Clinical issues and myths. *Social Work, 45*(2), 38–42.

Daley, J. (1993). Overcoming the barrier of words. In M. Gerteis, S. Edgman-Levitan, J. Daley, & T. L. Delbanco (Eds.), *Through the patient's eyes: Understanding and promoting patient-centered care* (pp. 72–95). San Francisco: Jossey-Bass.

Doherty, W. L., Schrott, H. G., Metcalf, L., & Iasiello-Vailas, L. (1983). Effect of spouse support and health beliefs on medication adherence. *Journal of Family Practice, 17,* 837–841.

Eisenberg, D. M., Kessler, R. C., Foster, C., Norlock, F. E., Calkins, D. R., & Delbanco, T. L. (1993). Unconventional medicine in the United States: Prevalence, costs, and patterns of use. *New England Journal of Medicine, 328,* 246–252.

Ellers, B. (1993). Innovations in patient-centered education. In M. Gerteis, S. Edgman-Levitan, J. Daley, & T. L. Delbanco (Eds.), *Through the patient's eyes: Understanding and promoting patient-centered care* (pp. 96–118). San Francisco: Jossey-Bass.

Garfield, S. L. (1980). *Psychotherapy: An eclectic approach.* New York: Wiley.

Garfield, S. L. (1986). Research on client variables in psychotherapy. In S. L. Garfield & A. E. Bergin (Eds.), *Handbook of psychotherapy and behavior change* (pp. 213–256). New York: Wiley.

Gerteis, M., Edgman-Levitan, S., Daley, J., & Delbanco, T. L. (1993). *Through the patient's eyes: Understanding and promoting patient-centered care*. San Francisco: Jossey-Bass.

Klein, R. H., & Carroll, R. A. (1986). Patient characteristics and attendance patterns in outpatient group psychotherapy. *International Journal of Group Psychotherapy, 36*, 115–132.

Mammo, A., & Weinbaum, D. F. (1993). Some factors that influence dropping out from outpatient alcoholism treatment facilities. *Journal of Studies on Alcohol, 52*, 92–101.

McCrady, B. S. (1987). Implications of neuropsychological research findings for the treatment and rehabilitation of alcoholics. In O. A. Parsons, N. Butters, & P. E. Nathan (Eds.), *Neuropsychology of alcoholism: Implications of diagnosis and treatment* (pp. 381–391). New York: Guilford Press.

Meichenbaum, D., & Turk, D. C. (1987). *Facilitating treatment adherence: A practitioner's guidebook*. New York: Plenum Press.

Miller, W. R. (1985). Motivation for treatment: A review with a special emphasis on alcoholism. *Psychological Bulletin, 98*, 84–107.

Miller, W. R. (1989). Matching individuals with interventions. In R. K. Hester & W. R. Miller (Eds.), *Handbook of alcoholism treatment approaches* (pp. 261-271). New York: Guilford Press.

Miller, W. R., & Rollnick, S. (1991). *Motivational interviewing: Preparing people to change addictive behavior*. New York: Guilford Press.

Miller, W. R., Zweben, A., DiClemente, C. C., & Rychtarik, R. G. (1994). *Motivational enhancement manual*. (NIH Publication No. 94-3723). Washington, DC: U.S. Government Printing Office.

Newman, C. F. (1994). Understanding client resistance: Methods for enhancing motivation to change. *Cognitive Behavior and Practice, 1*, 47–69.

Orlinsky, D., Grawe, K., & Parks, B. (1994). Process and outcome in psychotherapy. In A. Bergin & S. Garfield (Eds.), *Handbook of psychotherapy and behavior change* (4th ed., pp. 270-376). New York: Wiley.

Pekarkik, G. (1983). Follow-up adjustment of outpatient dropouts. *American Journal of Orthopsychiatry, 53*, 501–511.

Prochaska, J. O., Norcross, J. C., & DiClemente, C. C. (1994). *Changing for good*. New York: Morrow.

Seligman, M. E. P. (1993). *What you can change and what you can't: The complete guide to successful self-improvement*. New York: Fawcett Columbine.

Shaffer, H. J. (1992). The psychology of stage change: The transition from addiction to recovery. In J. H. Lowinson, P. Ruiz, & R. B. Millman (Eds.), *Substance abuse: A comprehensive textbook* (pp. 100–105). Baltimore, MD: Williams & Wilkins.

Siegel, C., Alexander, M. J., & Lin, S. (1984). Severe alcoholism in the mental health sector, II: Effects of service utilization on readmission. *Journal of Studies on Alcoholism, 45,* 510–516.

Sparr, L. F., Moffitt, M. C., & Ward, M. F. (1993). Missed psychiatric appointments: Who returns and who stays away. *American Journal of Psychiatry, 150,* 801–805.

Stark, M. J. (1992). Dropping out of substance abuse treatment: A clinically oriented review. *Clinical Psychology Review, 12,* 93–116.

Walker, R. D., Donovan, D. M., Kivlahan, D. R., & O'Leary, M. R. (1983). Length of stay, neuropsychological performance, and aftercare: Influences on alcohol treatment outcome. *Journal of Consulting and Clinical Psychology, 51,* 900–911.

Wartman, S. A., Morlock, L. L., Malitz, F. E., & Palm, E. A. (1983). Patient understanding and satisfaction as predictors of compliance. *Medical Care, 21,* 886–891.

Zweben, J. E. (1989). Recovery-oriented psychotherapy: Patient resistances and therapist dilemmas. *Journal of Substance Abuse Treatment, 6,* 123–132.

11

Reducing Risk of Relapse in Addiction

Emil Chiauzzi, PhD

Dr. Chiauzzi is Clinical Director, Addictions Treatment Program, Waltham-Weston Hospital, Waltham, MA.

KEY POINTS

- Although the treatment of addictions has expanded, relapse rates remain unacceptably high.

- Substance abuse relapse is often viewed incorrectly as an unpredictable, spontaneous occurrence. Many specific factors can be used to predict and prevent relapse.

- Relapse results from insufficient knowledge of biopsychosocial risk factors. Biologic risk factors include familial alcoholism and physical dependence, neurologic/neuropsychological impairment, and biochemical deficiencies. Examples of psychological risk factors are expectancy, cue reactivity, coping ability, and psychopathology. Areas of social risk factors are socioeconomic status, marital and family cohesion, employment status, and residential stability.

- Many beliefs regarding relapse are in fact myths whose inaccuracies result in many misconceptions. It is essential to understand the true nature of relapse behavior so that it may be dealt with successfully.

- Models of relapse include the moral, disease, self-medication, cognitive-behavioral, and biopsychosocial models.

- Relapse prevention techniques are presented, including psychoeducational approaches, cognitive remediation, skill building, lifestyle modification, and regulation.

INTRODUCTION

Despite the expansion of treatment for addictions, relapse rates remain unacceptably high. Relapse often is considered an unexpected occurrence, but careful study of this phenomenon reveals that it conforms to various biopsychosocial risk factors. The basic premises of this chapter are that relapse results from insufficient knowledge of these risk factors and that psychoeducational approaches can be used to reduce relapse potential. Many addicted persons link their relapse to one single factor, but the search for the "silver bullet" is likely to be fruitless. Instead, each relapse represents a convergence of multiple factors that reach "critical mass" before actual use.

Because risk factors and issues in relapse vary, several key areas must be examined: (a) relapse rates, (b) models of relapse, (c) relapse mythology, (d) biopsychosocial risk factors, (e) relapse prevention techniques, and (f) trends in relapse prevention. A clear understanding of these issues will assist both client and clinician in establishing a comprehensive treatment program.

RELAPSE RATES

Definitions of Relapse and Recovery:

The determination of relapse rates is difficult because definitions of "relapse" vary so widely. Litman, Stapleton, Oppenheim, and Peleg (1983) suggest that relapse can be viewed as:

- A discrete event initiated with a return to substance use

- A process that insidiously leads to the initiation of substance use

- A return to the same intensity of substance use

- Daily use for a specific number of sequential days

- A consequence of substance use, requiring re-admission for treatment

On the other end of the spectrum, a relapse can be considered to be secondary to life circumstances; that is, substance use is symptomatic of underlying dynamics or stressors. This approach places most attention on quality of life. The former abstinence-oriented approach is limited because simple abstinence does not necessarily create a meaningful life. To give an extreme example, according to Litman and colleagues (1983), a recovering alcoholic who is suicidal would be considered successful as long as he or she remains abstinent. On the other hand, the latter insight-oriented approach places inadequate emphasis on abstinence, which is necessary for any meaningful psychotherapy to occur.

To counter these limitations, present-day treatments combine these two definitions of relapse. Abstinence remains a goal, but the client is encouraged to develop self-knowledge, coping skills, and even a spiritual base. It is therefore important to establish a more inclusive definition of "recovery."

Bean-Bayog (1985) described three phases of recovery: (a) achieving sobriety, (b) maintaining abstinence and early recovery, and (c) advanced recovery. The addicted person begins by stopping substance use, then develops relapse prevention methods; after about 2 years, the person enters a period of reconstructive work aimed at exploring identity issues, intimacy, and family trauma.

The author envisions recovery as a progression through four similar phases: (a) abstinence (the first 6 months), (b) lifestyle change (months 6–18), (c) self-knowledge (months 18 and beyond), and (d) spirituality (unspecified). Abstinence is the most concrete phase because it involves specific behaviors that negate substance use; the results of abstinence can be seen quite readily. Lifestyle change involves broader interventions, such as moving to a safer locale, leaving a relationship, or switching jobs. Self-knowledge requires an objective self-analysis (also called a "fearless moral inventory" by Alcoholics Anonymous [AA] members) and would therefore require an even longer period of time. Psychotherapy would be likely at this phase, because the client begins to review important life events, themes, relationships, or personality issues. Finally, some people in recovery reach a state of spirituality; that is, a sense of meaning and direction in life. This is not necessarily religious in nature, but certainly involves questions such as "Who am I?" and "What is my purpose in life?" As recovering persons progress through these stages, the key questions become increasingly similar to those posed by nonaddicted people. As in the general population, not everyone reaches this phase; however, the person's recovery can still be a meaningful experience. Progression through these phases necessitates an increasing ability to integrate abstract concepts, which may not fit the cognitive style of some people.

Treatment Outcome:

Many outcome studies do not use broad definitions of relapse and recovery. Their results are generally based on the immediacy, amount, or frequency of use after treatment. When results are based on absolute abstinence, the treatment picture is discouraging. Hunt, Barnett, and Branch (1971) reported an average 1-year success rate of about 30%; Miller and Hester (1980) reported a 26% complete abstinence rate at 1 year. The Rand Report (Armor, Polich, & Stambul, 1978) found that only 7% of a total sample of 2000 patients were continuously abstinent for 4 years.

However, when broader indices of improvement are used, treatment results appear more promising. One review indicates that across various types and levels of treatment, clients were abstinent on the average of 80% or more of the days of follow-ups ranging from 18 to 24 months (McKay, Murphy, & Longabaugh, 1991). A major study of employee assistance program referrals to inpatient treatment found that drinking volume dropped from 6.3 to 1.5 drinks and number of drinking days in prior months dropped from 19.8 to 3.1 (Walsh et al., 1991). (For more information on employee assistance programs, see Thomas, 1996). McLellan and co-workers (1993) found 73% and 74% reductions in alcohol and drug use, respectively. These studies also report improvements in work performance and reductions in crime, family problems, and the use of medical benefits.

Socioeconomic factors may affect relapse rates: "good prognosis" (higher socioeconomic status) clients had success rates between 32% and 68%, whereas "poor prognosis" clients of lower socioeconomic status had rates between 0% and 18% (Baekland, 1977). This difference has been borne out in two later studies of private treatment centers, which found continuous abstinence rates of 66% (Wallace, McNeill, Gilfillan, MacLean, & Fanella, 1988) and 84% at 6-month follow-up (McLellan et al., 1993). The latter study suggested that middle-class, employed, insured men referred by employee assistance programs experienced the best response to treatment.

Relapse Rates Across Addictions:

Relapse rates across addictions are consistent. The results described above, which refer primarily to alcohol, are similar to those of cocaine, heroin, and nicotine. One study of adolescent cocaine abusers found a 76% relapse rate within the first 3 months (Wallace, 1989). About 66% of outpatient methadone-detoxified patients (Maddux & Desmond, 1986) and 50% of methadone maintenance graduates (Stimmel & Rabin, 1974) relapse. Approximately 50%–90% of opiate addicts discharged from public hospitals relapse (Stephens & Cottrell, 1972). Following treatment for nicotine addiction, about 70%–80% of persons return to smoking within 1 year (Hunt et al., 1971). About 25%–30% of treated smokers remain abstinent for 2–6 years (Colletti, Supnick, & Rizzo, 1982). The lure of cigarette smoking is extremely powerful: about 90% of smokers who consume *one* cigarette after a period of abstinence experience a full-blown relapse (Brandon, Tiffany, & Baker, 1986); and only one third of myocardial infarction patients who have been advised to quit smoking remain abstinent at 1 year (Perkins, 1988).

MODELS OF RELAPSE

Moral Model:

The moral model of relapse is best embodied within religious and legal principles. From a religious standpoint, the person who relapses is weak or a sinner. The relapser is therefore encouraged to admit his or her sins and adopt spiritual guidelines. A religious advisor would be the appropriate intervention agent in this situation.

The legal approach views the drinker or drug user as having violated social rules; he or she can therefore be considered a criminal. According to this model, substance-related rule-breaking therefore requires punishment, which allows the rule-breaker to pay his or her debt to society. Also, this approach may label the addicted person as "lazy" or "undesirable." Legal or social authorities are appropriate intervention agents.

Disease Model:

The disease model is the most prevalent approach in contemporary addictions treatment. This model provides a useful alternative to the moral model because it seeks to remove the stigma of addiction and place the addicted person within the treatment realm. The counselor is accordingly the primary intervention agent. Because addiction is considered a progressive and irreversible disease, any use is considered an expression of an innate inability to control intake. This model posits that any use can potentially trigger loss of control, so abstinence is the primary goal. However, this model may be limited due to the potential for self-fulfilling prophesy; that is, initial use may be construed as inevitably leading to loss of control, dismissing the possibility of interruption. In addition, the concept of "disease" may be construed as absolution of responsibility and render the addicted person passive in the recovery process.

Self-Medication Model:

Khantzian (1985) suggests that addicted people are predisposed to abuse substances because of painful affective states and psychopathologic conditions. Drugs are not chosen randomly — the addicted person selects those drugs that relieve unpleasant feelings. Opiate addicts may select heroin because it blunts underlying rage, whereas cocaine addicts may use cocaine to relieve depression. Mental health professionals are appropriate intervention agents with such individuals.

However, it is often difficult to establish "chicken and egg." Does the psychopathologic condition create the addiction or vice versa? It is critical to establish whether the psychopathologic condition is a precursor of, secondary to, or coexistent with the addiction. Next, it is crucial to educate the client about the primary importance of abstinence because effective mental health treatment cannot occur otherwise. Finally, many addicted clients do not meet criteria for any psychiatric diagnosis; thus, this model is primarily applicable to "dual diagnosis" patients.

Cognitive-Behavioral Model:

Marlatt and Gordon (1985) view addiction as an acquired habit pattern that can be modified by applied learning theory. The addicted person is encouraged to take responsibility for learning the skills necessary for maintaining abstinence. Less emphasis is placed on biologic factors and a greater reliance on cognitive-behavioral factors is stressed. Several cognitive factors figure prominently in this theory:

- Treatment readiness

- Self-efficacy

- Outcome expectancy

- Apparently irrelevant decisions

- Abstinence violation effect

Treatment readiness is viewed as a commitment to change and an understanding of the implications of such change, as opposed to an impulsive decision to stop substance use. Any counselor experienced in the addictions field has encountered many addicted clients who repeatedly apply short-term, superficial solutions to long-term problems.

Self-efficacy represents one's perception of competence in coping with a high-risk situation. For example, the development of coping skills such as relaxation or assertiveness may build one's confidence in refusing an offer for a drink.

Outcome expectancy represents one's perception of the potential results of such actions. Those who do not expect to be effective are not likely to perform the coping response, which will increase the risk of relapse.

Apparently irrelevant decisions occur along the path to relapse. Rather than being a discrete event, relapse is a consequence of a series of subtle and often unconscious decisions. For instance, the addicted person who allows a doctor to prescribe a painkilling medication for an injury (when there may be other alternatives) may be inviting a relapse.

Finally, an *abstinence violation effect* is said to occur when a person experiences an intense feeling of guilt, shame, and remorse when he or she has "slipped" into use of a substance.

These intense feelings then motivate further use. Rather than inducing guilt, Marlatt and Gordon (1985) suggest that the slip (or "lapse") should be viewed as an indicator of inadequate coping skills. The mistakes that the addicted person made can then be corrected through further education, training, and practice of needed coping skills.

Biopsychosocial Model:

Rather than applying a single theory or strategy to a highly diverse population of addicted persons, it is wise to evaluate such clients by using multiple perspectives. Because each client's addictive pathology involves a unique combination of biologic, psychological, and social factors, the application of a biopsychosocial model may provide needed flexibility for individualized treatment (Chiauzzi, 1991). The biopsychosocial model makes several assumptions:

- Counselors must assess biologic, psychological, and social factors to treat addiction in a comprehensive manner.

- The combination of these factors vary among addicted persons. Some clients have higher biologic risk (e.g., physical dependence), others have higher psychological risk (e.g., depression), and yet others have higher social risk (e.g., living in a drug-infested area).

- Because of the importance of psychological and social factors, people do not only become addicted to the drug itself, but also to the drug-taking experience.

- Such individualized assessment will allow "treatment matching" and thereby improve outcome.

- The need to assess and treat biologic, psychological, and social risk factors necessitates multidisciplinary treatment and cross-fertilization among disciplines.

Much research has been conducted on factors that predispose addicted people to relapse. The following sections examine the mythology and risk factors commonly associated with relapse.

RELAPSE MYTHOLOGY

Relapse is an Unpredictable Occurrence:

Those who promulgate the myth that relapse is an unpredictable outcome believe that the addicted person is at the mercy of unseen and powerful forces. A careful assessment typically finds that the relapser tends to overlook high-risk situations, substitute addictive behaviors, internal factors (such as negative personality traits), unresolved emotions, or inadequate knowledge of recovery. It is important to stress that relapse is a process and that substance use occurs at the *end* of the cycle, not the beginning.

Relapse Begins with the First Instance of Substance Use:

The first instance of substance use indicates that a biopsychosocial risk factor has been unattended. If one believes this myth, then one is likely to regard abstinence as sufficient. However, relapsers experience negative tendencies in behavior, affect, attitude, daily routine, and life events that encourage a return to substance use (Washton, 1989). The best example of these tendencies is the "dry drunk," the person who displays negative affect despite the absence of alcohol. The process of relapse usually involves a "window" of opportunity. Some relapsers are impulsive, in that a narrow window exists between thoughts of use and actual use. Others experience a wider window — the process of relapse requires a longer time span. However, in each case, a decision-making process needs to be uncovered and studied.

Relapse Results from a Lack of Willpower:

The willpower approach is based in a moral conceptualization of addiction. It suggests that mind can overcome matter — not by avoiding high-risk situations, but by confronting them. When an addicted person consistently resorts to willpower, he or she probably takes unnecessary risks. Those who adopt a careful and safe approach to recovery often report that willpower is unnecessary. As a result, relapse does not result from a lack of willpower but rather from an overreliance on it.

Relapse Negates Any Progress Made up to that Point:

This myth suggests an all-or-nothing approach to recovery. This may result from the AA practice of tracking one's time in recovery, thus leading a relapser back to the first day in recovery. However, each "day one" is different because the addicted person has had an opportunity to experience a period of recovery. One does not necessarily forget all that is learned through personal contacts, self-help groups, or treatment — the problem is that the addicted person does not know enough. As a result, treatments following a relapse should not simply repeat interventions but focus on mistakes or unlearned information. Recovery becomes a step-wise process rather than a win-or-lose situation.

Relapse is Caused by Negative Events in a Person's Life:

Relapse is not a random occurrence. But it is also overly simplistic to link relapse to particular negative events. An alcoholic in denial can regard just about any event as negative and find reason to drink. It is therefore preferable to assess perceptions of events. How else can we explain one alcoholic who drinks in response to a car that does not start, while another does not drink after experiencing the death of a loved one?

This myth is inaccurate for another reason: positive events are more risky than negative events for some people. For example, many use substances in response to job promotions, celebrations, or pleasant social situations. In fact, complacency is a risk factor for many people who have achieved early success in recovery.

Relapse Means That the Relapser is Not Motivated:

Negative outcomes in treatment often are explained by a lack of motivation on the client's part. However, many practitioners confuse motivation with compliance. Rather than residing in the client, motivation is better understood as a product of the clinician-client interaction (Miller, 1985). Counselor behaviors can significantly influence client behavior. Miller (1989) found that negative behaviors such as confrontation, counselor hostility, and poor prognosis are associated with drop-out and relapse. Better outcomes are associated with greater accessibility of treatment, provision of individualized feedback, goal setting, offering of treatment options, and presentation of a helping attitude.

BIOPSYCHOSOCIAL RISK FACTORS

The following summary of biopsychosocial risk factors is not meant to be exhaustive but is offered as a representation of major domains of assessment in determining relapse potential.

Biologic Risk Factors:

The research literature indicates three major areas of biologic risk: (a) familial alcoholism and physical dependence, (b) neurologic/neuropsychological impairment, and (c) biochemical deficiencies.

Goodwin (1988) distinguishes between familial and nonfamilial alcoholics: familial alcoholics tend to begin drinking at earlier ages and progress to more severe forms of alcoholism, whereas nonfamilial alcoholics engage in more self-medication—drinking to relieve anxiety or depression. Because familial alcoholics exhibit greater physical dependence (evidenced by tremulousness, blackouts, and morning drinking), they may be more likely to relapse. There is indeed evidence for this hypothesis, as a higher level of dependence may lead to greater perceived dangerousness of high-risk situations (Litman, Eiser, Rawson, & Oppenheim, 1977) and continuing alcohol problems (Polich, Armor, & Braiker, 1981).

A second biologic risk factor is impairment in neurologic or neuropsychological functioning. There may be neurologic deficits that precede alcoholism, such as the decreased amplitude of P300 waves in sons of alcoholics (Begleiter, Porjesz, Bihari, & Kissin, 1984). These waves are a measure of one's ability to identify relevant environmental cues, so a deficit may interfere with evaluating behavior. Other researchers have found a higher probability of hyperkinesis in children from alcoholic families (Tarter, Hegedus, & Gavaler, 1985).

Neuropsychological impairments also may be caused by alcoholism; 75%–95% of recovering alcoholics experience brain dysfunctions (Porjesz & Begleiter, 1983). Such "protracted withdrawal" also is experienced with opiate dependence (Satel, Kosten, Schuckit, & Fischman, 1993). Mood lability, decreased concentration, diminished cognitive functioning (such as impaired abstract reasoning and problem solving), insomnia, and distractibility are frequently found (Satel et al., 1993). The severity of these impairments may affect outcome: a lesser degree of dysfunction has been linked to longer abstinence (Abbot & Gregson, 1981), better participation in rehabilitation programs (O'Leary, Donovan, Chaney, & Walker, 1979), higher clinician ratings of prognosis (Leber, Parsons, & Nichols, 1985), and better postdischarge functioning (Walker, Donovan, Kivlahan, & O'Leary, 1983).

A third biologic risk factor is an abnormality in biochemistry. Space limitations do not allow for a complete review of these abnormalities, but several findings can be mentioned. Alcoholics and heroin addicts are thought to lack endorphins and may drink to produce tetrahydroisoquinolines, which are opiate-like metabolites of alcohol (Trachtenberg & Blum, 1987). Others hypothesize a decrease in norepinephrine in alcoholics, thus leading to a low internal level of arousal (Borg, Czarnecka, Kvande, Mossberg, & Sedvall, 1983). Alcoholics may try to correct this lack of arousal by sensation seeking through drinking. Finally, cocaine withdrawal symptoms have been correlated with depletion of dopamine (Dackis, Gold, & Pottash, 1987). Therefore, relapse may be a consequence of such deficiencies.

Although genetic and physiological factors heighten the risk of alcoholism and other addictions, psychological and social factors modulate the expression of such vulnerabilities (U.S. Department of Health and Human Services, 1993). At present, further research is necessary to determine the interactions that predict addiction and the protective factors (resilience) that prevent addiction.

Psychological Risk Factors:

The four most important areas of psychological risk for relapse are: (a) expectancy, (b) cue reactivity, (c) coping ability, and (d) psychopathology. Expectancies of the effects of one's preferred substance can be predictive of drinking behavior. These expectancies also are known as the "seven dwarves" because alcohol makes one sleepy, grumpy, dopey, bashful, and so forth (Leigh, 1989). Beliefs about alcohol effects on emotion can motivate drinking in alcoholics (Brown, Goldman, & Christiansen, 1985), and positive expectancies can increase the risk of relapse (Brown, 1985). Among those who develop alcohol problems, differences may exist in the manner in which information about alcohol is encoded, stored, and retrieved, which affects beliefs and behavior toward alcohol (U.S. Department of Health and Human Services, 1994).

Another important area is cue reactivity, which is a familiar concept to all addicted persons, but which has been surprisingly ignored in contemporary treatments. Alcoholics respond to alcohol cues with increased pupillary dilation (Kennedy, 1971), physiologic arousal (Kaplan, Meyer, & Stroebel, 1983), and salivation (Monti et al., 1987). Even after 30 days of residential treatment, opioid addicts continue to react physiologically to drug cues (Childress, McLellan, Ehrman, & O'Brien, 1988). Increased cue reactivity may be related to relapse potential (Niaura et al., 1988). The risk of cue reactivity does not require the actual presence of a substance. A recent study found that severely dependent alcohol abusers report less confidence in their ability to resist urges to drink heavily than do nonproblem drinkers when viewing a prime time television program with alcohol commercials (Sobell, Sobell, Toneatto, & Leo, 1993a).

A third area of psychological risk for relapse is the frequency of positive and negative life events. Billings and Moos (1983) reported that relapsed alcoholics experienced greater negative life events (such as deaths of friends or financial problems) than recovering alcoholics. Moos, Finney, and Chan (1981) found that relapsed alcoholics experienced more negative life events and fewer positive life events than community controls or recovering alcoholics.

A fourth psychological risk factor is psychopathology. About 78% of alcoholics meet lifetime criteria for a DSM-III Axis I or II diagnosis, and 65% meet current criteria (Ross, Glaser, & Germanson, 1988). The most common personality disorder diagnoses were affective (27%), anxiety (33%), and antisocial (37%). The presence of these disorders can affect outcome, because psychiatric severity is a powerful predictor of relapse (McLellan, Luborsky, Woody, O'Brien, & Druley, 1983). Relapsed patients have higher mean depression scores than abstinent patients at follow-up (Hatsukami, Pickens, & Svikis, 1981).

Social Risk Factors:

Four areas of social risk should be assessed: (a) socioeconomic status, (b) marital and family cohesion, (c) unemployment status, and (d) residential stability. Alcoholics of higher socioeconomic status fare better than alcoholics of lower socioeconomic status (Baekland, 1977). Addicted persons with higher-status occupations (white collar) and higher income achieve a better outcome than those with lesser resources (Westermeyer, 1989). Greater abstinence has been associated with being married (Westermeyer, 1989), greater expressiveness (Billings & Moos, 1983), and efficient problem solving (Kosten, Jalali, Steidl, & Kleber, 1987). Being employed has been consistently related to improved treatment outcome (Bromet & Moos, 1977), whereas being homeless is indicative of a poor prognosis (Poikolanien & Saila, 1986).

RELAPSE PREVENTION TECHNIQUES

Psychoeducational Approaches:

Relapse prevention is primarily an educational process. Furthermore, relapse has been viewed as a result of incomplete assessment (Monti, Abrams, Kadden, & Cooney, 1989). This is not surprising, because many addicted clients are limited in their ability to integrate important information, whether the inability is caused by emotional factors or the biochemical effects of substances. The counselor can improve efficiency of treatment by considering the following:

- Protracted withdrawal can produce memory deficits; repetition and concrete presentation are necessary.

- The myths about relapse must be debunked early because they can produce inaccurate expectations of treatment.

- Clients should receive information about the biologic, psychological, and social aspects of addiction and be encouraged to examine each area carefully.

- Treatment information is best retained if it is individualized so as to be relevant to the population being treated (e.g., adolescents may ignore medical information about alcoholism, whereas elderly alcoholics would not).

- Treatment information should be relevant to the natural environment to stimulate discussion about ways to transfer skills learned in treatment beyond discharge.

- Curiosity and original thinking should be rewarded rather than viewed as a departure from the "message" of recovery.

Cognitive Remediation:

Marlatt (1985) highlighted several areas important in cognitive remediation:

- Outcome expectancy

- Self-efficacy

- Stimulus control

- Apparently irrelevant decisions

- Abstinence violation effect

- Cognitive distortion

Outcome expectancy is critical to the client's perceptions of the substance and treatment. The substance is thought to produce a beneficial reaction to enhance coping with difficult situations. Education regarding these perceptions is important (e.g., countering the notion that alcohol use helps one's social functioning). In addition, counselors need to enhance outcome expectancies of treatment by reminding clients that past relapses do not "doom" them. In fact, the more attempts one has made at stopping addictive behavior, the greater the chances are that the next attempt will be successful (Rose & Hamilton, 1978). Assessing outcome from single attempts provides relatively uninspiring results; however, many people change their behavior over longer periods of time.

Self-efficacy can be enhanced by adopting a collaborative relationship with the client and removing any confrontive stance in problem solving. The focus is better placed on the acquisition of skills rather than willpower. Past relapses are cast as "mistakes" rather than as moral failings; accordingly, information, practice, and feedback are primary interventions.

Stimulus control involves a careful assessment of cues that are reliably related to substance use. These cues may include objects (bottles, needles), places (a favorite easy chair for drinking), people (drinking "buddies"), moods (depression, anxiety, elation), times of day ("quitting time"), or even music that one may listen to during times of substance use. Removal and avoidance of these cues are essential.

Tracing apparently irrelevant decisions may produce much information about the addicted person's thought process. Asking about an "average" day, the thoughts that arise when a workday is over, or the self-talk that is triggered by exposure to drinking friends can illuminate the critical "choice points" before relapse.

The abstinence violation effect should be framed as an indicator of inadequate coping skills rather than evidence of one's weakness. Because an abstinence violation effect can precipitate further substance use (especially when combined with an expectation that one will lose control over use), the distinction between a lapse (initial use) and relapse (a return to previous unhealthy patterns) should be made. The client should be encouraged to seek the "missing link" (the information, skill, or insight that could have prevented a past substance use).

The final area of cognitive remediation is cognitive distortion, which is based on the principles of cognitive therapy (Beck, Wright, Neuman, & Liese, 1993). Beck and colleagues delineated ways in which the *process* of thinking is disrupted, thus increasing the risk of substance use. These distortions are related to an addictive belief system that serves dysfunctional "core" beliefs related to personal survival, achievement, freedom, autonomy, or acceptability. In addition, many addicted persons do not fully assess all available information, thus rendering them prone to making inaccurate decisions when faced with substance-related situations. Cognitive distortions can be reduced if the resulting assumptions are avoided and *all* available information is evaluated. Through self-monitoring homework and cognitive-behavioral interventions, addicted persons can be taught to recognize these dysfunctional beliefs and cognitive distortions, replace them with healthy alternatives, and, ultimately, change addictive patterns.

Skill Building:

Skill building includes assertiveness, problem solving, and relaxation. The addicted person may need to develop drink or drug refusal skills, so assertiveness training can be used to develop direct, efficient responses to offers of alcohol or drugs.

D'Zurilla and Goldfried (1971) break down problem solving into five steps:

- Orientation (recognizing a problem)

- Definition (clearly stating the problem)

- Generation of alternatives ("brainstorming")

- Decision making (selecting the best alternative)

- Verification (evaluating the results)

Addicted persons frequently make poor decisions because every step of this process can be disrupted by active drug use. In fact, when given a problem to solve, many produce only one impulsive solution! Teaching this systematic process can prevent unhealthy responses in high-risk situations.

Relaxation skills can be used to reduce craving for substances, enhance coping with stressful life events, or counter feelings of anxiety, depression, or even boredom. Many addicted persons are surprised to find that they are able to exercise some control over bodily reactions without use of substances.

Lifestyle Modification:

Lifestyle modification can take several forms:

- Environmental change

- Social change

- Development of leisure interests that compete with substance use

- Alteration in lifestyle pacing

Environmental change may be necessary if one lives in a drug-infested neighborhood or near to drinking establishments. Social change may be necessary if one's primary social contact involves substance use or if involvement with a significant other increases relapse risk. Leisure interests offer a healthy escape from the emotional stress of recovery, but the clinician is advised to assess carefully the degree of substance use connected with past leisure interests. For example, activities such as fishing and playing billiards or softball often include drinking. Lifestyle pacing refers to the speed with which one conducts daily activities: some people are relatively unhurried and directionless, while others adopt a "type A" philosophy (marked by a high motivation level and goal-directed behavior). The concept of "balance," defined as an equilibrium between "wants" and "shoulds" (Marlatt & Gordon, 1985) is important to emphasize in early recovery.

Affect Regulation:

Emotional mismanagement is a principal factor in relapse (Chiauzzi, 1991). These difficult emotions may be rooted in psychopathology, such as major depression, anxiety disorders, or bipolar disorders, but also may be observed in a relatively normal range of experience. For example, many addicted clients exhibit loss of control over anger or are at high risk of using a substance when they experience positive emotions. When dealing with clients' emotions in relapse prevention, practitioners should bear in mind that:

- Emotions are not random; rather, they are situational. Therefore, identification of high-risk situations that precipitate troublesome emotions should be included in relapse prevention.

- Waiting passively for an emotion to diminish is less fruitful than developing a proactive plan for an activity that reduces the emotion — behavior drives emotion more quickly than emotion drives behavior.

- Identification of cognitive distortions can reduce unwanted emotional reactions.

- Identification of unresolved emotional events may

provide understanding about situations (or people) that can trigger such emotions; for example, people can "push buttons" for old resentments.

- Emotion can be expressed in many guises: vague somatic complaints (headaches, fatigue), escapist behavior (sleeping, reading, daydreaming), or apparently positive behavior that is intended to mask negative emotions (smiling while angry).

TRENDS IN RELAPSE PREVENTION

The use of relapse prevention strategies for addictive disorders represents only an initial attempt to develop a plan for reducing recurrence of psychopathologic symptoms. In fact, relapses are common in most psychopathologic disorders, and relapse prevention is now increasingly applied to obesity, depression, schizophrenia, panic disorder, obsessive-compulsive disorders, sexual deviance, and stuttering (Wilson, 1992). Of course, the definition of *relapse* varies greatly among these disorders, but the issues and techniques are similar. In addition, with increased emphasis on brief and cost-effective treatment, there will be a greater need to prevent the recurrence of symptoms and minimize hospitalization. These goals are more likely to be achieved if clients become active participants in treatment and recognize the relapse process more readily.

Another area worthy of investigation relates to the application or relapse prevention across stages of recovery. In a long-term follow-up of male alcohol abusers, Vaillant (1996) found that the risk of relapse drops dramatically after 5 years of abstinence. Therefore, it will be important to determine the ways in which relapse risk is altered over time. Rather than view recovery as a static experience, clinicians will increasingly apply relapse prevention principles and techniques differentially, depending on whether the client requires a concrete (early recovery) or analytic (later recovery) approach.

Treatment matching represents a third key area in the development of effective relapse prevention. The Institute of Medicine (1990) determined that "there is no single treatment approach that is effective for all persons with alcohol problems. A number of different treatment methods show promise in particular groups." As a result, future interventions should be better specified for special populations and subgroups of addicted clients. The findings of project MATCH, a recently-completed, multisite clinical trial comparing Twelve-Step Facilitation, Cognitive-Behavioral Coping Skills, and Motivational Enhancement Therapy, should prove helpful in directing matching strategies (Project MATCH Research Group, 1993).

Finally, relapse prevention requires medical, psychological, and social interventions, and cross-fertilization among disciplines will be necessary. The integration of psychotherapy and addiction approaches can maximize the best knowledge in each field. In addition, the input of people who transform their lives through "natural recovery" (changing addictive behavior without formal intervention) needs to be included. People who change their addictive behavior without seeking treatment often use methods similar to those who have received treatment; for example, changing social contacts, developing healthy recreational activities, and changing diet and exercise patterns (Shaffer & Jones, 1989; Sobell, Sobell, Toneatto, & Leo, 1993b). Approaches to relapse prevention that broaden areas of inquiry will likely transform addictions treatment into a more meaningful and, ultimately, more successful endeavor.

REFERENCES

Abbot, M. W., & Gregson, R. A. M. (1981). Cognitive dysfunction in the prediction of relapse in alcoholism. *Journal of Studies on Alcohol, 43,* 230–243.

Armor, D. J., Polich, J. M., & Stambul, H. B. (1978). *Alcoholism and treatment.* New York: Wiley.

Baekland, F. (1977). Evaluation of treatment methods in chronic alcoholism. In B. Kissin & H. Begleiter (Eds.), *The biology of alcoholism, IV. Treatment and rehabilitation of the chronic alcoholic* (pp. 385–440). New York: Plenum Press.

Bean-Bayog, M. (1985, March). *Psychotherapy and the sober alcoholic.* Presented at the Eighth Annual Alcoholism Symposium: Strategies and Objectives for Treatment Interventions, Boston.

Beck, A. T., Wright, F. D., Neuman, C. F., & Liese, B. S. (1993). *Cognitive therapy of substance abuse.* New York: Guilford Press.

Begleiter, H., Porjesz, B., Bihari, B., & Kissin, B. (1984). Event-related brain potentials in boys at high risk for alcoholism. *Science, 225,* 1493–1496.

Billings, A. G., & Moos, R. H. (1983). Psychosocial processes of recovery among alcoholics and their families: Implications for clinicians and program evaluators. *Addictive Behaviors, 8,* 205–218.

Borg, S., Czarnecka, A., Kvande, H., Mossberg, D., & Sedvall, G. (1983). Clinical conditions and concentrations of MOPEG in cerebrospinal fluid and urine of alcoholic patients during withdrawal. *Science, 213,* 1135–1137.

Brandon, T. H., Tiffany, S. T., & Baker, T. B. (1986). The process of smoking relapse. In F. M. Tims & C. G. Leukefeld (Eds.), *Relapse and recovery in drug abuse* (DHHS Publication No. ADM 86-1473). Washington, DC: U.S. Government Printing Office.

Bromet, E., & Moos, R. H. (1977). Environmental resources and the posttreatment functioning of alcoholic patients. *Journal of Health and Social Behavior, 18,* 326-338.

Brown, S. A. (1985). Reinforcement expectancies and alcoholism treatment outcome after a 1-year follow-up. *Journal of Studies on Alcohol, 46,* 304–308.

Brown, S. A., Goldman, M. S., & Christiansen, B. A. (1985). Do alcohol expectancies mediate drinking patterns of adults? *Journal of Consulting and Clinical Psychology, 53,* 512–519.

Chiauzzi, E. J. (1991). *Preventing relapse in the addictions: A biopsychosocial approach*. New York: Pergamon Press.

Childress, A. R., McLellan, A. T., Ehrman, R., O'Brien, C. P. (1988). Classically conditioned responses in opioid and cocaine dependence: A role in relapse? In B. A. Ray (Ed.), *Learning factors in substance abuse* (DHHS Publication No. ADM 88-1576). Washington, DC: U.S. Government Printing Office.

Colletti, G., Supnick, J. A., & Rizzo, A. A. (1982). Long-term follow-up (3-4 years) of treatment for smoking reduction. *Addictive Behaviors, 7*, 429-433.

Dackis, C., Gold, M. S., & Pottash, A. L. C. (1987). Central stimulant abuse: Neurochemistry and pharmacotherapy. In M. S. Gold & M. Galanter (Eds.), *Cocaine: Pharmacology, addiction, and therapy* (pp. 7-21). New York: Haworth Press.

D'Zurilla, T. J., & Goldfried, M. R. (1971). Problem solving and behavior modification. *Journal of Abnormal Psychology, 78*, 107-126.

Goodwin, D. W. (1988). *Is alcoholism hereditary?* (2nd ed.). New York: Ballantine Books.

Hatsukami, D., Pickens, R. W., & Svikis, D. (1981). Posttreatment depressive symptoms and relapse to drug use in different age groups of alcohol and other drug abuse populations. *Drug and Alcohol Dependence, 8*, 271-277.

Hunt, W., Barnett, L. W., & Branch, L. G. (1971). Relapse rates in addiction programs. *Journal of Clinical Psychology, 27*, 455-456.

Institute of Medicine. (1990). *Broadening the base for treatment for alcohol programs*. Washington, DC: National Academy Press.

Kaplan, R. F., Meyer, R. E., Stroebel, C. F. (1983). Alcohol dependence and responsivity to an ethanol stimulus as predictors of alcohol consumption. *British Journal of Addiction, 78*, 256-267.

Kennedy, D. (1971). *Pupilometrics as an aid in the assessment of motivation, impact of treatment, and prognosis of chronic alcoholics*. Unpublished doctoral dissertation, University of Utah.

Khantzian, E. J. (1985). The self-medication hypothesis of addictive disorders: Focus on heroin and cocaine dependence. *American Journal of Psychiatry, 142,* 1259–1264.

Kosten, T. R., Jalali, B., Steidl, J. H., & Kleber, H. D. (1987). Relationship of marital structure and interactions to opiate abuse relapse. *American Journal of Drug and Alcohol Abuse, 13,* 387–399.

Leber, W. R., Parsons, O. A., & Nichols, N. (1985). Neuropsychological test results are related to ratings of men alcoholics' therapeutic progress: A replicated study. *Journal of Studies on Alcohol, 46,* 116–121.

Leigh, B. C. (1989). In search of the seven dwarves: Issues of measurement and meaning in alcohol expectancy research. *Psychological Bulletin, 105,* 361–373.

Litman, G. K., Eiser, J. R., Rawson, N. S. B., & Oppenheim, A. N. (1977). Towards a typology of relapse: A preliminary report. *Drug and Alcohol Dependence, 2,* 157–162.

Litman, G. K., Stapleton, J., Oppenheim, A. N., & Peleg, M. (1983). An instrument for measuring coping behaviors in hospitalized alcoholics. *British Journal of Addiction, 78,* 269–276.

Maddux, J. F., & Desmond, D. P. (1986). Relapse and recovery in substance abuse careers. In F. M. Tims & C. G. Leukefeld (Eds.), *Relapse and recovery in drug abuse* (DHHS Publication No. ADM 86-1473). Washington, DC: U.S. Government Printing Office.

Marlatt, G. A. (1985). Cognitive factors in the relapse process. In G. A. Marlatt & J. R. Gordon (Eds.), *Relapse prevention: Maintenance strategies in the treatment of addictive behavior* (pp. 128–200). New York: Guilford Press.

Marlatt, G. A., & Gordon, J. R., (Eds.) (1985). *Relapse prevention: Maintenance strategies in the treatment of addictive behavior.* New York: Guilford Press.

McKay, J. R., Murphy, R. T., & Longabaugh, R. (1991). The effectiveness of alcoholism treatment: Evidence from outcome studies. In S. M. Mirin, J. T. Gossett, & M. C. Grob (Eds.), *Psychiatric treatment: Advances in outcome research* (pp. 143–158.). Washington, DC: American Psychiatric Press.

McLellan, A. T., Grissom, G. R., Brill, P., Durell, J., Metzger, D. S., & O'Brien, C. P. (1993). Private substance abuse treatments: Are some programs more effective than others? *Journal of Substance Abuse Treatment, 10,* 243–254.

McLellan, A. T., Luborsky L., Woody, G. E., O'Brien, C. P., & Druley, K. A. (1983). Predicting response to alcohol and drug abuse treatments: The role of psychiatric severity. *Archives of General Psychiatry, 40,* 620–626.

Miller, W. R. (1989). Increasing motivation for change. In R. K. Hester & W. R. Miller (Eds.), *Handbook of alcoholism treatment approaches* (pp. 67–80). New York: Pergamon Press.

Miller, W. R. (1985). Motivation for treatment: A review with special emphasis on alcoholism. *Psychological Bulletin, 98,* 84–107.

Miller, W. R., & Hester, R. K. (1980). Treating the problem drinker: Modern approaches. In W. R. Miller (Ed.), *The addictive behaviors: Treatment and alcoholism, drug abuse, smoking, and obesity* (pp. 11-141). New York: Pergamon Press.

Monti, P. M., Abrams, D. B., Kadden, R. M., & Cooney, N. L. (1989). *Treating alcohol dependence.* New York: Guilford Press.

Monti, P. M., Binkoff, J. A., Zwick, W. R., Abrams, D. B., Nirenberg, T. D., & Liepman, N. R. (1987). Reactivity of alcoholics and nonalcoholics to drinking cues. *Journal of Abnormal Psychology, 96,* 122-126.

Moos, R. H., Finney, J. W., & Chan, D. A. (1981). The process of recovery from alcoholism, I: Comparing alcoholic patients and matched community controls. *Journal of Studies on Alcohol, 42,* 383-402.

Niaura, R. S., Rohsenow, D. J., Binkoff, J. A., Monti, P. M., Pedraza, M., & Abrams, D. B. (1988). Relevance of cue reactivity to understanding alcohol and smoking relapse. *Journal of Abnormal Psychology, 97,*133-152.

O'Leary, M. R., Donovan, D. M., Chaney, E. F., & Walker, R. D. (1979). Cognitive impairment and treatment outcome with alcoholics: Preliminary findings. *Journal of Clinical Psychiatry, 40,* 397-398.

Perkins, K. A. (1988). Maintaining smoking abstinence after myocardial infarction. *Journal of Substance Abuse, 1,* 91-107.

Poikolanien, K., & Saila, S. L. (1986). Drunkenness arrests: Predictors of recurrence and effect of detoxification treatment. *Journal of Studies on Alcohol, 47,* 409–412.

Polich, J. M., Armor, D. J., & Braiker, H. B. (1981). *The course of alcoholism: Four years after treatment.* New York: Wiley.

Porjesz, B., & Begleiter, H. (1983). Brain dysfunction and alcohol. In B. Kissin & H. Begleiter (Eds.), *The biology of alcoholism, Vol 7. The pathogenesis of alcoholism: Biological factors* (pp. 415–483). New York: Plenum Press.

Project MATCH Research Group. (1993). Project MATCH: Rationale and methods for a multisite clinical trial matching patients to alcoholism treatment. *Alcoholism: Clinical and Experimental Research, 17,* 1130-1145.

Rose, G., & Hamilton, P. J. S. (1978). A randomized controlled trial of the effect on middle-aged men of advice to stop smoking. *Journal of Epidemiology and Community Health, 32,* 275–281.

Ross, H. E., Glaser, F. B., & Germanson, T. (1988). The prevalence of psychiatric disorders in patients with alcohol and other drug problems. *Archives of General Psychiatry, 45,* 1023–1031.

Satel, S. L., Kosten, T. R., Schuckit, M. A., & Fischman, M. W. (1993). Should protracted withdrawal from drugs be included in DSM-IV? *American Journal of Psychiatry, 150,* 695–704.

Shaffer, H. J., & Jones, S. B. (1989). *Quitting cocaine: The struggle against impulse.* Lexington, MA: Lexington Books.

Sobell, L. C., Sobell, M. B., Toneatto, T., & Leo, G. I. (1993a). Severely dependent alcohol abusers may be vulnerable to alcohol cues in television programs. *Journal of Studies on Alcohol, 54,* 85-91.

Sobell, L. C., Sobell, M. B., Toneatto, T., & Leo, G. I. (1993b). What triggers the resolution of alcohol problems without treatment? *Alcoholism: Clinical and Experimental Research, 17,* 217-224.

Stephens, R., & Cottrell, E. (1972). A follow-up study of 200 narcotic addicts committed for treatment under the Narcotic Rehabilitation Act (NARA). *British Journal of Addictions, 67,* 45–53.

Stimmel, B., & Rabin, J. (1974). The ability to remain abstinent upon leaving methadone maintenance: A prospective study. *American Journal of Drug and Alcohol Abuse, 1,* 379–391.

Tarter, R. E., Hegedus, A. M., & Gavaler, J. S. (1985). Hyperactivity in sons of alcoholics. *Journal of Studies on Alcohol, 46,* 259–261.

Thomas, J. C. (1996). *Substance abuse in the workplace: The role of employee assistance programs.* In *The Hatherleigh guide to treating substance abuse, part II.* New York: Hatherleigh Press.

Trachtenberg, M. C., & Blum, K. (1987). Alcohol and opioid peptides: Neuropharmacologic rationale for physical craving of alcohol. *American Journal of Drug and Alcohol Abuse, 13,* 365–372.

U.S. Department of Health and Human Services. (1994). *Eighth special report to the U.S. Congress on alcohol and health* (NIAAA Publication No. 94-3699). Rockville, MD: Author.

Vaillant, G. E. (1996). A long-term follow-up of male alcohol abuse. *Archives of General Psychiatry, 53,* 243-249.

Walker, R. D., Donovan, D. M., Kivlahan, D. R., & O'Leary, M. R. (1983). Length of stay, neuropsychological performance, and aftercare: Influences on alcohol treatment outcome. *Journal of Consulting and Clinical Psychology, 51,* 900–911.

Wallace, B. C. (1989). Psychological and environmental determinants of relapse in crack cocaine smokers. *Journal of Substance Abuse Treatment, 6,* 95–106.

Wallace, J., McNeill, D., Gilfillan, D., MacLean, K., & Fanella, F. (1988). Six-month treatment outcomes in socially stable alcoholics I: Abstinence rates. *Journal of Substance Abuse Treatment, 5,* 247–252.

Walsh, D. C., Hingson, R. W., Merrigan, D. M., Levenson, S. M., Cupples, A., Heeren, T., Coffman, G. A., Becker, C. A., Barker, T. A., Hamilton, S. K., McGuire, T. G., & Kelly, C. A. (1991). A randomized trial of treatment options for alcohol-abusing workers. *New England Journal of Medicine, 325,* 775–782.

Washton, A. M. (1989). *Cocaine addiction: Treatment, recovery, and relapse prevention*. New York: Norton.

Westermeyer, J. (1989). Nontreatment factors affecting treatment outcome in substance abuse. *American Journal of Drug and Alcohol Abuse, 15,* 13–29.

Wilson, P. H. (Ed.). (1992). *Principles and practice of relapse prevention*. New York: Guilford Press.

12

Interagency Collaboration: Improving Outcomes in the Treatment of Addictions

Michael D. McGee, MD

Dr. McGee is Medical Director of Massachusetts Biodyne, Inc. and Psychiatrist in Chief at the Solomon Mental Health Center, Lowell, MA.

KEY POINTS

- Interagency collaboration between clinical and social service agencies enables clinicians to better access the matrix of human services needed to support recovery from substance abuse.

- Benefits of organized strategic collaboration may include optimizing cost effectiveness and outcome effectiveness, increasing the availability of clinical and social services, decreasing the use of intensive treatment resources, fostering individual and program survival, and guiding the development of structures that more closely mirror the needs of patients.

- Barriers to collaboration may be financial, organizational, ideological, administrative, or attitudinal in nature.

- Effective collaboration requires organizational, administrative, and fiscal support. Managers must welcome innovation and flexibility in their support staff as well as act as role models. Leaders need to manage and depersonalize resistance to change as well as smooth emotional conflicts along the way. Collaboration requires clear and consistent communication of vision, priorities, mandates, and expectations from management.

- Various collaboration models are presented. An optimal approach involves a balance between integration and linkage.

INTRODUCTION

The lessons learned from the outcome literature on the treatment of addictions are both inspiring and humbling. We know that certain treatments work more effectively than others, for certain patients, in certain situations. At last, we are empowered with the knowledge required to practice individualized, clinically driven treatment guided by what we have learned.

We also know that improving treatment outcomes cannot be accomplished alone: no one of us can be all things to all people. Patients require more than psychotherapy to heal: recovery requires a range of social services and resources. They include a safe, stable, and supportive environment; fulfilling daytime structures; friends; family; and community. Enhancing interagency collaboration between clinical and social service agencies will allow clinicians to help their patients access more effectively the matrix of human services needed to support recovery.

THE BENEFITS OF COLLABORATION

Collaboration is defined as "a planned strategy in which two or more systems or agencies form a cooperative relationship around one or more functions designed to improve the achievement of mutual goals" (Yank, Fox, & Davis, 1991). Although informal collaboration occurs ubiquitously, we need more formal strategies because of the increased complexity in service delivery patterns, resource scarcity, and pressures for cost and outcome effectiveness (Taube & Burns, 1988).

The development of complex health and social service delivery systems has led to several problems, including barriers to access, fragmentation of care, impaired continuity, and failure to provide follow-up care (Nakao, 1986). The existing community resources often create redundancies as well as gaps in services, and the demand for individualized treatment requires coordination of complex psychosocial treatment plans to be executed by multiple agencies. Formal structures for interagency coordination of treatment are either underdeveloped or lacking. Multiagency treatment makes the management of accountability, outcome, satisfaction, and fiscal and clinical performance difficult, if not impossible. Resource scarcity requires coordination of existing resources and minimization of redundant services (Davis, 1991).

Organized strategic collaboration within a community can optimize cost effectiveness by decreasing redundancy through the development of complementary and cooperative services. Few efforts have been made, for example, to coordinate clinical services with self-help organizations. Such coordination can decrease the use of intensive treatment resources (Hansen, 1987).

Collaboration can optimize outcome effectiveness through improved case finding, referrals, enhancement of linkages between agencies and services, and improved follow-up care (Broskowski, Marks, & Budman, 1981). Collaboration makes available a wider array of both clinical and social services to patients and providers (Boudreau, 1991).

An organizing interagency body can guide the development of interagency system structures that more closely mirror the needs of patients. For example, a community consortium can facilitate the integration of gateway agencies into a care delivery system. This might include schools and medical settings, where most children with psychiatric needs can be identified and treated (Zahner, 1992). Almost half the patients with mental illnesses are treated by nonpsychiatric physicians in primary care settings. Almost 35% of psychotropic prescriptions are made by nonpsychiatrists, even though primary care clinicians greatly underdiagnose and treat psychiatric illnesses in primary care settings (Jones, 1987; Zimmerman & Wienckowski, 1991). Psychiatric clinicians who treat addictions in primary care settings as well as other crisis settings can provide triage, backup, and case management services for other agencies (Ellison & Wharff, 1985).

The Human Service Matrix:

We know that patients in recovery often need psychosocial treatment, occupational rehabilitation, and supportive and supervised residential treatment options to optimize the outcomes of therapy (Ford, 1992). Figure 11.1 represents a "human service matrix" on which clinicians can plot a patient's clinical and social service needs.

Cost- and outcome-effective treatment planning requires a flexible interaction of two axes: social support services and clinical support services. Through the development of the human service matrix, providers can equip themselves to provide truly clinically driven treatment by making available the broad range of services required for recovery. This matrix must be created through collaboration, partnership, and cooperation. Through collaborative interagency efforts, innovative services and modalities not yet available can be developed. Interagency strategic planning can facilitate the expansion of clinical modalities and social services that address multicultural issues, expand the range of residential support services available to match client/patient characteristics, and allow for matching the modality to individual problems based on our knowledge of the outcomes literature. Finally, human service consortia and associations can promote collaboration of clinical services with self-help and consumer advocacy services (Segal, Silverman, & Temkin, 1993).

A GLIMPSE AT THE HISTORY OF COLLABORATION

The mandate to collaborate was first articulated in the Mental Health Act of 1963, which required collaboration from community agencies receiving federal and state funding. Since then, there have been multiple acts and mandates, with a consistent emphasis by federal and state agencies on collaboration (Zimmerman & Wienckowski, 1991). In the 1970s and 1980s, there was increased public policy focus on human service coordination (Thacker & Tremaine, 1989). Several suc-

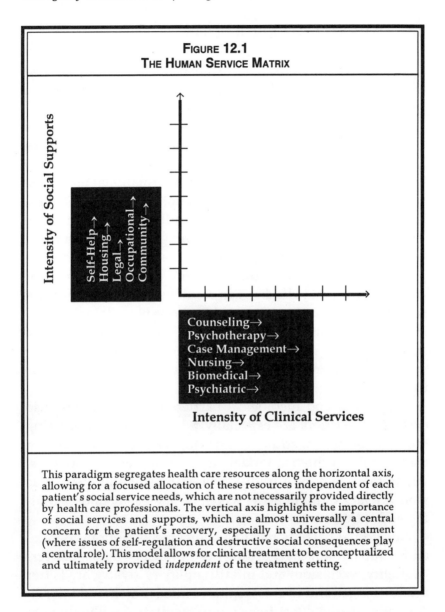

FIGURE 12.1
THE HUMAN SERVICE MATRIX

This paradigm segregates health care resources along the horizontal axis, allowing for a focused allocation of these resources independent of each patient's social service needs, which are not necessarily provided directly by health care professionals. The vertical axis highlights the importance of social services and supports, which are almost universally a central concern for the patient's recovery, especially in addictions treatment (where issues of self-regulation and destructive social consequences play a central role). This model allows for clinical treatment to be conceptualized and ultimately provided *independent* of the treatment setting.

cessful collaborations have resulted, including collaboration between state substance abuse and mental health agencies (Neligh, 1991) and state mental health and university training programs (Goldman, 1982; Yank, 1991). These efforts have allowed for joint program development and staffing, facilitation of recruitment, and improvement in the quality of care.

BARRIERS TO COLLABORATION

Over the past three decades, a great deal has been learned about the barriers to collaboration (Persky, Taylor, & Simpson, 1989; Sullivan, Richardson, & Spaulding, 1991; Thacker & Tremaine, 1989). Financial barriers include competitive forces and the unavailability of resources to support collaborative efforts. A consortium may fail because of a lack of basic funds for legal fees or for promotional and informational materials.

Developing new collaborative relationships means change. For this to occur, institutional and cultural inertia must be countered. A "this is the way we do things" approach can lead to blind spots. We are especially vulnerable to overlooking problems when a ready solution is not available. Functional and organizational blinders can result in failures to identify a need for collaboration. Oversights can especially arise from inadequate assessment and diagnosis as well as a paucity of adequately trained staff who can formulate a patient's treatment plan comprehensively from a biopsychosocial perspective.

Theoretical and ideological barriers to collaboration also exist. Such barriers are especially relevant when addressing the collaboration of addictions treatment programs with both traditional psychiatric models and social service agencies, where there may be a tradition of animosity and distrust as well as a lack of familiarity, which promotes misunderstanding and intolerance.

Attitudinal barriers must be overcome as well. Individual and group dynamics regarding power must be managed. Territoriality, exclusion, and interdisciplinary rivalry are better acknowledged and addressed than denied (Broskowski, 1980). A strong, shared constituency will facilitate a willingness to share control of the patient's care and well-being.

Finally, functional and organizational barriers should be addressed (Neligh, 1991). Administrative barriers such as rigid program boundaries, a limited array of special services, and inflexible funding patterns may hamper otherwise effective collaborative strategies.

Unfortunately, effective models for collaboration are not always readily available. Such efforts typically have been fragile, with success being the result of an individual's efforts and not based on sustaining structural changes (Neligh, 1991).

RISKS OF COLLABORATION

To collaborate is to enter into a relationship and, therefore, to accept the risks of interdependence. Collaborating agencies receive both the many benefits and the unavoidable problems of collaboration, including new dimensions of vulnerability, diminished autonomy, and threats to privilege, power, control, and status. As in any relationship, an agency's identity must change as a result of the process. Worthwhile collaboration requires the goodwill and collaborative skill of each participating agency. Effective managers must create conditions and contingencies that promote these qualities among participants.

INGREDIENTS FOR SUCCESSFUL COLLABORATION

Fortunately, collaborators have access to a relatively large body of research to learn what makes for successful collaboration (Faulkner, 1989; Goldman, Burns, & Burke; 1980; Prindaville, Sidwell, & Milner, 1983; Sullivan et al., 1991). Perhaps the most important factor is recognition of interdependence by key stakeholders. Collaboration is driven by parties who need one another, require shared resources, receive a mutual benefit from the relationship, and experience situations in which risk is shared. The better agency leaders can identify complementary goals and develop a framework of mutually accepted theories, values, and ideologies, the better will be the conditions for collaboration.

External contingencies often can drive collaboration. Thacker and Tremaine (1989) have described a mandate to address mental health and substance abuse issues through collaboration. Governmental and societal support can be crucial to instituting interagency relationships and providing funding incentives.

Organizational, administrative, and fiscal support are essential for effective collaboration. Senior administrative managers must contribute to a shared vision because collaboration will not survive without top-down support. Managers must welcome innovation and flexibility in their support staff as well as act as role models. Initial collaborative efforts must be supported by key personnel, especially while managers develop more enduring collaborative structures. Leaders must manage and depersonalize resistance to change as well as smooth emotional conflicts along the way. Because change involves loss, leaders must address issues surrounding the loss in a sensitive manner while acting as enthusiastic supporters for the rationale behind the change. Doing something that has never been done before requires clear and consistent communication of vision, priorities, mandates, and expectations from the leaders. Collaborating agencies must commit necessary personnel for collaboration activities as well as financial and other resources — for legal fees, marketing, care coordination and joint service initiatives, office operations and supplies, and so forth.

Not only is top-down support necessary, but a bottom-up "buy in" from staff members, consumers, and other providers must exist and be nurtured. Fears of exploitation must be quelled. Trust and mutual respect can be built by structuring regular forums for interaction among different agencies. This process will foster the eventual development of shared values and vision. Leaders must skillfully facilitate opportunities for collaboration and create rewarding contingencies. Ideally, effective collaboration will create a larger circle of identity, which will encompass the identities of individual agencies and providers. Forces that encourage an investment in the interagency identity will foster collaborative efforts.

Funding support is not only necessary for sustaining collaboration, but it may act as a motivational force. Because money talks, financial incentives (either direct or indirect) are an important — if not essential — element of success.

As in any complicated group endeavor, success depends on skillful management; in this case, success depends on effective interagency management. There must be a mission and a collective commitment to a set of interagency policies and procedures. Strategic planning and implementation must be guided by improved program evaluation and assessment of human service matrix needs.

Collaborators must create enduring interagency structures for access and referral, conflict resolution and problem solving, case management, and information systems. These tasks require a skilled interagency governing body and some degree of administrative and clerical support. Interagency policies and procedures should define common modes of communication and interaction (including personnel who will serve as interagency contacts) as well as clear mechanisms for problem–solving and conflict resolution.

Agencies should create interagency forums for resource development and advocacy. Managing the human service matrix calls for some investment in interagency quality improvement and quality assurance activities in fiscal, organizational, and clinical realms. Agencies may adopt common assessment and outcome tools or agree to use common quality assessment and quality improvement protocols and methodologies. If possible, sharing information systems data and developing common information platforms can greatly facilitate these activities. As agencies begin to speak the same quality language, common evaluation and accountability mechanisms will emerge to help managers monitor interagency performance.

Stakeholders in partnerships must have relatively equal control over decisions and outcomes to obtain effective interagency governance and control (Boudreau, 1991). Effective interagency managers will consistently promote collaboration between the agencies, facilitate understanding of systems, and model mutual advocacy. All these activities require effective networking and collaboration skills, including the ability to understand group dynamics and intergroup functioning as well as to build relationships with key leaders and stakeholders (Edgerton, 1994). Interagency managers will most likely include agency heads, county commissioners, community leaders, club and service organization leaders, church leaders, mental health service advocates and family members, teachers, and school administrators.

Ultimately, public support and advocacy must drive collaborative efforts. Patients, families, and friends can act either individually or through consumer advocacy organizations to promote collaboration. Leaders interested in collaborating will benefit from skillfully harnessing these forces.

As in any realm of human endeavor where something is being attempted for the first time, guidance, supervision, instruction, support, and technical assistance are extremely valuable. Potential collaborators should solicit the expertise of community members with effective collaboration skills, such as leaders of trade associations, coalitions, and voluntary professional associations. In addition, students of collaboration would do well to study the rich body of literature already available on this topic.

COLLABORATION MODELS

An agency can enhance the array of services available for its clients or patients by either linking and collaborating with other agencies or expanding its own range of services through integration (Kline, 1991). Choosing integration has the advantages of a greater ease in negotiating and coordinating services as well as a reduction in the barriers to access of services.

An optimal strategy ultimately involves the balance of integration and linkage, depending on the contingencies involved. Linkage may provide more options than a single agency can offer through integration, overcome social stigmas and resistance to mental health treatment, and diffuse certain patients' dependencies on a larger network of providers, thereby decreasing (at least somewhat) the intensity and vulnerability certain patients may feel.

However, linkage is more complicated, more difficult to coordinate, and requires a broader range of conditions for success that are not always within a given agency's control. Therefore, linkage efforts may lead to failure. The barriers to collaboration may not always be easy to overcome.

There are many models of linkage (Borus, 1975; Coleman & Patick, 1976; Morrill, 1972; Pincus, 1987). In fact, most providers have an extensive array of informal linkages based on personal and professional relationships. Typically, the coordination of treatment with self-help groups occurs in this manner (Segal et al., 1993). Treatment programs will often nurture these linkages by providing support to self-help groups in the form of meeting rooms, staff members, or community announcements.

Other professional interagency arrangements may include models of joint care, consultation, referral, and training. Agencies offering treatment of addictions can capitalize on these models by providing needed treatment in primary care settings and gateway agencies where patients with addictions often first appear, such as the YMCA, the courts, or social service offices. Agencies may enter into a contractual agreement for community education, information, and treatment referral. Such agencies also may provide a screening and information exchange specialist to a clinic or other organization. Mental health services can be provided directly in a primary care setting, or a clinician can provide consultation and continuing education to other health care providers (Persky et al., 1989). Agencies can collaborate to provide coordinated, joint care in one setting.

Interagency collaboration benefits from an interagency governing and coordinating body. This may be achieved by establishing a nonprofit corporation whose mission is to coordinate the multitude of services in the community. A successful example of this model is Baltimore Health Systems, Inc. (Collier, 1991). This government-funded corporation managed the funding of Baltimore's clinical and social services, restructured the financial system for funding and reimbursement, expanded the services continuum, created housing, established a case-advocacy program, and promoted community education and involvement for the Baltimore area.

The Galt Visiting Scholar Model is an example of a *consultant model* (Yank et al., 1991). In this model, an expert in a state/university-funded health system works through consultative recommendations to create structures for ongoing collaboration, implement new standards of care, and make suggestions for the reallocation of resources. This model offers the consultant a great deal of freedom, but with that freedom comes a relative lack of authority to implement often difficult changes.

The *coalition model* is represented by the Western Interstate Commission for Higher Education (Davis, 1991). This coalition of mental health service agencies was created to facilitate access to and provision of necessary resources in rural areas through restructuring of systems and management training. It was created as a response to consumer advocacy groups in the region, underscoring the importance of grassroots consumer support for collaboration efforts.

Many agencies have worked effectively through linchpin models, where agency heads enter into agreements to work with one another (Godard, 1991). They promote collaboration, for example, between state mental health agencies and university faculty. Linchpins facilitate the understanding of systems, provide for mutual advocacy, as well as model and manage the collaborative efforts for their agencies.

Agencies in the community should agree on some strategy, if possible, for structuring their collaborative effort. Coalitions and consortia can be structured not only as nonprofit corporations but also as voluntary associations, such as recovery or human service trade organizations.

Finally, legal and accreditation issues must be considered. Such organizations cannot be structured so as to be exclusionary because this would violate antitrust laws. Organizations should have some routine way of evaluating the outcome of their referrals to other agencies.

SUMMARY: TOWARD THE FUTURE

Providers of addictions treatment require more education regarding mental health and social services, the benefits of linkage, and training in linkage tasks, including case management, consultations, and referrals. Agencies need to provide financial support and incentives for effective linkage. Administrators will become increasingly motivated to obtain reimbursement for linkage activities and interagency case coordination as managed care and health care reform spurs the growing awareness of the need to collaborate to survive. Grassroots consumer advocacy and self-help groups are important players in this arena and should be regarded as allies. Volunteers and community service organizations are also important resources (Golden, 1991). Such groups can provide support for telephone help lines, staffing of drop-in resource rooms, assistance with transportation, and orientation to self-help groups.

Providers will do well to expand their range of vision beyond their office or agency and invest efforts into the coordination of their community human service matrix. Not only will this foster individual and program survival, it will ultimately benefit the patients we serve.

REFERENCES

Borus, J. F. (1975). The coordination of mental health services at the neighborhood level. *American Journal of Psychiatry, 132,* 1177–1181.

Boudreau, F. (1991). Partnership as a new strategy in mental health policy: The case of Quebec. *Journal of Health Politics, Policy and Law, 16,* 307–329.

Broskowski, A. (1980). *Evaluation of the Primary Health Care Project-Community Mental Health Center Initiative.* Rockville, MD: Department of Health and Human Services.

Broskowski, A., Marks, E., & Budman, S. H., (Eds.). (1981). The health-mental health connection: An introduction. *Linking health and mental health* (pp. 13–26). Beverly Hills, CA: Sage.

Coleman, J. V., & Patick, D. L. (1976). Integrating mental health services into primary medical care. *Medical Care, 14,* 654–661.

Collier, M. T. (1991). The linkage of Baltimore's mental health and public health systems. *Journal of Public Health Policy, 12*(1, Spring), 50–60.

Davis, M. (1991). Public-academic linkages in Western states. *Community Mental Health Journal, 27,* 411–423.

Edgerton, J. W. (1994). Working with key players for psychological and mental health public services. *American Psychologist, 49,* 314–321.

Ellison, J. A., & Wharff, E. A. (1985). More than a gateway: The role of the emergency psychiatry service in the community mental health network. *Hospital and Community Psychiatry, 36,* 180–185.

Faulkner, L. R. (1989). Oregon's state-university collaboration in a national context. In J. D. Bloom (Ed.), *New directions for mental health services* (pp. 29-39). San Francisco: Jossey-Bass.

Ford, J. (1992). Needs assessment for persons with severe mental illness: What services are needed for successful community living? *Community Mental Health Journal, 28,* 491–503.

Godard, S. (1991). Public-academic linkages: A 'linchpin' model. *Community Mental Health Journal, 27,* 489–500.

Golden, G. K. (1991). Volunteer counselors: An innovative, economic response to mental health service gaps. *Social Work, 36,* 230–232.

Goldman, H. H. (1982). Integrating health and mental health services: Historical obstacles and opportunities. *American Journal of Psychiatry, 139,* 616–620.

Goldman, H. H., Burns, B. J., & Burke, J. D. (1980). Integrating primary health care and mental health services: A preliminary report. *Public Health Reports, 95,* 535–539.

Hansen, V. (1987). Psychiatric service within primary care. *Acta Psychiatrica Scandinavica, 76,* 121–128.

Jones, L. R. (1987). Inside the hidden mental health network: Examining mental health care delivery of primary care physicians. *General Hospital Psychiatry, 9,* 287–293.

Kline, J. (1991). Contrasting integrated and linkage models of treatment for homeless, dually diagnosed adults. In J. D. Bloom (Ed.), *New directions for mental health services* (pp. 95–106). San Francisco: Jossey-Bass.

Morrill, R. (1972). A new mental health services model for a comprehensive neighborhood health center. *American Journal of Public Health, 62,* 1108–1111.

Nakao, K. (1986). Referral patterns to and from inpatient psychiatric services: A social network approach. *American Journal of Public Health, 76,* 755–760.

Neligh, G. (1991). The program for public psychiatry: State-university collaboration in Colorado. *Hospital and Community Psychiatry, 42,* 44–48.

Persky, T., Taylor, A., & Simson, S. (1989). The Network Trilogy Project: Linking aging, mental health, and health agencies. *Gerontology and Geriatrics Education, 9,* 79–88.

Pincus, H. A. (1987). Patient-oriented models for linking primary care and mental health care. *General Hospital Psychiatry, 9,* 95–101.

Prindaville, G. M., Sidwell, L. H., & Milner, D. E. (1983). Integrating primary health care and mental health services — a successful rural linkage. *Public Health Reports, 98,* 67–72.

Segal, S. P., Silverman, C., & Temkin, T. (1993). Empowerment and self-help agency practice for people with mental disabilities. *Social Work, 38,* 705–712.

Sullivan, M. E., Richardson, C. E., & Spaulding, W. D. (1991). University-state hospital collaboration in an inpatient psychiatric rehabilitation program. *Community Mental Health Journal, 27,* 441–453.

Taube, C. A., & Burns, B. J. (1988). Mental health services system re-search: The National Institute of Mental Health program. *Health Services Research, 22,* 837–955.

Thacker, W., & Tremaine, L. (1989). Systems issues in serving the mentally ill substance abuser: Virginia's experience. *Hospital Community Psychiatry, 40,* 1046–1049.

Yank, G. R. (1991). Virginia's experience with state-university collabora-tion. *Hospital and Community Psychiatry, 42,* 39–44.

Yank, G. R., Fox, J. C., & Davis, K. E. (1991). The Galt Visiting Scholar in Public Mental Health: A review of a model of state-university collabora-tion. *Community Mental Health Journal, 27,* 455–471.

Zahner, G. E. P. (1992). Children's mental health service needs and utilization patterns in an urban community: An epidemiological assess-ment. *Journal of the American Academy of Child and Adolescent Psychiatry, 31,* 951.

Zimmerman, M. A., & Wienckowski, L. A. (1991). Revisiting health and mental health linkages: A policy whose time has come. . . again. *Journal of Public Health Policy,* Winter, 510–524.

Name Index

A

Subject Index

A

antipsychotics, 38-41
anxiolytics, 33-35
Psychosis
induced by bupropion, 37
toxic, 139
Psychotherapy, 201, 244
resistance to, 192
Psychotropic substances,
See Drugs

Q

Questionnaires,
See Scales, questionnaires, and
inventories

R

Rand Report, 216
Rates of Patients Without Relapse
(*figure*), 73
Raves, 130, 141
dance party phenomenon, 131-
132
Rebound neural excitation, 65
Recency criteria, for caffeine
intoxication, 158
Recidivism, 52
Recovery, defined, 215
Recreation and leisure, 17
Relapse
defined, 69, 214-215
models of
biopsychosocial, 221-222
cognitive-behavioral, 219-221
disease, 218-218
moral, 218
self-medication, 219
mythology, 222-224
preventing, 20, 120, 122, 123
reducing the risk of, 213-235
risk of with alcoholism, 64, 66, 67
risk factors, 224-228
statistics, 69-70, 79
Relapse Rates (*figure*), 72
Relaxation skills, 232
Reliability
internal, 3, 4
interrater, 3
test-retest, 3
Remission, 10
Resistance, patient, factors in, 193-
195
ReVia (naltrexone), for treatment of

alcohol dependence, 63-83
Reward structures, group, 181-183
Risperdal (risperidone), 39-40
Risperidone (Risperdal), 39-40
Robert Wood Johnson Foundation,
132, 136
Role-playing, 118
Roles, family, 123

S

Sample Diet, Days 1 Through 4
(*table*), 59
Sample Record Sheet of Daily Caring
Behaviors (*figure*), 113
Scales
questionnaires and inventories
Addiction Severity Index, 10,
93, 96
Alcohol Use Inventory, 10
Child Behavior Checklist, 11
Constructive Thinking
Inventory, 13
Cornell Medical Index, 54
Diagnostic Interview for
Children and Adolescents,
12
Drug Use Screening Inventory
(DUSI-R), 5, 6, 8, 9, 19, 20,
21
Family Assessment Measure,
13
Family Environment Scale, 13
Global Assessment Scale, 96
Halstead-Reitan
Neuropsychological Test
Battery, 18
Kiddie Schedule for Affective
Disorders and
Schizophrenia, 12
Luria-Nebraska
Neuropsychological Test
Battery, 18
Metabolic Screening
Questionnaire, 54
Millon Behavioral Health
Inventory, 12
Mini Mental Status Exam, 18
Minnesota Multiphasic
Personality Inventory
(MMPI), 11
Multidimensional Personality
Questionnaire, 11
Pittsburgh Initial
Neuropsychological

Contributors

Jeffrey S. Bland, PhD
Founder and Chief Executive Officer, HealthComm, Inc., Gig Harbor, WA.

Fong Chan, PhD
Professor and Co-Director of the Rehabilitation Research and Training Center on Career Development, Department of Rehabilitation Psychology and Special Education, University of Wisconsin-Madison.

Emil Chiauzzi, PhD
Dr. Chiauzzi is Clinical Director, Addictions Treatment Program, Waltham-Weston Hospital, Waltham, MA.

Joseph Cunningham, MS
Doctoral student in the Clinical Psychology Program, Department of Psychology at the Illinois Institute of Technology, Chicago, IL.

Laura Dunlap, MA
Doctoral student in the Department of Rehabilitation Psychology and Special Education, University of Wisconsin-Madison.

Robert L. DuPont, MD
President of the Institute for Behavior and Health Inc, Rockville, MD; Clinical Professor of Psychiatry at Georgetown University School of Medicine, Washington, DC; and First Director of the National Institute on Drug Abuse (NIDA).

Kristine M. Eiring, MS
Doctoral student in the Department of Rehabilitation Psychology and Special Education, University of Wisconsin-Madison.

Mark S. Gold, MD, FCP, FAPA
Professor, Departments of Neuroscience, Psychiatry, Community Health & Family Medicine, University of Florida Brain Institute, Gainesville, FL.

Donald Kates, MS
Doctoral student in the Department of Rehabilitation Psychology and Special Education, University of Wisconsin-Madison.

Malcolm Lader, MD, PhD, DSc, FRCPsych
Professor of Clinical Psychopharmacology, Institute of Psychiatry, London, UK.

Susan Gallagher-Lepak, RN, MSN
Doctoral student in the Department of Rehabilitation Psychology and Special Education, University of Wisconsin-Madison.

Michael D. McGee, MD
Dr. McGee is Medical Director of Massachusetts Biodyne Inc, and Psychiatrist in Chief at the Solomon Mental Health Center, Lowell, MA.

Timothy J. O'Farrell, PhD
Associate Professor of Psychology in the Department of Psychiatry at Harvard Medical School, Boston, MA, and Associate Chief of the Psychology Service at the Veterans Affairs Medical Center in Brockton and West Roxbury, MA, where he directs the Counseling for Alcoholics' Marriages (CALM) Project and the Alcohol and Family Studies Laboratory.

Barbara W. Reeve, MD
Acting Chief of Psychiatry, Eastern Maine Medical Center, Bangor, ME, and maintains a private practice in Ellsworth, ME.

Paul Richard Smokowski, MSW
Student in the Doctoral Program in Social Welfare at the University of Wisconsin School of Social Work, Madison, WI.

Ralph E. Tarter, PhD
Professor of Psychiatry and Neurology, University of Pittsburgh [PA] Medical School; and Director, Center for Education and Drug Abuse Research (CEDAR) — CEDAR, a consortium between St. Francis Medical Center and the University of Pittsburgh.

John S. Wodarski, PhD
The Janet B. Wattles Research Professor and Director of the Doctoral Program and Research Center, State University of New York at Buffalo, School of Social Work, Buffalo, NY.

For information on other books in
The Hatherleigh Guides series, call the
Marketing Department at Hatherleigh
Press, 1-800-367-2550, or write:
Hatherleigh Press
Marketing Department
420 E. 51st St.
New York, NY 10022